Glossary of Insurance Terms

Sales and Reference Material
6th Edition, Revised

At press time, this edition contains the most complete and accurate information currently available. Owing to the nature of license examinations, however, information may have been added recently to the actual test that does not appear in this edition. Please contact the publisher to verify that you have the most current edition.

This publication is designed to provide accurate and authoritative information in regard to the subject matter covered. It is sold with the understanding that the publisher is not engaged in rendering legal, accounting, or other professional services. If legal advice or other expert assistance is required, the services of a competent professional should be sought.

We value your input and suggestions. If you found imperfections in this product, please let us know by sending an email to **errata@kaplan.com**. Please include the title, edition, and PPN (reorder number) of the material.

We are always looking for ways to make our products better to help you achieve your career goals.

07	08	10	09	08	07	06	05	04	03	02	01
J	F	M	A	M	J	J	A	S	O	N	D

Before You Begin

Kaplan Financial's sixth edition of *The Glossary of Insurance Terms* is a completely new volume. It covers many areas of the insurance business and also includes a variety of noninsurance terms that are related to insurance in some manner. We hope this glossary will be a valuable addition to any business library and a helpful resource for anyone who needs to understand the meaning of terms and concepts generated by the ever-changing insurance industry. It is designed to be used not only by insurance professionals and commercial insurance buyers, but also by consumers who need to better understand their own insurance coverages.

The glossary is divided into sections, in alphabetical sequence. Abbreviations and acronyms (if any) appear at the beginning of each section, followed by an alphabetical presentation of terms. Each term is set in bold type. To help you gain a quick reference point, definitions are immediately followed by one or more abbreviations for general categories of insurance, set in parentheses. The abbreviations for the reference categories used in this glossary are as follows:

AN	=	*ANNUITIES*
AU	=	*AUTOMOBILE*
AV	=	*AVIATION*
C	=	*CRIME*
EP	=	*ESTATE PLANNING*
G	=	*GENERAL*
H	=	*HEALTH*
IM	=	*INLAND MARINE*
LE	=	*LEGAL*
LA	=	*LIABILITY*
LI	=	*LIFE*
OM	=	*OCEAN MARINE*
PR	=	*PENSION AND PROFIT SHARING*
P	=	*PROPERTY*
R	=	*REINSURANCE*
S	=	*SURETY*
WC	=	*WORKERS' COMPENSATION*

Some terms are cross-referenced with other terms that appear in the glossary. In this case, the referenced terms are also set in bold type. Cross-referencing is used for terms that have the same or similar meanings, terms that differ from related terms, and terms that are opposites.

This new edition of the glossary includes hundreds of new and revised terms. Many of these items have been added because of the introduction of new policy forms and coverages, important legal developments, and the changing business environment.

Diligent efforts have been made by Kaplan Financial staff to provide you with an up-to-date and comprehensive glossary of insurance terms. However, this glossary is not put forth as the final authority on any given term, and we recognize that we may have overlooked a few items. Insurance terminology is subject to a never-ending developmental process, which means that definitions change with time and usage. New terms are developed with each passing year. For these reasons, we welcome and encourage constructive criticism about items in the glossary as well as suggestions about terms that should be included. Such information will be accumulated and taken into consideration in our preparation of future editions.

About the Authors

The original *Glossary of Insurance Terms* was compiled by John S. Bickley, PhD, and the late Robert W. Osler. Both men served on operating committees of the Commission on Insurance Terminology (CIT), which worked to develop more precise insurance definitions during 1958–1971, and both sought to continue the efforts of the commission.

Thomas E. Green, CPCU, CLU, has done much of the editorial work on the glossary. Mr. Green has enjoyed a long and distinguished career in the insurance field. He graduated from the University of Wisconsin, where he majored in insurance. In 1950, he joined the Wausau Insurance Companies, where he has held various positions, including director of educational planning and services. Tom became a CPCU in 1964 and a CLU in 1968. In 1971, he was awarded the Associate in Management designation by the Insurance Institute of America. Over the years, Tom has been a member of the American Society for Training and Development, the Education Committee of the Alliance of American Insurers, and the Insurance Advisory Task Force of the NAIC Uniform Licensing Committee. He has served as president of the Northern Wisconsin Chapter Society of CPCU and as president of the Insurance Company Education Director Society (now called Society for Insurance Training and Education). Tom has also been a member of the Society of CPCU Curriculum Liaison Committee. He became national director of the Society of CPCU in 1984 and regional vice president in 1986.

Kaplan Financial has been producing and publishing specialized reference manuals and training and study materials for the insurance industry for more than 30 years. Members of its full-time editorial staff have diverse backgrounds in the insurance industry.

Contents

Alphabetical Listings

A

ABBREVIATIONS AND ACRONYMS

AAI. *See* Alliance of American Insurers. **(G)**

AAIS. *See* American Association of Insurance Services. **(G)**

ACAS. Associate of the Casualty Actuarial Society. *See* **Fellow of the Casualty Actuarial Society. (LA)**

AD&D. *See* **accidental death and dismemberment insurance. (H, LI)**

ADL. *See* **activities of daily living standards. (H)**

A&H, A&S. Accident and health insurance, and accident and sickness insurance. Once commonly used as generic designations for the entire field now called health insurance. *See* **health insurance. (H)**

AIA. *See* American Insurance Association. **(G)**

AIDS. *See* acquired immunodeficiency syndrome. **(H, LI)**

ARC. *See* AIDS-related complex. **(H, LI)**

ARIA. *See* American Risk and Insurance Association. **(G)**

ARM. *See* Associate in Risk Management. **(G)**

ASO. *See* administrative services only. **(H, LI)**

PRESENTATION OF TERMS

A (or judgment) rates. Rates that are not backed up by loss experience statistics. They are based on the judgment of the underwriter on an individual risk basis. **(G)**

abandonment. A relinquishing of ownership of lost or damaged property by the insured to the insurer so that a total loss may be claimed. Abandonment is prohibited in most other types of property insurance. **(OM)**

abandonment clause. A clause in fire insurance policies and other property forms that prohibits the insured from abandoning partially damaged property to the insurer to claim a total loss. **(PR)**

absolute assignment. Assignment by a policyowner of all control of and rights in the policy to a third party. **(G)**

absolute beneficiary. *See* irrevocable beneficiary. **(LI)**

absolute liability. A type of liability that arises from extremely dangerous operations. An example would be in the use of explosives. A contractor would almost certainly be liable for damages caused by vibrations of the earth following an explosive detonation. With absolute liability, it is usually not necessary for a claimant to establish that the operation is dangerous. *See also* strict liability. **(LA)**

accelerated benefits. Riders on life insurance policies that allow the life insurance policy's death benefits to be used to offset expenses incurred in a convalescent or nursing home facility. **(H, LI)**

accelerated endowment. A dividend option allowing dividend accumulations to be applied to convert a life insurance policy into an endowment or to shorten the endowment term. **(LI)**

accelerated option. A provision whereby an insured may use accumulated policy dividends and the cash value of a life insurance contract to pay up the policy or to mature it as an endowment. **(LI)**

accelerative endowment. An option to use life insurance policy dividends to mature a policy as an endowment before the regular maturity date. **(LI)**

acceptance. In insurance, acceptance occurs when an applicant for insurance receives the policy from the company and, in the case of general insurance, pays the premium. In life insurance, because the initial premium is almost always submitted with the application, issuance of the policy by the company constitutes acceptance. **(LE)**

access. The availability of medical care to a patient. This can be determined by such factors as location, transportation, and type of medical services in the area. **(H)**

accident. An unplanned event, unexpected and undesigned, that occurs suddenly and at a definite place. *See also* occurrence. **(G)**

accident and health insurance (A&H). An older name for health insurance. *See* health insurance. **(H)**

accident and sickness insurance (A&S). An older name for health insurance. *See* **health insurance. (H)**

accident frequency. The rate of the occurrence of accidents, often expressed in terms of the number of accidents over a period. It is one method used for measuring the effectiveness of loss prevention services. *See also* **accident severity. (G)**

accident insurance. A form of insurance against loss by accidental bodily injury to the insured. **(H)**

accident prevention. *See* **loss prevention service. (G)**

accident severity. A measure of the severity or seriousness of losses, rather than the number of losses. It is measured in terms of time lost from work rather than the number of individual accidents. It is another way of measuring the effectiveness of loss prevention services. *See also* **accident frequency. (G)**

accident year experience. Measures premiums and losses related to accidents that occurred during a 12-month period. **(G)**

accidental bodily injury. Traumatic damage to the body, of external origin, unexpected and undesigned by the injured person. *See also* **accidental means. (G)**

accidental death and dismemberment. A policy or a provision in a disability income policy that pays either a specified amount or a multiple of the weekly disability benefit if the insured dies, loses his sight, or loses two limbs as the result of an accident. A lesser amount is payable for the loss of one eye, arm, leg, hand, or foot. **(H)**

accidental death benefit. An extra benefit that generally equals the face of the contract or principal sum, payable in addition to other benefits in the event of death as the result of an accident. *See also* **double indemnity** and **multiple indemnity. (H, LI)**

accidental death insurance. A form that provides payment if the death of the insured results from an accident. It is often combined with dismemberment insurance in a form called accidental death and dismemberment. *See also* **accidental death and dismemberment. (H, LI)**

accidental means. Unexpected or undesigned cause of an accidental bodily injury. Under a definition of accidental means, the mishap itself must be accidental, not just the resulting injury. An example would be an individual chopping wood. If the axe slipped out of his hand and cut his foot, it would have been accidental means. However, if his finger got in the way of the axe, it would not have been. **(G)**

accommodation line. Business accepted from an agent or broker that would normally be rejected according to strict underwriting standards but that is accepted because of the overall profitability of the agent's or customer's other business. For example, an insurer might accept coverage on property that would not normally meet its underwriting standards if the other lines of insurance that it carries for the customer were profitable. **(G)**

account current. A monthly financial statement provided to an agent by an insurer showing premiums written, cancellations, endorsements, and commissions. **(G)**

account premium modification plan. A rating plan for fire, property damage, and time element coverages. The maximum credit or surcharge is 25%, and it is available to risks that develop a three-year premium of at least $5,000. **(PR)**

accounts receivable insurance. Insurance against the loss that occurs when an insured is unable to collect outstanding accounts because of damage to or destruction of the accounts receivable records by a peril covered in the policy. **(PR)**

accredited service. All service, by an employee, recognized under a pension plan as being allowable or creditable in calculating the amount of benefits due. **(PE)**

accrete. A Medicare term that means the process of adding new members to a health plan. **(H)**

accrued benefit. The amount of retirement benefit accumulated on behalf of a participating employee. **(PE)**

accrued liability. The amount of money needed to offset the employee's accumulated benefits under a retirement plan. Accrued liability equals the difference between the present value of the future benefits and the present value of future contributions. **(PE)**

accumulated actuarial benefit. The sum of benefits assigned to credited service before a specified date and that is determined pursuant to the actuarial valuation method in use. **(PE)**

accumulated earnings tax. A tax penalty that is imposed on corporate earnings that are retained by the corporation for nonbusiness-related needs. **(G)**

accumulated plan benefit. The portion of a participant's retirement benefit that is attributable pursuant to the plan to the participant's period of credited service before a specified date. **(PE)**

accumulation at interest. A dividend option where interest is paid on accumulated dividends and compounded annually at a guaranteed minimum interest rate. **(LI)**

accumulation period. The period before retirement during which an annuitant makes payments or investments in an annuity. Such payments will accumulate on a tax-deferred basis. **(AN)**

accumulation units. Issuances to owners of variable annuities during the accumulation period as evidence of the annuitant's participation in the separate account. **(AN)**

accumulation value. A term used in universal life policies to describe the total of all premiums paid and interest credited to the account before deductions for any expenses, loans, or surrenders. **(LI)**

accumulations (or accumulation benefits). Percentage additions to policy benefits when the contract is continuously renewed. **(LI)**

acquired immunodeficiency syndrome (AIDS). An infectious and incurable disease caused by the human immunodeficiency virus (HIV). **(H, LI)**

acquisition cost. The expenses incurred by an insurer or reinsurance company that are directly related to putting the business on the books of the company, including clerical work, medical examiners' fees, inspection costs, and so forth. The largest portion of this cost is usually the agent's or sales representative's commission or bonus. **(G)**

act of God. An event arising out of natural causes with no human intervention that could not have been prevented by reasonable care or foresight. Examples are floods, lightning, and earthquakes. **(G)**

action. A lawsuit involving the right of one party to recover from another person in a court of law. **(LE)**

active malfunction. A products insurance term. If the product, instead of bringing a benefit to the user, actually damages the user's property, it is an active malfunction. An example is a pesticide that, when applied to a crop, damages the crop. Active malfunctioning is covered. **(LA)**

actively at work. Most group health insurance policies state that if an employee is not actively at work on the day the policy goes into effect, coverage will not begin until the employee returns to work. **(H)**

activities of daily living (ADL). Everyday living functions and activities performed by individuals without assistance. These functions include mobility, dressing, personal hygiene, and eating. **(H)**

activities of daily living (ADL) standards. Used to assess the ability of an individual to live independently, measured by the ability to perform unaided such activities as eating, bathing, toiletry, dressing, and walking. ADL standards are sometimes discussed as a way to measure or define eligibility for long-term care. **(H)**

actual cash value. An amount equivalent to the replacement cost of lost or damaged property at the time of the loss, less depreciation. With regard to buildings, there is a tendency for the actual cash value to closely parallel the market value of the property. *See also* **market value. (G)**

actual charge. The actual amount charged by a physician for medical services rendered. **(H)**

actual total loss. *See* total loss. **(G)**

actuarial. Having to do with insurance mathematics. **(G)**

actuarial asset value. The value assigned by the actuary to the assets of a plan for the purposes of an actuarial valuation. **(PE)**

actuarial equivalence. Two different series of payments or values are in actuarial evidence when they have an equal actuarial present value under a given set of actuarial assumptions. **(PE)**

actuarial experience gain or loss. The effect on the unfunded supplemental actuarial value of deviations between the past events that would have occurred according to the actuarial assumptions and those that actually occurred. **(PE)**

actuarial present value. The single amount as of a given evaluation date that results from applying actuarial assumptions to an amount or series of amounts payable or receivable at various times, with the amount(s) referred to being adjusted where appropriate to reflect expected changes from the valuation date to the date of expected payment or receipt by reason of expected salary changes, cost of living adjustments, or other changes and adjusted to reflect the time value of money (through discounts for interest) and the probability of payment (by means of decrements such as for death, disability, withdrawal, or retirement) between the valuation date and the expected date of payment or receipt. **(PE)**

actuarial valuation method. A procedure, using actuarial assumptions, for measuring the expected value of benefits and assigning such value to periods. **(PE)**

actuarially sound. When the amount of money in a pension fund and the current level of contributions to the fund are sufficient to meet the liabilities that have already accrued and that are accruing on a current basis. **(PE)**

actuary. A specialist trained in mathematics, statistics, and accounting who is responsible for rate, reserve, and dividend calculations and other statistical studies. **(G)**

acute care. Skilled, medically necessary care provided by medical and nursing personnel in order to restore a person to good health. **(H)**

additional drug benefit list. Prescription drugs listed as commonly prescribed by physicians for patients' long-term use. Subject to review and change by the health plan involved. Also called drug maintenance list. **(H)**

additional insured. A person other than the named insured who is protected under the terms of the contract. Usually, additional insureds are added by endorsement or referred to in the wording of the definition of *insured* in the policy itself. **(G)**

additional living expense insurance. A contract to reimburse the insured for increased living costs when loss of property forces the insured to maintain temporary residence elsewhere. Examples of these types of expenses are the cost for a hotel or motel, the extra cost for restaurant meals, and the cost of using a laundromat. The term *extra expense insurance* is defined with regard to additional expenses incurred by businesses. *See also* **loss of use. (PR)**

additional monthly benefit. Riders added to disability income policies to provide additional benefits during the first year of a claim while the insured is waiting for Social Security benefits to begin. **(H)**

additur. A situation in which the court increases a previous jury award. *See also* **remittitur. (LE)**

adhesion. This is a characteristic of a unilateral contract that is offered on a take it or leave it basis. Most insurance policies are contracts of adhesion because the terms are drawn up by the insurer and the insured simply adheres. For this reason, ambiguous provisions are often interpreted by courts in favor of the insured. *See also* **manuscript policy. (G)**

adjustable life. A form of life insurance that allows changes on the policy face amount, the amount of premium, period of protection, and the length of the premium payment period. *See also* **flexible premium adjustable life insurance policy. (LI)**

adjustable premium. The right of an insurer to change the premium rate on classes of insureds or blocks of business at the time of policy renewal. **(H, LI)**

adjusted community rating (ACR). Community rating adjusted by factors specific to a particular group. Also known as factored rating. **(H)**

adjusted gross estate. In the calculation of federal estate taxes, it is equal to the gross estate less specific deductions. **(EP)**

adjusted net worth. The capital, surplus, and voluntary reserves of an insurer, plus an estimated value for business on the books and unrealized capital gains, less the potential income tax on such gains. **(G)**

adjuster. A representative of the insurer who seeks to determine the extent of the firm's liability for loss when a claim is submitted. *See also* claim representative. **(G)**

adjuster, average. *See* average adjuster. **(OM)**

adjuster, independent. *See* independent adjuster. **(G)**

adjuster, public. *See* public adjuster. **(G)**

adjustment bureau. A firm organized to provide adjustment services to insurers not wishing to create their own claims division. **(G)**

administration bond. A bond furnished by the executor or administrator of an estate. It guarantees that the estate will be settled in accordance with the terms of the will or, if there is no will, in accordance with the law. It guarantees the fidelity of the executor or administrator. **(S)**

administrative services only. The services provided by an insurer, such as providing claim forms and processing claims, when the insurer is not the party funding the loss payments. *See also* self-funded plan. **(H, LI)**

administrator. A person appointed by a court as a fiduciary to settle the financial affairs and the estate of a deceased person. *See also* executor. **(LE)**

admiralty liability. All laws relating to liability resulting from any kind of maritime activity. This would include common law and statutory law, such as the Jones Act and the Seamen's Remedies. **(OM)**

admiralty proceeding. A type of proceeding involving questions of maritime suit. Any insurance claims involving ocean marine insurance would generally be settled by an admiralty court. **(OM)**

admissions/1,000. The number of hospital admissions for each 1,000 members of the health plan. **(H)**

admits. The number of admissions to a hospital (including outpatient and inpatient facilities). **(H)**

admitted (or allowed) assets. Assets whose values are permitted by state law to be included in the annual statement of the insurer. **(G)**

admitted company. An insurance company authorized and licensed to do business in a given state. **(G)**

admitted liability. A coverage for guests in an aircraft. In the event of an accident, with this coverage, guests can recover without having to go through a determination as to whether the insured was liable. It is written with a limit per seat in the aircraft. **(AV)**

adult day care. A group program for functionally impaired adults, designed to meet health, social, and functional needs in a setting away from the adult's home. **(H)**

advance funding. Periodically setting aside a predetermined sum of money to fund future retirement benefits of a pension plan. **(PE)**

advance payment. Premiums paid in advance of the current policy period, including the amount tendered with an application by an applicant for life insurance. **(G)**

advance premium. *See* deposit premium. **(G)**

adverse selection. The tendency of poorer than average risks to buy and maintain insurance. Adverse selection occurs when insureds select only coverages that are most likely to have losses. **(G)**

adverse underwriting decision. Any decision involving individually underwritten insurance coverages resulting in termination of existing insurance, declination of an application, or writing the coverage only at higher rates. For property and casualty insurance, it also includes placing the coverage with a residual market mechanism or an unauthorized insurer. **(G)**

advertising injury. Injury arising out of libel or slander; violation of the right to privacy; misappropriation of advertising ideas; or infringement of copyright, title, or slogan committed in the course of advertising goods, products, or services. *See also* **personal injury. (LA)**

affiant. The person who executes an affidavit. **(LE)**

affidavit. A written or printed declaration or statement of fact, made voluntarily and confirmed by the oath or affirmation of the party making it, and taken before an officer having authority to administer such oath. **(LE)**

affiliated companies. Insurers linked together through common stock ownership or through interlocking directorates. **(G)**

affirmed. When an appellate court declares that a judgment, decree, or order is valid and right and must stand as rendered in the lower court. **(LE)**

after charge. A charge sometimes included in fire rates for commercial buildings. It is usually added for conditions that can be corrected by the insured, such as failure to have the proper types of fire extinguishers. **(PR)**

aftercare. Individualized patient services required after hospitalization or rehabilitation. **(H)**

age change. The date on which a person's age, for insurance purposes, changes. In most life insurance contracts, this date is midway between the insured's natural birth dates. Health insurers frequently use the age of the previous birth date for rate determinations. On the date of age change, a person's age may change to that of the last birth date, the nearer birth date, or the next birth date, depending on the way in which the rating structure has been established by that particular insurer. **(H, LI)**

age limits. The ages below which or above which an insurer will not write certain forms of insurance or above which it will not continue a policy presently in force. **(G)**

agency. (1) When one person acts on behalf of another person, an agency is created; the first person is the agent and the second person is the principal. The principal generally can be held responsible for acts of its agents. **(LE)**. (2) An insurance sales office that is directed by a general agent, manager, independent agent, or company manager. **(G)**

agency company. An insurance company that produces business through an agency network. *See also* **direct writer. (G)**

agency contract (or agreement). The document that establishes the legal relationship between an agent and an insurer. **(G)**

agency plant. The total force of agents representing an insurer. **(G)**

agency system. *See* **independent agency system. (G)**

agent. One who solicits, negotiates, or effects contracts of insurance on behalf of an insurer. The agent's right to exercise various functions, authority, and obligations and the obligations of the insurer to the agent are subject to the terms of the agency contract with the insurer, to statutory law, and to common law. **(G)**

agent, general. *See* general agent. **(H, LI)**

agent, independent. *See* independent agent. **(G)**

agent, policywriting. *See* policywriting agent. **(G)**

agent, recording. *See* recording agent. **(PR)**

agent, special. *See* special agent. **(G)**

agent, state. *See* state agent. **(G)**

agent's appointment. Official authorization from an insurance company granting an agent the authority to act as its agent. In most states, agents must be appointed by at least one insurer in addition to being licensed by the state. **(G)**

agent's authority. The authority and power granted to an agent by the agency contract. The agent is also clothed with additional power under the legal concept of apparent agency. *See also* **apparent agency. (G)**

agent's balance. A periodic statement of the sums due and owed to an agent under the agent's contract with an insurer. **(G)**

agent's commission. The method by which an insurance company compensates its agents for placing insurance. The commission is usually a percentage of the premium for the policy. *See also* **commission. (G)**

agent's license. A certificate of authority from the state that permits the agent to conduct business. **(G)**

agent's qualification laws. Education, experience, and other requirements imposed by the state upon persons desiring to be licensed as agents. **(G)**

age/sex factor. Compares the age and sex risk of medical costs of one group relative to another. An age/sex factor above 1.00 indicates higher than average risk of medical costs due to that factor. Conversely, a factor below 1.00 indicates a lower than average risk. This measurement is used in underwriting. **(H)**

age/sex rates (ASR). Separate rates are established for each grouping of age and sex categories. Preferred over single and family rating because the rates and premiums automatically reflect changes in the age and sex content of the group. Also sometimes called table rates. **(H)**

aggregate excess of loss reinsurance. A form of excess of loss reinsurance that indemnifies the ceding company against the amount by which its losses incurred during a specific period, usually 12 months, exceed either (1) a predetermined dollar amount, or (2) a percentage of the company's premiums (loss ratio) for that period. This is commonly referred to as **stop loss reinsurance** or **excess of loss ratio reinsurance**. **(R)**

aggregate funding method. Accumulating money for a pension plan by actuarially determining the present value of all future benefit payments, deducting whatever funds may be on hand with the trustee or insurance company, and distributing the balance as a cost over the future. **(PE)**

aggregate indemnity. A maximum dollar amount that may be collected by the claimant for any disability, for any period of disability, or under the policy as a whole. **(H)**

aggregate limit. Usually refers to liability insurance and indicates the amount of coverage that the insured has under the contract for a specific period, usually the contract period, no matter how many separate accidents occur. **(G)**

aggregate products liability limit. This limit represents the amount of money an insurer will pay during the term of a policy for all products liability claims it covers. **(LA)**

agreed amount clause. Under this clause, the insured and the insurer agree that the amount of insurance carried will automatically satisfy the coinsurance clause. The effect is to eliminate the necessity of determining whether the amount carried is equal to the stated percentage of the actual cash value indicated in the coinsurance clause. **(PR)**

agreement. One of the elements of a legal contract. When an offer made by one party has been accepted by the other, with mutual understanding by both, an agreement exists. **(LE)**

AIDS-related complex (ARC). The term given to a variety of symptoms and opportunistic infections and conditions that frequently manifest themselves in patients suffering from AIDS (or acquired immunodeficiency syndrome), which is caused by the human immunodeficiency virus. **(H, LI)**

alcoholic beverage control laws. *See* dram shop laws. **(LE)**

alcoholic beverage liability insurance. *See* dram shop liability insurance. **(LE)**

aleatory contract. A contract in which the number of dollars to be given up by each party is not equal. Insurance contracts are of this type because the policyholder pays a premium and may collect nothing from the insurer or may collect a great deal more than the amount of the premium if a loss occurs. **(G)**

alien insurer. An insurer formed under the laws of a country other than the United States. A US company selling in other countries is also an alien insurer. **(G)**

alienated. In insurance, this term describes property that an insured no longer owns or holds title to. Generally, a public liability policy will cover the insured's liability for premises alienated by him. **(G)**

all or nothing rider. A rider to a health insurance policy that provides additional benefits in the event no benefits are payable under Social Security. If Social Security benefits are payable, no additional benefit is paid under the rider. **(H)**

Alliance of American Insurers (AAI). An association of insurance companies working together in the following areas of common interest: (1) government affairs affecting insurance; (2) education of the employees of member companies; (3) loss prevention; and (4) other insurance activities. **(G)**

allied health personnel. Health personnel who perform duties that would otherwise have to be performed by physicians, optometrists, dentists, podiatrists, nurses, and chiropractors. Also called paramedical personnel. **(H)**

allied lines. Various insurance coverages for additional types of losses, and against loss by additional perils, that are closely associated with and usually sold with fire insurance. Examples include coverage against loss by perils other than fire, coverage for sprinkler leakage damage, and business interruption coverage. The fire insurance field consists of coverages for fire and allied lines. **(PR)**

allocated benefits. Payments authorized for specific purposes with a maximum specified for each. In hospital policies, for instance, there may be scheduled benefits for x-rays, drugs, dressings, and other specified expenses. **(H)**

allocated funds. Qualified plan funds that are identified in the name of specific plan participants. **(PE)**

allocation formula. In a profit-sharing trust, the formula under which the employer's contributions are credited to employees. **(PE)**

allowable charge. The lesser of the actual charge, the customary charge, and the prevailing charge. It is the amount on which Medicare will base its Part B payment. **(H)**

allowable costs. Charges that qualify as covered expenses. **(H)**

allowed assets. *See* admitted assets. **(G)**

all risk insurance. The term was once used to mean insurance against loss of or damage to property arising from any cause except those that are specifically excluded. Today, all risk-type policies are known as special coverage forms. *See also* **open peril** and **named perils. (G, PR)**

alternative delivery systems. Systems that cover health care costs, other than on the usual fee-for-service basis. Could include HMOs, IPAs, PPOs, and so forth. **(H)**

Alzheimer's disease. A progressive, irreversible disease characterized by degeneration of the brain cells and severe loss of memory causing the individual to become dysfunctional and dependent on others for basic living needs. **(H)**

ambiguity. Terms or words in an insurance policy that make the meaning unclear or that can be interpreted in more than one way. The general rule of law is that any ambiguity in the policy is construed against the insurer and in favor of the insured. This is because the contract is one of adhesion—that is, the insured must adhere to what the insurer has written. If the insurer does not make its contract clear, it is responsible. **(G)**

ambulatory care. Similar to outpatient treatment in that it is care that does not require hospitalization. **(H)**

ambulatory setting. Institutions such as surgery centers, clinics, or other outpatient facilities that provide health care on an outpatient basis. **(H)**

amendment. A formal document that corrects or revises an insurance master policy. *See also* **endorsement** and **rider. (G)**

American Academy of Actuaries. A society concerned with the development of education in the field of actuarial science and with the enhancement of standards in the actuarial field. Members may use the designation MAAA (Member, American Academy of Actuaries). **(G)**

American agency system. *See* independent agency system. **(G)**

American Association of Insurance Services (AAIS). An association of insurance companies performing various technical functions for its members and subscribers. AAIS is licensed to operate in all states, the District of Columbia, and the Commonwealth of Puerto Rico. AAIS offers program services; files rates, rules, and forms on behalf of member and subscriber companies; acts as an official statistical agent; and offers a variety of professional services for its member companies. **(G)**

American College. An educational institution within the life insurance business. It confers the Chartered Life Underwriter designation and is concerned with continuing agents' training and with research and publication in areas related to the life insurance business. It also sponsors specialty life insurance courses and offers a college degree in financial services. It was formerly known as the American College of Life Underwriters (ACLU). **(LI)**

American Council of Life Insurance, Inc. An association made up of several previously independent insurance groups. It is concerned with legislative matters, intercompany communications, and the exchange of information. **(LI)**

American Experience Table of Mortality. A statement of expected mortality rates based on data accumulated in 1868 from a large number of insured persons. This table was widely used by life insurers until the 1950s to establish rates. **(LI)**

American Institute for Chartered Property and Casualty Underwriters, Inc. An insurance educational organization that establishes insurance standards and fosters educational work. Properly qualified individuals who pass a series of examinations given by this body receive the designation Chartered Property and Casualty Underwriter (CPCU). **(G)**

American Insurance Association (AIA). The informational, educational, technical, and legislative organization of the capital stock insurance companies in the property and liability fields. **(G)**

American Lloyd's. *See* Lloyd's Association. **(G)**

American Risk and Insurance Association. An association of insurance educators and others interested in insurance study and research. **(G)**

amortization. A method of spreading a fixed sum, together with accumulating interest, over a period of years. **(PE)**

amortized value. The value of bonds purchased by an insurance company which are eligible for amortization. For example, if a 10-year bond were purchased at $50 more than its face value, that $50 would be amortized or spread over the 10-year period. Each year the bonds would be valued at $5 less than the year before. **(G)**

amount at risk. The difference between the face amount of a whole life insurance contract and the cash value it has built up. The net amount at risk declines throughout the life of the contract, whereas the policy reserve increases along with the cash value. It is the amount the insurer would have to draw from its own funds rather than the policy reserve were the contract to become a death claim. **(LI)**

amount subject. The maximum amount that underwriters estimate can possibly be lost under the most unfavorable circumstances in any given loss, such as a fire or tornado. *See also* **probable maximum loss. (PR)**

ancillary. Additional services (other than room and board charges) such as x-rays, anesthesia, laboratory work, and so forth. Fees charged for ancillary care such as x-rays, anesthesia, and laboratory work. This term may also be used to describe the charge made by a pharmacy for prescriptions that exceed the health insurance plan's maximum allowable cost (MAC). **(H)**

ancillary benefits. Benefits for miscellaneous hospital charges. **(H)**

anniversary. *See* policy anniversary. **(G)**

annual additions. The total of employer contributions, voluntary employee contributions, and forfeited additions of terminated participants that equals the total annual contribution to a qualified retirement plan. **(PE)**

annual payment annuity. An annuity that was purchased by the payment of annual premiums for a specified period. **(AN, LI)**

annual (or yearly) renewable term (ART). (1) Term life insurance that may be renewed annually without evidence of insurability until some stated age. (2) A form of life, and sometimes health, reinsurance in which the reinsurer assumes only the mortality risk, which is usually calculated as the face amount of reinsurance minus the terminal reserve. **(H, LI)**

annual report. The insurer's published statement to its stockholders (or policyholders, in the case of a mutual insurance company), giving pertinent financial information and reviewing the year's activities. **(G)**

annual return/report (Form 5500). A required annual report reflecting the pension plan's operation for the year, to be submitted to the IRS and the Department of Labor. **(PE)**

annual statement. A report to the state insurance department of the year's financial results. The insurer's income and expenses are stated in detail, as well as its assets and liabilities. **(G)**

annuitant. The person who is covered by an annuity and who will normally receive the benefits of the annuity. **(AN)**

annuity. (1) An amount of money payable yearly, or by extension, at other regular intervals; (2) An agreement by an insurer to make periodic payments that continue during the survival of the annuitant(s) or for a specified period. **(AN)**

annuity certain. An annuity that pays income for a fixed number of years regardless of whether the insured lives or dies. If it pays for life after the certain period, it is called an annuity certain and for life thereafter. **(AN)**

annuity due. An annuity under which the benefits are paid at the beginning of the benefit period rather than at the end. **(AN)**

annuity option. A method of liquidating and distributing an annuity's principal and interest so that it lasts for the lifetime of the annuitant. **(AN)**

annuity period. The period, usually at retirement, during which the annuitant begins to receive annuity payments or benefits from the insurance company. **(AN)**

annuity with period certain. An annuity that pays throughout the life of the insured but that also guarantees to pay income for a specific number of years regardless of whether the insured lives or dies. If the insured is living at the end of the time specified in the policy, benefits continue beyond the guaranteed period until the death of the insured. **(AN)**

answer. A statement made by the defendant and filed with a court to respond to a complaint or action that has been brought against the defendant. It states why the defendant should not be held liable. **(LE)**

anticoercion law. A provision usually contained in a section of the state code titled Unfair Trade Practices or a similar name, declaring the use of coercion to be an unfair practice and, hence, a violation of the state law. **(G)**

antiselection. *See* adverse selection. **(G)**

app. A trade expression for the insurance application. *See* **application. (G)**

apparent agency. *See* presumption of agency. **(G)**

apparent authority. Authority of an agent that is created when the agent oversteps actual authority and when inaction by the insurer does nothing to counter the public impression that such authority exists. **(G)**

appeal. The right of a party who has received an adverse decision to take the case to a higher court for review. **(LE)**

appellant. The person making an appeal to the higher court. **(LE)**

appellate. Refers to courts that hear appeals for review of decisions rendered by a lower court. **(LE)**

appellee. Also called the respondent. The person against whom the appellant is making his appeal. **(LE)**

applicable credit amount. A credit that can be applied against the federal gift or estate taxes. Formerly known as the unified credit. **(EP)**

application. A form on which the prospective insured states facts requested by the insurer and on the basis of which, together with information from other sources, the insurer decides whether to accept the risk, modify the coverage offered, or decline the risk. *See* **app. (G)**

appointment. *See* agent's appointment. **(G)**

apportionment. The method of dividing a loss among insurers in the same proportions as their participation when two or more companies cover the same loss. **(G)**

appraisal. An evaluation of property made to ascertain either the appropriate amount of insurance to be written or the amount of loss to be paid. **(G)**

approved. The condition that exists when the person or object to be insured meets the underwriting standards of the insurer. **(G)**

approved charge. Amounts paid under Medicare as the maximum fee for a covered service. **(H)**

approved health care facility or program. A facility or program that has been approved by a health care plan as described in the contract. **(H)**

approved pension plan. A pension plan qualifying for tax exemptions under provisions of the Internal Revenue Code. **(PE)**

approved roof. A term used in building construction. It indicates a roof made of fire-resistive materials such as tile or asphalt shingles. **(G)**

appurtenant structures. Buildings on the same premises as the main building insured under a property insurance policy. Most dwelling property insurance policies cover appurtenant structures under most circumstances. **(PR)**

arbitration clause. The provision in a property insurance contract stating that if the insurer and insured cannot agree on an appropriate claim settlement, each will appoint an appraiser, and these appraisers will select a neutral umpire. A decision by any two of the three prescribes a settlement and binds both parties to it. **(PR)**

Archer Medical Savings Account (MSA). An employer-funded account linked to a high-deductible medical indemnity plan. Usually, the employer raises the plan deductible (usually by 300% to 400%) and, in turn, returns a portion of the premium savings to employees as contributions to the medical savings account. Employees can use the contributions to pay for health care expenses throughout the year, and at the end of the year may withdraw whatever remains in the account as cash. **(H)**

Armstrong Investigation. A study authorized by the New York state legislature in 1905 that reviewed the operations and practices of life insurers operating in the state. Numerous changes in policy forms and investment practices came from the study and were eventually reflected in other state codes. **(LI)**

arson. The willful and deliberate burning of property. **(LE)**

assailing thieves. Those other than the crew using force or violence to steal a ship or its cargo. Such action is an insured peril under an ocean marine contract. **(OM)**

assessed value. The value of real estate or personal property as determined by a governmental unit, such as a city, for the purpose of determining taxes. **(G)**

assessment company, society, or insurer. An insurer who retains the right to assess policyholders' additional amounts if premiums are insufficient for operations. In some cases, an assessment insurer may not charge a stipulated premium at all but will merely assess participants in the plan a pro rata share of each claim filed plus expenses. **(G)**

asset share value. The value of a book of business to an insurer, assuming that the business has been in force long enough to show true mortality rates. This value must be known by the insurer to make rates and also to sell the business. If assets share values do not grow properly, either the rates have been too low or the expenses have been too high. **(LI)**

assets. The items on the balance sheet of the insurer that show the book value of property owned. Under state regulations, not all property or other resources can be admitted in the statement of the insurer, which gives rise to the term *nonadmitted assets. See also* **nonadmitted assets. (G)**

assigned risk. A risk that is not ordinarily acceptable to insurers and that is, therefore, assigned to insurers participating in an assigned risk pool or plan. Each participating company agrees to accept its share of these risks. **(G)**

assignee. A person to whom policy rights are assigned in whole or in part by the original policyowner. **(LE)**

assignment. An authorization to pay Medicare benefits directly to the provider. Medicare payments may be assigned to participating providers only. **(H)**

assignment. Transfer by the policyowner of legal rights or interest in the policy contract to a third party. Most policies cannot be assigned without the permission of the insurer. **(LE)**

assignment. The transfer of the ownership rights of a life insurance policy from one person to another. The term also refers to the document that effects the transfer. **(LI)**

assignment of benefits. A method whereby the person receiving the medical benefits assigns the payment of those benefits to a physician or hospital. **(H)**

Associate in Risk Management. A professional designation granted by the American Institute for Property and Casualty Underwriters to individuals who have completed a series of examinations. **(G)**

association. *See* **pool** and **syndicate. (G)**

association group insurance. Technically, group insurance issued to an association rather than to an employer or a union. **(H, LI)**

Association of Life Insurance Counsel. An organization of life company attorneys that seeks to increase knowledge in areas of the law affecting life insurance. **(LI)**

assume. To accept from another insurer all or part of the risk of an insured loss. **(R)**

assumed interest rate (AIR). An assumed value assigned to the annuitant's account during the annuity period. It is an estimated return for the separate account. Monthly annuity payments are based on the AIR in relation to the actual rate of return experienced by the separate account of a variable annuity. **(AN)**

assumed liability. *See* contractual liability. **(LA)**

assumption. An amount accepted by the reinsurer. **(R)**

assumption certificate. A statement of coverage by the reinsurer under which payment is guaranteed to a party not in privity with the reinsurance contract. *See also* cut-through clause. **(R)**

assumption of risk. One of the common-law defenses available to an individual. For example, one person riding with another in an automobile has generally assumed the risk and, therefore, has no action against the driver of the vehicle should an accident occur. This is a common-law concept and has been modified by recent case law and by statute in some jurisdictions. **(LE)**

assurance. *See* insurance. **(G)**

assured. *See* insured. **(G)**

assurer. *See* insurer. **(G)**

atomic energy reinsurance. *See* mutual atomic energy reinsurance pool. **(LA)**

attachment. A court order allowing one person to take something of value belonging to another into custody for a particular purpose. For example, if an individual is at fault in an automobile accident, the insured person may receive a court order attaching the first individual's automobile in settlement of the claim. The purpose of the attachment is to make sure something of value is available to settle the claim if the individual is held liable. **(LE)**

attained age. The age an insured has reached on a given date. **(LI)**

attending physician's statement (APS). A source of medical information used when underwriting a life or health insurance policy, usually obtained from the proposed insured's doctor. **(H, LI)**

attested will. A formal type of will that is produced (e.g., handwritten or typed), signed by the testator, and witnessed. **(EP)**

attorney-in-fact. The individual who manages a reciprocal insurance exchange and to whom each subscriber gives authority to exchange insurance on the subscriber's behalf with other subscribers. *See also* **reciprocal insurance exchange. (G)**

attractive nuisance. An artificial structure or condition, rather than a naturally occurring part of the land or property, that is especially attractive to children and capable of resulting in harm to them. Property owners are legally obligated to protect trespassing children against harm caused by attractive nuisances. **(LE)**

audit. A survey of the insured's payroll records to determine the premium that should be paid for the coverage furnished. Used in workers' compensation and general liability policies. **(LA, WC)**

audit bureau. A stamping office. A central office or bureau to which agents and companies send certain daily reports and endorsements for auditing before transmittal to the insurer. **(G)**

authorization. The amount of insurance an underwriter will agree to accept on a risk of a given class on specific property. It is given for the guidance and information of agents. **(G)**

authorized insurer. An insurer authorized by the state to transact business in that state for specific types of insurance. **(G)**

automatic cover. Coverage given automatically by a policy, usually for a specified period and limited amount, to cover increasing values and newly acquired and changing interests. **(G)**

automatic increase in insurance endorsement. *See* inflation guard endorsement. **(PR)**

automatic premium loan. A provision in a life policy authorizing the insurer to use the loan value to pay any premiums still due at the end of the grace period. **(LI)**

automatic reinstatement clause. A stipulation in a property insurance policy stating that after a partial loss covered by the policy has been paid, the original limit of the policy will be automatically reinstated. **See also loss clause. (PR)**

automatic reinsurance. (1) This form of reinsurance, also known as treaty reinsurance, is one whereby an insurer must cede that portion of a risk that is above the limit established by contract, and the reinsurer must accept all risks ceded to it. **(H, LI)**. (2) Reinsurance of specified types of risks that is automatically ceded and accepted within the terms of the contract, called a treaty, without consideration of each one individually. The reinsurance takes effect as soon as the original contract is in force. *See also* **obligatory reinsurance** and **facultative reinsurance. (R)**

automobile fleet. Refers to a number of automobiles under the same ownership. For insurance purposes, a fleet usually consists of five or more self-propelled units and generally qualifies for certain premium reductions and rating plans. **(AU)**

automobile insurance. A type of insurance that protects the insured against losses involving automobiles. Different coverages can be purchased depending on the needs and wants of the insured (e.g., the liability coverages of bodily injury liability, property damage liability, and medical payments, and the physical damage coverages of collision and comprehensive). **(AU)**

automobile insurance plans. The name used to identify assigned risk plans for auto insurance. *See* **assigned risk. (AU)**

average adjuster. One whose primary work is the adjusting of ocean marine losses. **(OM)**

average benefit test. A coverage or discrimination test for a qualified plan stating that at least 50% of the lower paid employees must benefit from the plan and that the average benefit provided must be at least 70% of the benefit provided for the higher-paid employees. **(PE)**

average clause. A clause providing that similar items in one location or several locations that are insured by a policy will be covered in the proportion that the value of each bears to the value of all. Previously known as the pro rata distribution clause and the average distribution clause. *See also* **pro rata distribution clause. (PR)**

average cost per claim. The total cost of administrative and/or medical services divided by the number of units of exposure, such as costs divided by number of admissions, cost divided by number of outpatient claims, and so forth. **(H)**

average indexed monthly earnings (AIME). A wage indexing formula based on earnings listed in the records of the Social Security Administration; used to compute Social Security benefits for retirement, survivor benefits, and disability income benefits. **(PE)**

average length of stay (ALOS). The total number of patient days divided by the number of admissions and discharges during a specified period, which equals the average number of days in the hospital for each person admitted. **(H)**

average rate. A rate for a policy established by multiplying the rate for each location by the value at that location and dividing the sum of the results by the total value. **(PR)**

average weekly wage. A term generally used in workers' compensation laws. It is the basis for determining weekly benefits under such laws. **(WC)**

aviation accident insurance. A form of insurance that protects individuals as passengers or pilots, usually on scheduled aircraft, or that covers the flight travel of the employees of a company under a master policy. **(LI)**

aviation hazard. The extra hazard of death or injury resulting from participation in aeronautics, usually as other than a fare-paying passenger in licensed aircraft. This generally requires an extra premium rating or waiver of certain benefits or coverage. **(LI)**

aviation insurance. A type of policy that protects an insured against losses connected with the use of an airplane. Coverage can be purchased depending on the needs and desires of the insured and can include the liability coverages of bodily injury, property damage, passenger bodily injury, and medical payments, as well as physical damage or hull coverage. Hull coverage can be written to provide either broad or limited coverage. Coverage can also be written for airports, aircraft dealers, airlines, and hangarkeepers liability. **(AV)**

avoidance of risk. Taking steps to remove a hazard, engage in an alternative activity, or otherwise end a specific exposure. One of the four major risk management techniques. *See* **risk management. (G)**

B

BI. (1) *See* **bodily injury liability**. This is what these letters most often refer to in the liability field. **(LA)**. (2) *See* **business interruption insurance** and **business income coverage form**. This is what these letters most often refer to in the property field. **(PR)**

PRESENTATION OF TERMS

backdating. A procedure for making the effective date of a policy earlier than the application date. Backdating is often used to make the age at issue lower than it actually was to get a lower premium. State laws often limit to six months the time to which policies can be backdated. **(H, LI)**

bail bond. A form of bond given to guarantee that a person released from legal confinement will appear as required in court, or the penalty of the bond will be forfeited to the court. In insurance policies, bail bond fees are covered under an automobile policy. **(S)**

bailee. A person or concern that has possession of personal property entrusted to that person by the owner. An example would be a laundry that has custody of customers' clothing for washing or dry cleaning. Bailees are required to exercise the same care with the property of others as they would with their own property. **(LE)**

bailees customer insurance. Insurance purchased by a bailee to protect the personal property of customers against loss caused by specific perils. An example would be a carpet cleaner who buys coverage to protect customers against loss or damage to their carpets while in the store's care. **(IM)**

bailees liability coverage. Coverage that meets the needs of a bailee's liability. The bailee's legal responsibility is to exercise care appropriate to the circumstances of the bailment. In addition, most bailees want to carry enough insurance to make good any loss to property in their custody, whether or not they are legally liable. **(IM)**

bailment. The personal property of one person being held by another with the intent that it will be returned to the original owner. Cars in a garage for repairs would be an example of a bailment. **(LE)**

bailor. A person who owns property that has been entrusted to another. The owner of a fur coat who has entrusted it to a furrier for storage would be a bailor. **(LE)**

balance sheet. An accounting term that refers to a listing of the assets, liabilities, and surplus of a company or individual as of a specific date. **(G)**

bank loan plan. *See* financed insurance. **(LI)**

bankers blanket bond. A type of insurance coverage purchased by banks to pay for losses caused by the dishonesty of employees as well as losses caused by people other than employees as the result of burglary, robbery, larceny, theft, forgery, and mysterious disappearance. **(C)**

barratry. A fraudulent breach of duty on the part of a master of a ship causing loss to the owner of the ship or the owner of the cargo. **(OM)**

base capitation. The total amount that covers the cost of health care per person, minus any mental health or substance abuse services, pharmacy, and administrative charges. **(H)**

base premium. *See* subject premium. **(R)**

basic auto policy. Once used to insure commercial vehicles, motorcycles, motor scooters, and a variety of substandard risks. This policy had broad eligibility rules, but the scope of coverage was narrower than modern auto policies. Most automobile risks today are insured by business or personal auto policies, with appropriate endorsements. **(AU)**

basic coverage form. Any of the commercial or personal lines property forms that provide basic coverages. These forms generally provide the most limited coverage, which is surpassed by broad forms and special forms. **(PR)**

basic extended reporting period. An automatic tail for reporting claims after expiration of a claims-made liability policy. It is provided without charge and consists of two parts: a **mini tail** covers claims made within 60 days after the end of the policy, and a **midi tail** covers claims made within five years after the end of the policy period arising out of occurrences reported no later than 60 days after the end of the policy. **(LA)**

basic form rates. Under the latest commercial lines program, basic form rates are arrived at by adding group I and group II rates together. *See also* **group I rates** and **group II rates**. **(PR)**

basic hospital expense insurance. Hospital coverage providing benefits for room and board and miscellaneous hospital expenses for a specified number of days during hospital confinement. **(H)**

basic limit. Usually refers to liability policies and indicates the lowest amount for which a policy can be written. This amount is either prescribed by law or company policy. **(G)**

basic limits of liability. Minimum amounts of insurance. The term is usually used in reference to bodily injury and property damage limits that are either the lowest amounts that can be written at the published or manual rates, the minimum amount of insurance an insurer is willing to underwrite, or the minimum amount of insurance required by law (e.g., automobile insurance financial responsibility laws). **(AU, LA)**

basic medical expense insurance. Basic medical coverage for doctor visits, diagnostic x-rays, laboratory tests, and emergency treatments. Usually written without deductibles and coinsurance provisions, but benefits are limited to specified dollar amounts. *See also* **major medical insurance**. **(H)**

basic premium. A fixed cost charged in a retrospective rating plan. It is a percentage of the standard premium and is designed to give the insurer the money needed for administrative expenses and the agent's commission plus an insurance charge. *See also* **retrospective rating**. **(G)**

basic rate. The manual rate from which discounts are taken or to which charges are added to reflect the individual circumstances of a risk. **(G)**

bed days/1,000. The number of inpatient hospital days per 1,000 members of the health plan. **(H)**

below market loan. A demand loan with interest paid below the federal rate; typically, part of an executive loan program provided by an employer. **(PE)**

bench error. A term used in products insurance that describes a loss that occurs in the production process. For example, if production workers mistakenly use the wrong ingredients in a chemical formula, a bench error has occurred. Bench errors are covered. **(LA)**

beneficiary. A person who may become eligible to receive or is receiving benefits under an insurance policy other than a participant. *See also* **irrevocable beneficiary, revocable beneficiary, primary beneficiary, secondary beneficiary, tertiary beneficiary,** and **contingent beneficiary. (LI)**

benefit. The amount to be paid to a participant of a retirement plan or to the participant's beneficiary at retirement, at death, or at termination of service. **(PE)**

benefit, flat dollar. A certain monthly benefit given to all employees regardless of length of service or standard of living. Everybody receives the same amount. **(PE)**

benefit, flat percentage. A monthly pension benefit determined by a fixed percentage of compensation. Although it recognizes the employee's standard of living, it ignores the employee's length of service. **(PE)**

benefit levels. The maximum amount a person is entitled to receive for a particular service or services as spelled out in the contract with a health plan or insurer. **(H)**

benefit package. A description of the services the insurer or health plan offers to those covered under the terms of a health insurance contract. **(H)**

benefit period. Defines the period during which a Medicare beneficiary is eligible for Part A benefits. A benefit period is 90 days and begins the day the patient is admitted to a hospital and ends when the individual has not been hospitalized for a period of 60 consecutive days. **(H)**

benefits. The financial reimbursement and other services provided insureds by insurers under the terms of an insurance contract. An example would be the benefits listed under a life or health insurance policy or benefits prescribed by a workers' compensation law. **(G)**

benefits of survivorship. *See* **survivorship benefits. (LI)**

betterment. *See* **improvements and betterments insurance. (PR)**

bid bond. A bond filed with a bid for a construction or other project guaranteeing that if the contractor has the low bid and is awarded the job, the required performance bond will be furnished. **(S)**

billed claims. The amounts submitted by a health care provider for services provided to a covered individual. **(H)**

binder. An agreement executed by an agent or insurer (usually the latter) putting insurance into force before the contract has been written or the premium paid. This term is not usually used in life insurance. *See also* **cover note. (G)**

binding receipt. *See* conditional binding receipt. **(H, LI)**

birthday rule. One method of determining which parent's medical coverage will be primary for dependent children; the parent whose birthday falls earliest in the year will be considered as having the primary plan. **(H)**

birth rate. The number of births related to the total population in a given group during a period. It is usually expressed as births per 100,000 people in one year. **(G)**

blackout period. The period during which a surviving spouse no longer receives survivors benefits (after the youngest child is no longer eligible) and before he is eligible for retirement benefits. **(LI)**

blanket bond. A type of fidelity bond that covers losses caused by the dishonesty of all employees as opposed to bonds that specifically identify only certain employees to be covered. *See also* **blanket position bond, commercial blanket bond, name position bond,** and **name schedule bond. (C)**

blanket contract. *See* blanket insurance. **(G)**

blanket crime policy. A policy that once provided a package of coverages for employee dishonesty, loss of money and securities inside and outside the premises, depositor's forgery, loss of money orders, and loss due to counterfeit paper currency. This policy has been replaced by modern commercial crime coverage forms. **(C)**

blanket fidelity bond. *See* blanket bond. **(C)**

blanket honesty bond. *See* commercial blanket bond. **(S)**

blanket insurance. (1) A contract of health insurance that covers all of a class of persons not individually identified in the contract. **(H)**. (2) A form of property insurance that covers, in a single contract, either multiple types of property at a single location or one or more types of property at multiple locations. **(PR)**

blanket medical expense. A policy or provision in a health insurance contract that pays all medical costs, including hospitalization, drugs, and treatments, without limitation on any item except for possibly a maximum aggregate benefit under the policy. It is often written with an initial deductible amount. **(H)**

blanket position bond. A blanket fidelity bond in which the amount of coverage applies separately to each position covered. *See also* **commercial blanket bond**, which provides a single amount of coverage for any one loss, regardless of the number of employees involved in the loss, and **blanket bond. (C)**

blasting and explosion exclusion. Exclusion of liability for damages from blasting or explosions. Rates for the types of construction work followed by the letter **X** in the manual exclude this coverage. If it is desired, an additional rate must be charged. **(LA)**

block policy. An open perils (all risk) policy that derives its name from the French term *en bloc*, meaning all together. It provides coverage on stock, property being transported, property in bailment, and the property of the insured on the premises of others. **(PR)**

blowout and cratering. Industry terms having to do with accidents that can arise from drilling operations. Generally, they are either excluded under the liability policy or can be added by endorsement for an additional premium, depending on the judgment of the underwriter. **(LA)**

Blue Cross. Blue Cross plans are hospital expense prepayment plans designed primarily to provide benefits for hospitalization coverage, with certain restrictions on the type of accommodations to be used. **(H)**

Blue plan. A generic designation for companies that usually write a service, rather than a reimbursement, contract and that are authorized to use the designation Blue Cross or Blue Shield and the insignia of either. **(H)**

Blue Shield. Blue Shield plans are prepayment plans offered by service organizations covering medical and surgical expenses. **(H)**

board certified. A physician or other professional who has passed an examination that certifies him as a specialist in a particular medical area. **(H)**

board eligible. A professional person or physician who is eligible to take a specialty examination. **(H)**

bobtailing. Using the truck-tractor after unloading the trailer and not driving for trucking purposes. **(AU)**

bodily injury liability (BI). A legal liability that may arise as a result of the injury or death of another person. **(LA)**

boiler and machinery insurance. Insurance against the sudden and accidental breakdown of boilers, machinery, and electrical equipment. Coverage can be extended to cover consequential losses and loss from interruption of business. Also called equipment breakdown protection coverage. **(PR)**

bond. A three-party contract guaranteeing that if one person, the principal, fails to perform as specified or proves to be dishonest, the person to whom the duty is owed, the obligee, will be financially protected by the issuer of the bond, the surety. **(S)**

bond, contract. *See* contract bond. **(S)**

bond, court. *See* court bond. **(S)**

bond, fidelity. *See* fidelity bond. **(S)**

bond, fiduciary. *See* fiduciary bond. **(S)**

bond, forgery. *See* forgery bond. **(S)**

bond, maintenance. *See* maintenance bond. **(S)**

bond, performance. *See* contract bond. **(S)**

bond, permit. *See* permit bond. **(S)**

bond, public official. *See* public official bond. **(S)**

bond, surety. *See* suretyship. **(S)**

book of business. A total of all insurance accounts written by a company or agent. It may be treated in different ways. Examples include an insurer's book of automobile business, an agent's overall book of business, and an agent's book of business with each insurer. **(G)**

book value. Refers to the value of assets as shown in the official accounting records of the company. **(G)**

bordereau. (1) A written report of individual cessions, usually detailed to show such items as reinsurance premiums or reinsurance losses with respect to specific risks. (2) A memorandum containing information concerning documents that accompany it. Used extensively in passing reinsurance from one insurer to another under a reinsurance agreement and by property and liability general agents for passing information to various insurers on coverages written. **(G, R)**

borderline risk. An insurance prospect of doubtful quality from an underwriting point of view. **(G)**

Boston plan. Plan under which insurers agree that they will not reject property coverage on residential buildings in a slum area. Instead, they will accept the coverage until there has been an inspection and the owner has had an opportunity to correct any faults. Boston was the first city to originate such a plan, and many other cities have followed, including New York, Oakland, Cleveland, and Buffalo. **(PR)**

bottomry. A contract of insurance by which a ship or its cargo is pledged as collateral for a loan required to support a maritime venture. If the ship or cargo is lost, the loan is canceled and the borrower does not have to repay the loan. **(OM)**

boycott. An unfair trade practice that occurs when someone in the insurance business refuses to have business dealings with another until he complies with certain conditions or concessions. **(G)**

branch manager. An executive who manages a branch office for an insurer or an agency. *See also* **regional office. (G)**

branch office. *See* **regional office. (G)**

brick construction. Refers to a building in which at least 75% of the exterior walls are of some type of masonry construction (i.e., brick, stone, or hollow masonry tile; poured concrete or reinforced concrete; or hollow masonry block). **(G)**

brick veneer construction. Refers to a building in which the outside walls are constructed of wood with a facing of a single layer of brick. **(G)**

brief. A statement prepared by an attorney, to be filed with a court, that highlights the principal issues of a case. **(LE)**

broad form. A term generally used to designate policies that provide insurance for multiple types of perils over and above the usual basic perils or additional coverages beyond standard coverages. **(LA, PR)**

broad form nuclear energy liability exclusion endorsement. A form that must be attached to every general liability coverage part. It excludes coverage for any loss resulting from the hazardous properties of nuclear material related to the operations of a nuclear facility. **(LA)**

broad form personal theft policy. Theft coverage on personal property at private residences, usually on an open perils (all risk) basis. This type of coverage is most often part of a homeowners contract. A limited form of the broad form personal theft policy is known as the personal theft policy. **(C)**

broad form property damage endorsement. An endorsement to a general liability policy that deletes the exclusion referring to property in the care, custody, or control of the insured and replaces it with a less restrictive exclusion. **(LA)**

broad form storekeepers insurance. A form of coverage for small storekeepers. It includes several specific crime perils on the same basis as a storekeepers burglary and robbery policy, plus open perils (all risk) protection on money, securities, and depositors' forgery, and a small limit on employee dishonesty. *See also* **storekeepers burglary** and **robbery insurance. (C)**

broad theft coverage endorsement. This form may be attached to a dwelling policy to provide theft coverage for a named insured who is an owner occupant. **(PR)**

broker. One who represents an insured in the solicitation, negotiation, or procurement of contracts of insurance and who may render services incidental to those functions. By law, the broker may also be an agent of the insurer for certain purposes such as delivery of the policy or collection of the premium. **(G)**

broker of record. A broker who has been designated to handle certain insurance contracts for the policyholder. **(G)**

brokerage. (1) The fee or commission received by a broker. (2) Insurance placed by brokers contrasted with that placed by agents. **(G)**

brokerage business. Business offered to an insurer by a broker, which is sometimes called excess or surplus business. **(G)**

brokerage department. A department of an insurer whose purpose is to deal with brokers in the placing of insurance. **(G)**

broker/agent. One acting as an agent of one or more insurers and as a broker in dealing with one or more other insurers. **(G)**

builder's risk coverage form. A commercial property coverage form specifically designed for buildings in the course of construction. **(PR)**

building and personal property coverage form. A commercial property coverage form designed to insure most types of commercial property (buildings, or contents, or both). It is the most frequently used commercial property form and has replaced the general property form, special building form, special personal property form, and others. **(PR)**

building code. Municipal or other governmental ordinances regulating the type of construction of buildings within its jurisdiction. **(G)**

bullion. Refers to precious metals, such as gold, in the form of ingots or bars. **(G)**

bumbershoot policy. A liability policy similar to the umbrella policy that includes coverage related to ocean marine risks. In addition to general liability coverage, protection and indemnity can be provided, as can liability under the Longshoremen's and Harbor Workers' Act. Collision coverage can be provided, and general average and salvage charges can be included. A shipyard would be interested in a bumbershoot policy. **(LA)**

bureau, rating. *See* rating bureau. **(G)**

burglary. Breaking and entering into the premises of another with felonious intent, leaving visible signs of forcible entry or exit. **(C)**

burglary insurance. Insurance against loss caused by burglars. In personal lines, burglary insurance is provided by homeowners policies and theft endorsements, which may be added to dwelling policies. In commercial lines, a variety of commercial crime coverage forms include burglary insurance. **(C, PR)**

burning cost ratio. *See* pure loss cost ratio. **(R)**

burning ratio. The ratio of losses suffered to the amount of insurance in effect. **(G)**

business. (1) In property, liability, and health lines, it usually refers to the volume of premiums. **(G)**. (2) The face amount of life insurance written. **(LI)**

business auto coverage form. The latest commercial automobile insurance coverage form, which may be written as a monoline policy or as part of a commercial package. This form has largely replaced the business auto policy. **(AU)**

business auto policy. A policy that provided liability and physical damage coverages on commercial vehicles. In most jurisdictions, this policy has been replaced by the business auto coverage part. **(AU)**

business income coverage form. A commercial property form providing coverage for indirect losses resulting from property damage, such as loss of business income and extra expenses incurred. It has replaced earlier business interruption and extra expense forms. **(PR)**

business insurance. (1) Commercial insurance. The term is generally used to refer to insurance for businesses or commercial establishments as opposed to insurance for the personal protection of individuals. **(G)**. (2) Life and health policies written for business purposes, such as key employee, sole proprietorship, partnership, and corporation. **(H, LI)**

business interruption insurance. A time element coverage that pays for loss of earnings when operations are curtailed or suspended because of property loss due to an insured peril. Now referred to as business income insurance. *See* **business income coverage form. (PR)**

business interruption insurance, contingent. Now referred to as coverage for business income from dependent properties. *See* **business income coverage form** and **dependent properties. (PR)**

business liability. The term used to describe the liability coverages provided by the businessowners liability coverage form. It includes liability for bodily injury, property damage, personal injury, advertising injury, and fire damage. **(LA)**

business overhead expense. A disability income policy that indemnifies the business for certain overhead expenses incurred when the businessowner is totally disabled. **(H)**

business personal property. Traditionally known as *contents*, this term actually refers to furniture, fixtures, equipment, machinery, merchandise, materials, and all other personal property owned by the insured and used in the insured's business. **(PR)**

business risk exclusion. Also known as the (product) failure to perform exclusion. In products insurance, no coverage is provided for a product that does not meet the level of performance, quality, fitness, or durability warranted or represented by the insured. Coverage is provided, however, if liability results from a **bench error** or an **active malfunction**. *See also* the definitions of those two terms. **(LA)**

businessowners policy. A package policy that provides broad property and liability coverage in a single contract and is designed for small- and medium-sized mercantile, office, or apartment risks. **(LA, PR)**

buy-back deductible. A deductible that may be eliminated for an additional premium to provide first-dollar coverage. **(G)**

buy-sell agreement. (1) An agreement among part-owners of a business stating that under stated conditions—that is, disability or death—the person withdrawing from the business or the person's heirs are legally obligated to sell their interest to the remaining part-owners, and the remaining part-owners are legally obligated to buy at a price fixed in the agreement. (2) A similar agreement between an owner or part-owner of a business and a nonowner, such as a key employee. **(LI)**

buyers guide. A consumer publication that describes the type of coverage being offered and provides general information to help an applicant for life or health insurance compare different types of policies and reach a decision about whether the proposed coverage is appropriate. Also known as a shoppers guide. **(H, LI)**

bypass trust. Also referred to as the B trust, a trust that contains estate assets that will bypass the surviving spouse and pass directly to other family members. **(EP)**

C

CAS. *See* Casualty Actuarial Society. **(G)**

CCRCs. *See* continuing care retirement communities (CCRCs). **(H)**

CGL. *See* commercial general liability coverage part. **(LA)**

CLU. *See* Chartered Life Underwriter. **(LI)**

CMS. *See* Centers for Medicare and Medicaid Services. **(H)**

COB. Coordination of benefits. *See* nonduplication of benefits. **(H)**

COBRA. *See* Consolidated Omnibus Budget Reconciliation Act of 1986. **(H)**

CPCU. *See* Chartered Property and Casualty Underwriter. **(G)**

CREF. *See* College Retirement Equities Fund. **(LI)**

CSI 1961. *See* Commissioners' Standard Industrial Mortality Table, 1961. **(LI)**

CSO. *See* Commissioners' Standard Ordinary. **(LI)**

PRESENTATION OF TERMS

cafeteria plans. An employee benefit that provides a series of flexible health care benefits from which an employee may choose, including a cash only option. **(H)**

calendar year. January 1 through December 31 of the same year. Many deductible amount provisions are on a calendar year basis under major medical plans. Also, benefits under basic hospital surgical and medical plans are usually stated as so much for each calendar year. **(H)**

calendar year experience. This measures the premiums and losses entered on accounting records during the 12-month calendar. **(G)**

cancelable. A contract of insurance that may be terminated by the insurer or insured at any time. Practically every form of insurance is cancelable, except life insurance and health insurance policies designated as either guaranteed renewable or noncancelable and guaranteed renewable. Some states also regulate when or whether automobile policies can be canceled. **(G)**

cancellation. Termination of a contract of insurance in force by voluntary act of the insurer or insured in accordance with the provisions in the contract or by mutual agreement. **(G)**

cancellation, flat. *See* flat cancellation. **(G)**

cancellation, pro rata. *See* pro rata cancellation. **(G)**

cancellation, short rate. *See* short rate cancellation. **(G)**

capacity. The largest amount of insurance or reinsurance available from a company. In a broader sense, it can refer to the largest amount of insurance or reinsurance available in the marketplace. **(G)**

capital stock. The shares of ownership in a corporation. **(G)**

capital stock insurer. *See* stock insurer. **(G)**

capital sum. The maximum lump sum payable in the event of accidental death or dismemberment. **(G)**

capital transaction. The sale of a capital asset, such as stock, that results in the transaction being taxed as ordinary income and not as a dividend. **(G)**

capitation (CAP). A rate paid, usually monthly, to a health care provider. In return, the provider agrees to deliver the health services agreed upon to any covered person. **(H)**

captive agent. One who sells insurance for only one company as opposed to an agent who represents several companies. *See also* **exclusive agency system. (G)**

captive insurer. A legally recognized insurance company organized and owned by a corporation or firm whose purpose is to use the captive to write its own insurance at rates lower than those of other insurers. Usually, it is a nonadmitted insurer that has the right, under special circumstances, to reinsure with an admitted insurer. **(G)**

care, custody, and control. Most liability insurance policies exclude coverage for damage to property in the care, custody, or control of the insured. In some cases, this type of coverage is not available; in other cases, it can be purchased through certain forms of inland marine insurance, such as installation floaters, and in some cases this exclusion can be made less restrictive by adding a broad form property damage endorsement. **(LA)**

cargo insurance. A policy covering the cargo being transported by a carrier. **(IM, OM)**

carpenter cover. *See* spread loss reinsurance. **(R)**

carrier. (1) Usually a commercial insurer contracted by the Department of Health and Human Services to process Medicare Part B claims payments. **(H)** (2) Sometimes used to designate the insurer. The term *insurer* is preferred because of the possible confusion of *carrier* with transportation. *See also* **insurer. (G)**

carrier replacement. This refers to a situation where one carrier replaces one or more carriers. **(H)**

carryover provision. In major medical policies, allowing an insured who has submitted no claims during the year to apply any medical expenses incurred during the last three months of the year toward the new calendar year's deductible. **(H)**

case management. The assessment of a person's long-term care needs and the appropriate recommendations for care, monitoring, and follow-up as to the extent and quality of services to be provided. **(H)**

case manager. A person, usually an experienced professional, who coordinates the services necessary under the case management approach. **(H)**

case mix. The number of cases requiring different needs and uses of hospital resources. **(H)**

cash flow plans. Premium payment schemes that allow the insured to retain a large part of the premium and pay it out over a period such as a year. **(G)**

cash flow underwriting. The use of rating and premium collection techniques by insurance companies to maximize interest earnings on premiums. **(G)**

cash refund annuity. A form of annuity contract that provides that if, at the death of the annuitant, installments paid out have not totaled the amount of the premium paid for the annuity, the difference will be paid to a designated beneficiary in a lump sum. **(LI)**

cash surrender value. The amount of cash owed to an insured who surrenders cash value life insurance. Such surrender, with consequent termination of all insurance benefits, is sometimes called cashing out or cashing in a policy. *See also* **nonforfeiture values. (LI)**

cash value (1). *See* actual cash value. **(G)** (2) *See* **cash surrender value. (LI)**

Casualty Actuarial Society (CAS). A professional society for actuaries in areas of insurance work other than life insurance. This society grants the designation of Associate and Fellow of the Casualty Actuarial Society (ACAS and FCAS). **(LA, PR)**

casualty insurance. The type of insurance that is primarily concerned with the legal liability for losses caused by injury to persons or damage to the property of others. Many casualty insurers also write surety bonds. Casualty insurers write forms of insurance not considered property forms. *See also* **property insurance. (LA)**

catastrophe hazard. The hazard of large loss by reason of occurrence of a peril to which a very large number of insureds are subject. An example would be widespread loss resulting from a hurricane or tornado. **(G)**

catastrophe policy. This is an older name for major medical. *See* major medical. **(H)**

catastrophe reinsurance. A form of excess of loss reinsurance that, subject to a specified limit, indemnifies the ceding company against an amount of loss in excess of a specified amount as the result of an accumulation of losses resulting from a catastrophic event or a series of catastrophic events. **(R)**

causes of loss. Under the latest commercial property forms, this term replaces the earlier term *perils insured against.* **(C, IM, PR)**

causes of loss forms. Commercial property forms stating the perils insured against, additional coverages provided, and exclusions that apply. There are three causes of loss forms—**basic, broad,** and **special. (PR)**

caveat emptor. Let the buyer beware. **(G)**

cease and desist order. An order of the state insurance commissioner or of a court requiring that a company or person stop engaging in a particular act or practice, usually involving insurance trade practices. **(LE)**

cede. (1) To transfer to a reinsurer all or part of the insurance or reinsurance written by a ceding company. (2) The act of buying reinsurance. **(R)**

ceding company. The insurer that cedes all or part of the insurance or reinsurance it has written to another insurer. A company that has placed reinsurance, distinguished from the company that accepts it. **(R)**

Centers for Medicare and Medicaid Services. The federal agency that administers the Medicare and Medicaid programs. **(H)**

certificate. *See* certificate of insurance or participation. **(G)**

certificate of authority (COA). (1) Issued by the state, it licenses the operation of a health maintenance organization. **(H)** (2) A certificate showing the powers that an insurer grants to its agents. (3) A certificate issued by a state department of insurance showing the power of an insurer to write contracts of insurance in that state. **(G)**

certificate of convenience. A term used in some jurisdictions to refer to a temporary license or permit empowering a person to act as an agent even though not fully licensed according to the law. Usually, this certificate is granted to an agent who is studying for a licensing examination. It might also be issued to the administrator or executor of the estate of an insurance agent, who must have the authority of an agent to settle the estate, or to someone acting for an agent during a disability or an absence, such as military duty. **(G)**

certificate of insurance. (1) A statement of the coverage and general provisions of a master contract in group insurance that is issued to individuals covered in the group. (2) A form verifying that a policy has been written and stating the coverage in general, often used as proof of insurance in loan transactions and for other legal requirements. **(G)**

certificate of need (CON). Issued by a governmental body. It certifies that the proposed facility will meet the needs of those for whom it is intended. Such need might involve constructing a new health facility, offering a new or different health service, or acquiring new medical equipment. **(H)**

certificate of reinsurance. A short-form documentation of a reinsurance transaction. **(R)**

certiorari. A writ issued by a higher court to a lower court asking the lower court to forward the record of a particular case in question. **(LE)**

cession. The unit of insurance transferred to a reinsurer by a ceding company. It also refers to the process of ceding insurance to a reinsurer. **(R)**

cestui que vie. The person whose life measures the duration of a trust, gift, estate, or insurance contract. Thus, in life and health insurance, it is the person on whose life or health the policy is written, commonly called the insured, policyholder, or policyowner. **(H, LE, LI)**

change of occupation. A provision in a health insurance policy that allows the insurer to adjust policy benefits if the insured has changed to a more hazardous occupation. **(H)**

charter. (1) Usually the same as articles of incorporation. This is the grant of rights from a state or federal government, such as the right to incorporate and transact business. **(G)** (2) To rent or lease a ship or boat. **(OM)**

Chartered Life Underwriter (CLU). A designation granted by the American College of Life Underwriters upon successful completion of a series of examinations. **(LI)**

Chartered Property and Casualty Underwriter (CPCU). A designation granted by the American Institute of Property and Casualty Underwriters upon successful completion of a series of examinations. **(LA, PR)**

chattel. All personal property items. **(LE)**

chattel mortgage. A type of mortgage for which the collateral is personal property rather than land or buildings. **(G)**

chemical dependency services. The services required in the treatment and diagnosis of chemical dependency, alcoholism, and drug dependency. **(H)**

chemical equivalents. Drugs that contain identical amounts of the same ingredients. **(H)**

Christian Science Organization. A religious organization certified by the First Church of Christ, Scientist. The organization may also be Medicare certified as a hospital or skilled nursing facility. **(H)**

churning. An illegal practice whereby insurance agents unnecessarily replace existing life insurance for the purpose of earning additional (higher) first-year commissions. **(LI)**

civil commotion. An uprising of a large number of people, usually resulting in damage to property. This term is generally used to describe one of the extended coverage perils in the extended coverage endorsement. **(PR)**

Civilian Health and Medical Program of the Uniformed Services (CHAMPUS). *See* TRICARE. **(H)**

claim. A demand made by the insured, or the insured's beneficiary, for payment of the benefits provided by the contract. **(G)**

claim expense. The expense of adjusting a claim, such as investigation and attorneys' fees. It does not include the cost of the claim itself. **(G)**

claim report. A report filed by an agent setting forth the facts of a claim. *See also* **loss report. (G)**

claim representative. *See* adjuster. **(G)**

claimant. The person making a demand for payment of benefits. **(G)**

claims-made coverage. A policy providing liability coverage only if a written claim is made during the policy period or any applicable extended reporting period. For example, a claim made in the current year could be charged against the current policy even if the injury or loss occurred many years in the past. If the policy has a retroactive date, an occurrence before that date is not covered. *See also* **occurrence coverage. (LA)**

claims reserve. Amounts set aside to meet costs of claims incurred but not yet finally settled. An example might be a workers' compensation case where benefits are payable for several years. At any given point in time, the reserve would be the funds kept on the basis of the estimate of what the claim will cost when finally settled. **(G)**

class (or classification). A group of insureds with the same general characteristics and who are, therefore, grouped together for rating purposes. Class rates apply to dwellings and apartments because they usually have the same general characteristics and are exposed to the same perils. **(G)**

class action suit. A legal device allowing a group of individuals with a claim against a company or an individual to join together as plaintiffs in a single suit. **(LE)**

class rate. A rate for risks of similar hazard. Class rates, for example, apply to dwellings. **(PR)**

classified insurance. Life or health insurance on risks that do not meet the standards for the regular manual rate. *See also* **substandard. (H, LI)**

clause. A section of a policy contract or endorsement dealing with a particular subject. For instance, a subrogation clause deals with the rights of the insurer in the event of payment of a loss under the contract. **(G)**

cleanup fund. A term commonly used to designate policies whose express purpose is to pay final expenses at death. **(LI)**

clear space clause. A clause requiring that insured property, such as stacks of lumber, be stored at some particular distance from each other or from other property. **(PR)**

clerical error. A provision in a group health insurance policy that provides that if there is an error or omission in the administration of a group policy, the person's insurance is considered to be what it would be if there had been no error or omission. **(H)**

close corporation. A corporate form of business controlled and operated by a small, close group of persons such as family members. The corporation's stock is not sold to outsiders. **(G)**

closed panel. A situation in which covered insureds must select one primary care physician. That physician is the only one allowed to refer the patient to other health care providers within the plan. Also called closed access or gatekeeper model. **(H)**

codicil. A change or amendment to a will. **(EP)**

coding. A method of putting information into a numerical form for statistical use. Most information on policies is coded and then put into reports. **(G)**

coercion. An unfair trade practice that occurs when someone in the insurance business applies physical or mental force to persuade another to transact insurance. **(G)**

cognitive impairment. A deficiency in the ability to think, perceive, reason, or remember that results in loss of the ability to take care of one's daily living needs. **(H)**

coinsurance clause. A provision stating that the insured and the insurer will share all losses covered by the policy in a proportion agreed upon in advance (i.e., 80/20 would mean that the insurer would pay 80% and the insured would pay 20% of all losses). *See also* **percentage participation. (H)**

coinsurance clause. A clause under which the insured shares in losses to the extent that he is underinsured at the time of loss. The insurer grants a reduced rate to the insured, provided the insured carries insurance of 80%, 90%, or 100% to value. If, at the time of loss, the insured carries less coverage than required, the loss must be shared. For example, if an insured has a building worth $100,000 and carries an 80% coinsurance clause, it means that the insured agrees to carry at least $80,000 of insurance. If the insurance carried is just $60,000, any loss under the policy would be paid for on the basis of the comparison of $60,000 (amount carried) divided by $80,000 (amount agreed upon in advance) times the amount of the loss. Thus, in the event of a $10,000 loss, the insured would only receive 75% of a loss, or $7,500. **(PR)**

cold lead advertising. An illegal method of marketing insurance policies (often associated with Medicare supplement policies) that fails to disclose in a conspicuous manner that a purpose of the method of marketing is solicitation of insurance or other similar coverage and that further contact will be made by an insurance agent, other producer, or insurer. **(H)**

collapse. Literally, to cave in or give way. See **blasting and explosion exclusion** for information on how the coverage is handled under a liability policy. **(LA)**

collateral assignment. Assignment of a life insurance policy or its value as security for a loan. In the event of default, the creditor would receive proceeds or values only to the extent of the creditor's interest. **(LI)**

collateral source. A rule that allows a plaintiff to recover damages even if the plaintiff has already recovered damages from a source other than the defendant. **(LE)**

collateral split dollar. A split-dollar plan in which the employee controls the policy and pledges it as collateral for a series of employer loans to pay the premiums. **(PE)**

collection book. The debit agent's record book showing the amount collected on each policy, the week of the collection, and the policy period for which the premium has been paid. **(LI)**

collection commission. A percentage of premiums collected that is paid to an agent as the commission on collections of debit life insurance premiums. **(LI)**

collection fee. An industrial life insurance agent's fee that serves as compensation for making policy premium collections for which no commission is paid. **(LI)**

College Retirement Equities Fund (CREF). A separate organization affiliated with the Teachers Insurance Annuity Association. It introduces and sells a variable annuity to college and university personnel. **(AN, LI)**

collegia. Groups of associations in ancient Rome that were influential historically in the development of life insurance and pensions. They were the forerunners of mutual benefit societies or friendly societies. **(LI)**

collision, convertible. *See* convertible collision insurance. **(AU)**

collision insurance. A form of automobile insurance that covers loss to the insured's own vehicle caused by its collision with another vehicle or object or its upset but that does not cover bodily injury or property damage liability arising out of the collision. **(AU)**

collusion. An agreement, usually secret, between two or more persons to defraud or deprive another or others of their property or rights. **(G)**

combination. A term used to describe an agent, agency, or insurer that sells both industrial life insurance and ordinary life policies. **(LI)**

combination annuity. A contract that combines both the guarantees of a fixed annuity and the nonguarantees and investment risk of a variable annuity. **(AN)**

combination business interruption extra expense insurance. A policy that provides both business interruption and extra expense coverages in a single contract. This has been replaced by the latest business income forms. *See* business income coverage form. **(PR)**

combination plan. In pensions, this is a term applied to the combining of life insurance contracts with a fund called a side fund or auxiliary fund. The purpose is to increase the amount of money available for a pension or annuity at some future date. **(LI)**

combination plan reinsurance. A form of combined reinsurance that provides that in consideration of a premium, which is a fixed percentage of the ceding company's subject premium on the business covered, the reinsurer will indemnify the ceding company for the amount of loss of each risk in excess of a specified retention and subject to a specified limit and, after deducting the excess recoveries on each risk, the reinsurer will indemnify the ceding company against a fixed quota share percentage of all remaining losses. **(LI)**

combination policy. A policy made up of the contracts of two or more insurers in which each provides a different kind of insurance. This was once commonly used in automobile insurance when state law limited casualty companies to the writing of liability insurance and fire insurance companies to physical damage insurance. Combination policies are rarely written today. **(AU)**

Combined Annuity Mortality Table. A mortality table that was published in 1928 for use in determining rates for group annuities. **(LI)**

combined ratio. The sum of an expense ratio and a loss ratio. An underwriting profit occurs when the combined ratio is under 100%, and an underwriting loss occurs when the combined ratio is over 100%. **(G)**

combined single limit. A single limit of protection for both bodily injury and/or property damage, contrasted with split limits, where specific limits apply to bodily injury and property damage separately. **(LA)**

commercial blanket bond. This type of bond covers the insured against the dishonesty of all regular employees. A single amount of coverage applies to any one loss, regardless of the number of employees involved in the loss. *See also* **blanket bond** and **blanket position bond. (C)**

commercial crime insurance. Crime coverage that may be written as a monoline policy or part of a commercial package. Covers various crime exposures of businesses, such as employee dishonesty, burglary, theft, robbery, forgery and alteration, and computer fraud. Newer forms allow the insured to select a variety of coverages within a single form, replacing the separate crime coverage forms that were previously offered. **(C)**

commercial general liability (CGL) coverage part. General liability coverage that may be written as a monoline policy or part of a commercial package. CGL now means commercial general liability forms, which have replaced the earlier comprehensive general liability forms. The latest forms include all sublines and provide very broad coverage. Two variations are available—occurrence and claims-made coverage. **(LA)**

commercial lines. This term is used to refer to insurance for businesses, professionals, and commercial establishments. *See also* **business insurance** and **personal lines. (G)**

commercial package policy (CPP). A commercial lines policy that contains more than one type of commercial insurance. Most commercial policies may be included in the CPP, with the exception of ocean marine, aviation, workers' compensation, and businessowners. **(G)**

commercial policy. In health insurance, this term originally applied to policy forms intended for sale to individuals in commerce, as contrasted with industrial workers. Currently, the term is used loosely to mean all policies that do not guarantee renewability. **(H)**

commercial property coverage. Property coverage that may be written as a monoline policy or part of a commercial package. **(PR)**

commingling. An illegal practice that occurs when an agent mixes personal funds with the insured's or insurer's funds. **(G)**

commission. The portion of the premium paid to the agent as compensation for services. *See also* **first-year commission, renewal commission, level commission system, unlevel commission system, contingent commission,** and **graded commission. (G)**

commission. An allowance made by the reinsurer to the original insurer for part of the original insurer's acquisition and other costs. It may also include a profit factor. **(R)**

commission of authority. A document outlining the powers delegated to an agent by an insurer. **(G)**

Commissioner of Insurance. The title of the head of most state insurance departments. In some states, the title Director or Superintendent of Insurance is used instead. **(G)**

Commissioners' Disability Table. A morbidity table approved by the National Association of Insurance Commissioners for use in setting legal minimums for disability income insurance policy reserves. **(LI)**

Commissioners' Industrial Extended Term Mortality Table. An industrial mortality table approved by the NAIC for evaluation and computation of extended term insurance in industrial policies, where additional mortality margins are deemed necessary. This is a companion table to the CSI 1961. **(LI)**

Commissioners' Standard Industrial Mortality Table, 1961. An industrial mortality table approved by the NAIC as a standard for evaluation and for computation of nonforfeiture values for industrial policies. **(LI)**

Commissioners' Standard Ordinary (CSO). A mortality table approved by the NAIC as a standard for evaluation and for computation of nonforfeiture values for ordinary life policies. **(LI)**

Commissioners' Values. An annual list of securities published by the NAIC. The values are to be used in recording security values on insurance company balance sheets. **(G)**

common accident. An accident in which two or more persons are injured. **(LI)**

common carrier. An individual or organization that offers its services to the public for carrying persons or property from one place to another for payment. A common carrier cannot refuse to carry goods for one customer as opposed to another. **(IM)**

common disaster. A situation in which the insured and the beneficiary appear to die simultaneously with no clear evidence of who died first. **(LI)**

common disaster clause. A clause sometimes added to a life insurance policy that provides a means for the insurer to distribute the proceeds of the policy in the event of a common disaster. **(LI)**

common law. The unwritten law developed primarily from judicial case decisions based on custom and precedent. It developed in England and constitutes the basis for the legal systems of most of the states in the United States. **(LE)**

common-law defenses. Pleas that can defeat an injured worker's suit for injuries against the employer in the absence of a workers' compensation law or employers liability legislation. The three defenses are contributory negligence, assumption of risk, and fellow servant rule. **(LA)**

common-law liability. Responsibility based on common law for injury or damage to another's person or property that rests on an individual because of the individual's actions or negligence. This is opposed to liability based on statutory law. **(G)**

common policy conditions. Under the latest commercial lines program, a form including six common conditions that apply to all coverage parts attached to a commercial policy. **(G)**

common policy declarations. Under the latest commercial lines program, a common declaration page that is part of every commercial policy. It shows information applicable to the entire policy (e.g., policy number, insurer, insured, total premium, and forms attached). Each individual coverage part may also have its own declarations page. **(G)**

common stock. A security that provides an ownership or equity position in a company. Shareholders may receive dividends if declared by the board of directors. **(PE)**

community property. Common or statutory law that holds that husband and wife are each entitled to one-half of the total earnings and the property of both parties to the marriage. It is applicable in the states of Arizona, California, Idaho, Louisiana, Nevada, New Mexico, Texas, and Washington. **(LE)**

community rating. Under this rating system, the charge for insurance to all insureds depends on the medical and hospital costs in the community or area to be covered. Individual characteristics of the insureds are not considered at all. **(H)**

commutation. The exchange of one thing for another. In insurance, it is usually the exchange of installment benefits for a lump sum. **(G)**

commutation clause. A clause that provides for estimation, payment, and complete discharge of all future obligations for reinsurance loss or losses incurred, regardless of the continuing nature of certain losses. This clause is found particularly in Lloyd's treaties. **(G)**

commutation rights. The right of a beneficiary to receive in one sum the unpaid payments remaining under an installment option that was selected for the settlement of the proceeds or values of a life insurance policy. **(LI)**

commute. In insurance, it means to determine as of a given date the single sum that is the equivalent of a series of sums due at various future dates, with allowances for interest that would have been earned on the unpaid portion of the series of payments. **(G)**

commuted value. The amount of a single sum payment, as determined under the definition of **commute**. **(G)**

comparative negligence. In some states, the negligence of both parties to an accident is established in proportion to the degree of their contribution to the accident. Several states have comparative negligence laws, and each one varies somewhat from the others. This is in contrast to contributory negligence, which is a general common-law rule. *See also* **contributory negligence. (LE)**

compensation-related loan. A below-market loan between an employer and employee. **(PE)**

compensatory damages. Damages recoverable or awarded for injury or loss sustained. In addition to actual loss or injury, this term may include amounts for expenses, loss of time, bodily suffering, and mental suffering but does not include punitive damages. **(LE)**

competency. This is one of the elements that must be present to have a legal contract. It relates to the fitness or ability of either of the parties to the contract. An example of incompetency would be an alcoholic or a mental incompetent. **(LE)**

competitive medical plan (CMP). This refers to permission given by the federal government that allows an organization to write a Medicare risk contract. **(H)**

competitive state fund. This term refers to a fund established by a state to write workers' compensation insurance in competition with private insurers. **(WC)**

completed operations insurance. A form of insurance issued particularly to various types of contractors. It covers a contractor's liability for accidents arising out of jobs or operations that have been completed. *See also* **products-completed operations insurance. (LA)**

completion bond. This is a bond issued to a mortgagee. It guarantees that the construction for which the mortgagor has borrowed money will be completed and will be able to serve as collateral for the mortgage upon completion. **(S)**

composite rate. (1) One rate for all members of the group, regardless of their status as single or members of a family. **(H)** (2) A single rate with a single basis of premium (e.g., payroll or sales). For this single rate, the insured is covered for a variety of hazards, such as premises and operations, completed operations, products liability, and automobile. Its primary value is to make it simpler for the policy's premium to be computed. **(AU, LA)**

composition roof. A roof of either asbestos or asphalt shingles. The term is most frequently used in connection with construction factors used in determining the rate for property insurance. **(G)**

comprehensive coverage. Traditional name for physical damage coverage for losses by fire, theft, vandalism, falling objects, and various other perils. On personal auto policies, this is now called other than collision coverage. On commercial forms, it continues to be called comprehensive coverage. **(AU)**

comprehensive general liability. A policy covering a variety of general liability exposures, including premises and operations (owners, landlords, and tenants liability insurance or manufacturers and contractors liability insurance), completed operations, products liability, and owners and contractors protective. Contractual liability and broad form coverages could be added. In most jurisdictions, the comprehensive general liability policy has been replaced by the newer commercial general liability forms, which include all the standard and optional coverages of the earlier forms. *See also* **commercial general liability (CGL) coverage part. (LA)**

comprehensive glass insurance policy. A policy that covers the insured against loss by breakage of glass from almost any peril. Fire is usually excluded because it is covered under any basic property policy, and war is also excluded. This policy has largely been replaced by newer commercial forms. **(PR)**

comprehensive major medical. A plan of insurance that has a low deductible, high maximum benefits, and a coinsurance feature. It is a combination of basic coverage and major medical coverage that has virtually replaced separate hospital, surgical, and medical policies, each having its own deductible requirements. *See also* **major medical insurance. (H)**

comprehensive personal liability. This coverage protects individuals and families from liability for nearly all types of accidents caused by them in their personal lives, as opposed to business lives. It is most commonly a part of the protection provided by a homeowners policy. **(LA)**

comprehensive policy. In automobile and liability insurance, this is an open perils (all risk) coverage with certain named exclusions. **(AU, LA)**

comprehensive 3D policy. *See* **dishonesty, disappearance, and destruction policy. (C)**

compromise and release agreement. A settlement practice under which an injured worker agrees to a compromised liability amount (usually a lump sum) in exchange for releasing the employer from further liability. **(WC)**

compulsory insurance. Any form of insurance required by law. For example, some states have compulsory automobile insurance laws, and some have compulsory disability benefits laws. **(G)**

computation base years. A calculation that is the total of the computation elapsed years less the five lowest earnings years for Social Security tax purposes. **(EP)**

computation elapsed years. The total number of years since 1950 or attainment of age 21, if later, up to age 62, during which Social Security taxes have been paid. **(EP)**

computer fraud. Fraudulent theft or transfer of money, securities, or other property resulting from the use of any computerized equipment or systems. **(C)**

computer fraud coverage form. A commercial crime coverage form that protects against loss of money, securities, and property other than money and securities resulting from computer fraud. Separate crime coverage forms have been largely replaced by newer crime policies that provide multiple coverage options in a single policy. **(C)**

concealment. The failure to disclose a material fact. *See* **material fact.** **(LE)**

concurrent causation. A term referring to two or more perils acting concurrently (at the same time or in sequence) to cause a loss. This created problems for property insurers when one of the perils was covered and one was not, and it led to recent revisions in policy language. **(PR)**

concurrent insurance. Two or more policies with the same conditions and coverages that cover the same interest in the same property. If an insured has two or more property insurance policies, the policies should be concurrent (similar) or the property will not be insured properly. **(PR)**

concurrent review. A case management technique that allows insurers to monitor an insured's hospital stay and to know in advance whether there are any changes in the expected period of confinement and the planned release date. **(H)**

conditional binding receipt. This is the more exact terminology for what is often called a binding receipt. It provides that if a premium accompanies an application, the coverage will be in force from the date of application or medical examination, if any, whichever is later, provided the insurer would have issued the coverage on the basis of the facts revealed on the application, medical examination, and other usual sources of underwriting information. A life and health insurance policy without a conditional binding receipt is not effective until it is delivered to the insured and the premium is paid. **(H, LI)**

conditional sales floater. A type of policy designed to cover property that has been sold on an installment or conditional sales basis. It covers the interest of the seller. **(IM)**

conditional vesting. A form of vesting in a contributory pension plan under which entitlement to a vested benefit is conditional upon non-withdrawal of the participant's contribution. *See also* **vesting. (LI)**

conditionally renewable. A contract that provides that the insured may renew it to a stated date or an advanced age, subject to the right of the insurer to decline renewal only under conditions stated in the contract. **(H)**

conditions. These are provisions of an insurance policy that state either the rights and duties of the insured or the rights and duties of the insurer. Typical conditions have to do with such things as the insured's duties in the event of loss, cancellation provisions, and the right of the insurer to inspect the property. **(G)**

condominium association coverage form. A commercial property form designed to cover the joint insurance needs of members of a condominium association who collectively own commercial property. **(PR)**

condominium unit owners coverage form. A commercial property form designed to cover the individual needs of commercial (not residential) condominium unit owners. **(PR)**

confining. A form of disability or sickness that confines the insured indoors, usually at home or in a hospital. Many policies state that coverage is afforded only if the insured is confined. **(H)**

consent order. A disciplinary action in which the party at fault (usually an insurance company or agent) agrees to discontinue a particular practice (usually an unfair trade or claims practice) through a written agreement with the insurance department. Consent orders (also known as consent decrees) may or may not involve a fine. **(G)**

consequential loss (or damage). (1) An indirect loss arising out of the policyholder's inability to use the property over a period of time, as opposed to a direct loss that happens almost instantaneously. Business interruption, extra expense, rents insurance, and leasehold interest are the most common coverages included under the category of consequential loss coverages. (2) A loss not directly caused by a peril insured against, such as spoilage of frozen foods caused by fire damage to the refrigeration equipment. *See also* **indirect loss** and **direct loss. (PR)**

conservation. The insurance company's efforts to prevent current policies from lapsing. **(G)**

conservator. Someone appointed to manage an insurer deemed by law or court action to be in danger of failure. **(LE)**

consideration. The exchange of values on which a contract is based. In insurance, the consideration offered by the insured is usually the premium and the statements contained in the application. The consideration offered by the insurer is the promise to pay in accordance with the terms of the contract. **(LE)**

consignee. This is a person to whom materials or goods are delivered for resale. The consignee pays the owner after the goods have been sold. **(G)**

Consolidated Omnibus Budget Reconciliation Act (COBRA) of 1986. Legislation providing for a continuation of group health care benefits under the group plan for a period when benefits would otherwise terminate. Continuation rights apply to enrolled persons and their dependents in companies with 20 or more employees. Coverage may be continued for up to 18 months if the insured person terminates employment or is no longer eligible. Coverage may be continued for up to 36 months in nearly all other cases, such as loss of dependent eligibility because of death of the enrolled person, divorce, or attainment of the limiting age. **(H)**

consortium. The companionship of a spouse. If a spouse is injured through the fault of another, part of the damages could include the value of the spouse's services or companionship that was lost because of the accident. **(LE)**

conspiracy. A combination of two or more persons who by concerted action seek to accomplish an unlawful purpose or to accomplish a lawful purpose by unlawful means. **(LE)**

construction bond. This bond protects the owner of a building or other structure under construction in case the contractor cannot complete the job. If the contractor defaults, the insurer is obligated to see that the work is completed. **(S)**

constructive delivery. Intentionally relinquishing control over a policy and turning it over to someone acting for the policyowner, such as when an insurer mails the policy to its own agent for delivery to the policyowner. Legally, an insurance policy is considered delivered when mailed or turned over to the policyowner or someone acting on his behalf. **(LE)**

constructive performance. A situation in which an act has not actually been completed but conduct has gone so far as to show intent to complete the act. **(LE)**

constructive total loss. A partial loss of sufficient degree to make the cost of repairing the damaged property more than the property is worth. For example, an old automobile might suffer damage that could be repaired, but the cost of repairs would be more than the actual cash value of the automobile. **(G)**

Consumer Credit Insurance Association (CCIA). A trade association for insurers of credit insurance in the areas of life and health. **(H, LI)**

Consumer Protection Act. A law passed by many states that protects a policyholder from the misconduct, misrepresentation, or sharp trade practices of insurers, brokers, and agents. **(LE)**

consumer report. A report ordered on an insured or applicant under which information about the person's credit, character, reputation, personal characteristics, or lifestyle is obtained primarily through institutional sources. *See also* **investigative consumer report. (G)**

contents rate. The fire insurance rate on the contents of a building rather than on the building itself. **(PR)**

contestable clause. A provision in an insurance policy setting forth the conditions under which, or the period during which, the insurer may contest or void the policy. After that time has lapsed—normally two years—the policy cannot be contested. **(LI)**

contingency reserve. A reserve in an insurer's annual statement, in addition to the legal requirements, to provide for unexpected contingencies or losses. **(G)**

contingency surplus. *See* contingency reserve. **(G)**

contingent annuitant. A person(s) named to receive annuity benefits if the primary annuitant is deceased at the time benefits become payable. **(AN)**

contingent annuity. An annuity in which payment of benefits is contingent upon the occurrence of an uncertain event, such as death of a person not an annuitant. For example, an annuity might be purchased to pay benefits to a wife in the event of the death of her husband. **(AN)**

contingent beneficiary. A person(s) named to receive policy benefits if the primary beneficiary is deceased at the time the benefits become payable. **(LI)**

contingent business interruption insurance. Coverage for the loss of earnings of an insured because of a loss to another business that is one of the insured's major suppliers or customers. This insurance is now known as business income from dependent properties. *See* **business income coverage form** and **dependent properties. (PR)**

contingent (or profit) commission. An allowance payable to the ceding insurer, in addition to the normal ceding commission, based on the net profit derived from a reinsurance treaty. **(R)**

contingent fund. A reserve to cover possible liabilities resulting from an unusual event. **(G)**

contingent interest. An interest in personal property that is dependent on some future event. **(EP, LE)**

contingent liability. A liability imposed because of accidents caused by persons other than employees for whose acts an individual, partnership, or corporation may be responsible. For example, an insured who hires an independent contractor can be held liable for negligence in some cases. **(LA)**

contingent trust. A revocable living trust that becomes operational only upon a specified occurrence or contingency. **(EP)**

contingent vesting. In pensions, a form of vesting under which entitlement to a vested interest is conditional on circumstances surrounding the employee's termination of service or conduct after termination. *See also* **vesting. (LI)**

continuation. Allows terminated employees to continue their group health insurance coverage under certain conditions. **(H)**

continuing care retirement communities (CCRCs). Residential communities set up to provide residents with easy access to health care. **(H)**

continuing education requirement. State-level requirement that insurance licensees periodically complete a minimum number of hours of insurance-related education to be eligible for license renewal. **(G)**

continuous premium whole life policy. A whole life policy that stretches the premium payments over the insured's lifetime (to age 100). Also known as straight life. *See also* **limited payment whole life** and **single premium whole life. (LI)**

contract. (1) An agreement entered into by two or more persons, under which one or more of them agree, for a consideration, to do or refrain from doing acts in accordance with the wishes of the other party(ies). (2) In insurance, the agreement by which an insurer agrees, for a consideration, to provide benefits, reimburse losses, or provide services for an insured. A policy is the written statement of the terms of the contract. (3) An agreement under which an agency or agent does business with an insurer. **(G)**

contract bond. A guarantee of the faithful performance of a construction contract and the payment of all material and labor bills incidental thereto. A bond covering faithful performance only is known as a performance bond, and one covering payment of labor and materials only is a payment bond. **(S)**

contract carrier. A transportation company that carries, for payment, the goods of certain customers only, as contrasted with a common carrier who carries goods for the public in general. **(IM)**

contract of adhesion. A contract that one party must accept or reject in toto, without bargaining over the wording. An insurance contract is an example because the contract is developed by the insurer and the insured must accept it as it is. **(LE)**

contract of insurance. The contract whereby an insurer agrees to indemnify an insured for losses, provide other benefits, or render services to or on behalf of the insured. The contract of insurance is often called an insurance policy, but the policy is merely the evidence of the agreement. **(LE)**

contract year. This period runs from the effective date to the expiration date of the contract. **(H)**

contractual (or assumed) liability insurance. This insurance protects the insured in the event a loss occurs for which the insured has assumed liability, express or implied, under a written contract. For example, under most construction agreements with a municipality, the contractor agrees to hold the municipality harmless for any accidents arising out of the job. Contractual liability insurance would thus protect the contractor from any loss for which the municipality would be liable in connection with the construction. **(LA)**

contributing location. A location upon which the insured depends as a source of materials or services. One of the four types of dependent properties for which business income coverage may be written. **(PR)**

contribution. (1) The share of a loss payable by an insurer when contracts with two or more insurers cover the same loss. *See also* **apportionment.** (2) The insurer's share of a loss under a coinsurance or similar provision. (3) The amount of the premium for group insurance or a pension plan paid by the employee. **(G)**

contribution clause. *See* **coinsurance clause.** Both are similar in effect, but contribution clause is identified mostly with business interruption forms. **(G)**

contribution formula. As used under a qualified profit-sharing trust or money-purchase plan, the formula that spells out when and in what amounts the employer will make contributions to the trust. **(PE)**

contributory. A general term used to describe a plan of employee coverage in which the employee pays at least part of the premium. **(H, LI)**

contributory negligence. If an injured party fails to exercise proper care and in some way contributes to his injury, the doctrine of contributory negligence will probably negate or defeat the claim, even though the other party is also negligent. *See also* **comparative negligence. (LE)**

contributory retirement plan. Plan in which the participant pays part of the cost of purchasing the annuity or building up the fund from which benefits are paid. **(PE)**

control. Authority given to an agent or broker by a policyowner to place the insurance where the agent or broker sees it. **(G)**

control provision. A policy provision found most frequently in juvenile contracts, providing that ownership control is to be exercised for a stated or indefinite duration by a person other than the one whose life is insured. **(LI)**

controlled business. This term refers to the amount of insurance countersigned, issued, or sold by a producer covering the life, property, or interests of that producer, members of the producer's immediate family, or the producer's employer or employees. Many states limit the amount of controlled business that may be written, and if the premium or commissions on controlled business exceed a given percentage (usually 50%) of all business, the producer's license may be suspended, revoked, or not renewed. **(G)**

controlled insurance. *See* **control** and **control provision.** An insurance account that an agent or broker can control by influencing the buyer, as contrasted with controlling it by actual agreement. **(G)**

convention (or statement) blank. The uniform annual financial statement required by all United States insurance jurisdictions as prescribed by the National Association of Insurance Commissioners. It must be filed annually in an insurer's home state and every state in which it is licensed to do business. Nearly all insurance accounting practices are geared to it. **(G)**

convention values. Values assigned to insurers' assets in the convention blank. **(G)**

conversion. (1) Wrongful use of property by one in lawful possession of it. (2) Change of one policy form to another, usually without evidence of insurability. This term usually refers to life or health insurance contracts. **(G)**

conversion fund (supplemental). A fund used with ordinary life or limited payment life that augments the cash value at retirement to provide monthly retirement income. **(PE)**

conversion privilege. The right of an individual to convert a group health or life policy to an individual policy should the individual cease to be a member of the group. Usually, this can be done without a physical examination. **(H, LI)**

convertible. A policy that may be changed to another form by contractual provision and without evidence of insurability. Most term policies are convertible into permanent insurance. **(LI)**

convertible collision insurance. Automobile collision insurance with a deductible that, after claims exceeding the deductible have been paid, converts to full coverage for all losses thereafter. Rarely written today. **(AU)**

cooperative insurance. Insurance issued by a mutual association, such as a fraternal society, an employee association, an industrial association, or a trade union. **(G)**

coordination of benefits (COB). (1) *See* nonduplication of benefits. **(H)** (2) A group policy provision that helps determine the primary carrier in situations where an insured is covered by more than one policy. This provision prevents an insured from receiving claims overpayments. **(H, LI)**

co-pay. *See* co-payment. **(H)**

co-payment. This is an arrangement in which the covered person pays a specified amount for various services and the health care provider pays the remainder. The covered person usually must pay his share when the service is rendered. Similar to coinsurance, except that coinsurance is usually a percentage of certain charges, whereas the co-payment is a dollar amount. **(H)**

co-payment provision. Often used with major medical policies. The co-payment provision states what percentage of a claim the company will pay and what percentage the insured will pay. For example, an 80% co-payment provision would provide that the insurer pay 80% of claims and the insured pay 20%. **(H)**

corridor. In universal life insurance, it is necessary to maintain a certain level of pure insurance protection in excess of the accumulation value to qualify as life insurance for income tax purposes. This portion of the pure insurance protection is called a corridor. **(LI)**

corridor deductible. A major medical provision that provides for a deductible, or corridor, that applies after full payment of basic hospital and medical expenses up to a stated amount, and before additional expenses are shared on a coinsurance basis. For example, a policy might pay 100% of the first $2,000 of expenses, followed by a $500 corridor deductible paid by the insured, followed by a sharing of additional expenses on the basis of 80% payable by the insurer and 20% payable by the insured. **(H)**

cosmetic procedures. Procedures that improve appearance but are not medically necessary. **(H)**

cost basis. Money that has already been taxed; used in reference to taxation of investment dollars. **(PE)**

cost contract. An agreement between a provider and the Health Care Financing Administration to provide health services to covered persons based on reasonable costs for service. **(H)**

cost of insurance. The amount a policyowner pays to an insurer, minus what he gets back from the insurer. This expression is used when determining the true cost of permanent forms of life insurance to a policyowner. It considers the fact that premiums are paid in but also that an actual cash value is being built up, which is the portion that the insured will get back from the insurance. **(LI)**

cost of insurance charge. Another term to describe the charge for the pure insurance protection element of a life insurance contract. It is also known as the mortality charge. **(LI)**

cost-of-living benefit. An optional disability benefit where the monthly benefit will be increased annually once the insured is on claim for 12 months. **(H)**

cost-of-living rider. Designed to adjust policy benefits in relation to the change in the economic climate. The majority of such riders are tied to changes in the Consumer Price Index (CPI). The amount of insurance may be automatically increased, without evidence of insurability, at predetermined periods for a maximum amount. **(LI)**

cost sharing. A situation in which covered persons pay a portion of the health costs, such as deductibles, coinsurance, or co-payment amounts. **(H)**

co-surety. One of a group of sureties directly participating in a bond with obligations joint and several. **(S)**

countersignature. The signature of a licensed agent or representative on a policy. **(G)**

countersignature law. Refers to the laws in some states requiring that any insurance contract in a state be countersigned by a representative of the insurer located in that state. **(LE)**

countrywide rates. For each major division of the *Commercial Lines Manual*, a section called Countrywide Rates contains rates and minimum premiums. State rates are used for coverages for which there are no countrywide rates or to modify countrywide rates. **(G)**

countrywide rules. For each major division of the *Commercial Lines Manual*, a section called Countrywide Rules contains rules and rating factors applicable to coverages in that division. **(G)**

coupon policy. A life insurance policy, usually 20-pay life or some other limited payment period, with attached coupons that may be cashed in for a specified amount at the time of the payment of each annual premium. **(LI)**

court bond. Any bond required of a litigant to enable him to pursue a remedy in court. **(G)**

cover. (1) A contract of insurance. (2) To effect insurance—that is, to cover an insured, as for automobile insurance effective as of a given time. (3) To include within the coverage of a contract of insurance. For example, one could cover additional buildings under a property insurance contract. **(G)**

cover note. Similar to a binder, but binders are usually issued by companies and delivered to agents. A cover note is usually written by an agent, and it informs the insured that coverage is in effect. *See also* **binder**. In reinsurance, a cover note is a statement issued by an intermediary or broker indicating that coverage has been effected. **(G)**

coverage. The scope of the protection provided under a contract of insurance. **(G)**

coverage part. Any one of the individual commercial coverage parts that may be attached to a commercial policy. Under the latest commercial lines program, a coverage part may be issued as a monoline policy or may be combined with others as part of a package policy. **(G)**

coverage trigger. A mechanism that determines whether a policy covers a particular claim for loss. For example, the difference between the coverage triggers of liability occurrence forms and claims-made forms is that loss must occur during the policy period in the first case and the claim must be made during the policy period in the second case. **(LA)**

covered expenses. Health care expenses incurred by an insured or covered person that qualify for reimbursement under the terms of a policy contract. **(H)**

covered loss. Illness, injury, death, property loss, legal liability, or any other situation or loss for which an insurance company will pay benefits under a policy when such event occurs. **(G)**

covered person. An insured person under a contract of insurance. **(H)**

Coverdell Education Savings Account. A tax-advantaged account designed to help parents and students save for education expenses. Distributions are tax free if they are used for qualified education expenses, such as tuition, books, and fees. **(EP)**

crash coverage. A type of coverage that is optional under an aviation policy. It provides coverage for damage to an airplane caused by a crash and is usually referred to as hull coverage or physical damage coverage. **(AV)**

credentialing. Approving a provider on the basis of certain criteria to provide or participate in a health plan. **(H)**

credit card forgery. Protects the insured against losses caused by forgery in the use of credit cards or the alteration of them or of any other written instruments connected with them. **(C)**

credit carried forward. The transfer of credit or profit from one accounting period to another under a spread loss or other form of long-term reinsurance. **(R)**

credit carryover. Each year, an employer is allowed to contribute 15% of payroll toward a profit-sharing plan and deduct it from taxable income. If the contribution is less than 15% in a particular year, the unused percentage can be made up in succeeding years. However, deductible contributions are limited to a total amount not greater than 25% of the participants' payroll: 15% for the current year's contribution plus 10% for credit carryover. **(PE)**

credit health insurance. A group disability income insurance contract whereby a creditor is protected in the event of the total disability of a debtor. The policy will pay benefits equal to the monthly installment of the debtor. **(H)**

credit insurance. Insurance on a debtor in favor of a creditor to pay off the balance due on a loan in the event of the death or disability of the debtor. Liability insurance for abnormal loss from bad debts. **(H, LI)**

credit life insurance. A group life insurance contract whereby a creditor is protected in the event of death of the insured before the indebtedness is paid in full. **(LI)**

credit report. A confidential report made by an independent individual or organization that has investigated the reputation and record of an applicant for insurance. *See also* **consumer report. (G)**

creditor. The person to whom a debt is owed. *See also* **debtor. (LE)**

crime. A public wrong, a violation of criminal law. The state is the entity that brings charges against one who commits a crime, and the matter is adjudicated in a criminal court. *See also* **tort. (LE)**

criticism. A correction suggested by a rating or auditing bureau to an insurer. **(G)**

Cromie rule. A method or guide used to apportion losses under policies that are nonconcurrent (i.e., not identical as to coverage provided). **(PR)**

crop insurance. Provides protection against damage to growing crops by such perils as hail, windstorm, and fire. Traditionally, crop-hail coverage was the most common coverage sold. In recent years, premiums for broad multi-peril crop insurance (MPCI) have exceeded those for the crop-hail business. **(PR)**

cross purchase. A form of business life insurance in which each party to a mutual agreement (usually to buy out a disabled or deceased co-owner) insures each of the other parties. **(LI)**

cross-purchase agreement. A binding buy-sell agreement most commonly used with a partnership, in which each partner agrees to purchase the business interest of a deceased or disabled partner. **(PE)**

crude death (or mortality) rate. The ratio of total deaths to total population during any given period. *See also* **mortality rate. (LI)**

Crummey privilege. The annual withdrawal privilege offered by a trust to trust beneficiaries in order for the trust property to remain qualified for the gift tax exclusion. **(EP)**

cumulative liability. (1) The liability of a surety bonding company for the accumulation of loss under its own bond and under a bond which it replaced before a loss under the replaced bond was discovered. **(S)** (2) The accumulation of the liability of a reinsurer that has been assumed under several policies from several ceding companies covering different lines of insurance, all of which are involved in a common event or disaster. **(R)**

current disbursement. The funding and disbursement of pension benefits as they become due. Also known as pay-as-you-go. In the long run, this is the most costly method of funding pension plans. **(LI)**

current future service. The amount of pension payable for each year of future participation in the pension plan. **(LI)**

current ratio. The ratio of current assets to current liabilities. Bond underwriters like this ratio to be 2:1 on the balance sheets of contractors for whom they are considering contract bonds. **(S)**

current service benefit. The portion of a participant's pension benefit that relates to credited service in a contemporary period, usually 12 months. **(LI)**

current service cost. The cost in a pension plan to make provision for annuity credits earned by employees in the current year. **(PE)**

current value. The fair market value of a security or other property as determined by the trustees or a named beneficiary, according to the terms of the plan. **(PE)**

currently insured status. A provision of Old Age, Survivors, Disability, and Health Insurance. The requirements for being currently insured are fewer than those for being fully insured, and the former entitles a worker's dependents to survivor benefits in the event of the worker's death. *See also* **fully insured. (G)**

custodial care. Care that is primarily for meeting personal needs such as help in the activities of daily living (e.g., bathing, dressing, eating, and taking medicine). It can be provided by someone without professional medical skills or training but must be according to a doctor's orders. *See also* **activities of daily living. (H)**

custodian. Under commercial crime insurance coverages, the named insured or any of the insured's partners or employees while having care and custody of insured property inside the insured's premises. **(C)**

customary charge. Used to determine Medicare benefit amounts, this usually means the average fee charged for a particular medical service in the geographic area during the preceding year. *See also* **allowable charge** and **prevailing charge. (H)**

custom house bonds. Bonds required by US customs in connection with the payment of duties or the production of bills of lading. **(S)**

cut rate. This term generally applies to insurance companies that charge premiums below a normal or average rate. **(G)**

Cutoff. The termination provision of a reinsurance contract stating that the reinsurer is not liable for loss as a result of occurrences taking place after the date of termination. **(R)**

cut-through clause. *See* **assumption certificate. (R)**

D

DA. *See* deposit administration. **(LI)**

D&B. *See* Dun and Bradstreet, Inc. **(G)**

DBL. *See* disability benefits law. **(H)**

DEFRA. Deficit Reduction Act of 1984. **(G)**

DIC. *See* difference in conditions. **(PR)**

DOC. *See* drive-other-car endorsement. **(AU)**

PRESENTATION OF TERMS

D ratio. A factor used in workers' compensation experience rating plans. It is the ratio of smaller losses (those less than $2,000), plus the discounted value of large losses, compared with the total losses that might be expected of an insured in a particular type of business. **(WC)**

daily report. An abbreviated statement of pertinent policy information with copies for the insurer, the agent, and others. It is usually the top page of a policy. **(G)**

damages. The amount required to pay for a loss. **(LE)**

data processing coverage. A special form providing protection for loss due to the breakdown of data processing systems. It also includes coverage for the additional expense of putting the system back into operation. **(PR)**

date of issue. The date stated in a policy as the date on which the contract was issued by the insurer. This is not necessarily the effective date of the policy. **(G)**

date of service. The date that the health service was provided. **(H)**

death benefit. The amount stated in a policy contract as payable upon the death of the person whose life is being insured (cesti que vie). *See also* **principal sum. (LI)**

death benefit only (DBO) plan. A plan in which part of an employee's salary is deferred and paid upon the contingency of death. **(LI, PE)**

death rate. *See* mortality rate. **(LI)**

debit. (1) The amount of premium charged or debited to an agent to be collected. (2) The book of business represented by such premiums. (3) The territory where most of the insureds are located. (4) The total number of individual or home service insureds assigned to a given agent for collection of weekly or monthly premiums and for servicing, commonly referred to as people in my debit. **(LI)**

debit agent. An agent who works on the debit system. **(LI)**

debit life insurance. *See* industrial life insurance. **(LI)**

debit system. The system of collecting insurance premiums weekly or monthly by an agent. **(LI)**

debris removal clause. A provision that may be included in a property policy contract to provide the insured with indemnification for expenditures incurred in the removal of debris produced by the occurrence of an insured peril. Ordinarily a property policy covers only the direct damage caused by an insured peril. **(PR)**

debtor. One who owes a legal obligation or money to another. *See also* creditor. **(LE)**

decedent. Same as deceased. **(G)**

declaration. A formal written statement in which an individual avows under oath certain facts as personally known to him specifying of the facts constituting the plaintiff's cause of action against the defendant. **(LE)**

declarations. A term used in insurance other than life or health to denote the portion of the contract in which is stated such information as the name and address of the insured, the property insured, its location and description, the policy period, the amount of insurance coverage, applicable premiums, and supplemental representations by the insured. **(LA, PR)**

declination. Rejection of an application for insurance by the insurer. **(G)**

decreasing term. A form of life insurance that provides a death benefit that declines throughout the term of the contract, reaching zero at the end of the term. **(LI)**

decreasing term insurance. A term life insurance policy for which the death benefit decreases but the premium remains level for the policy term. *See also* **increasing term insurance, level term insurance, and term insurance. (LI)**

deductible. The portion of an insured loss to be borne by the insured before any recovery may be made from the insurer. **(G)**

deductible, calendar year. A deductible that specifies that one deductible needs to be satisfied for a calendar year regardless of the number of claims. **(H)**

deductible carryover credit. During the last three months of a calendar year, charges incurred for health services can be used to satisfy the deductible for the following calendar year. These credits may be applied whether or not the prior calendar year's deductible had been met. **(H)**

deductible clause. A contract provision that sets forth the deductible. **(G)**

deductible, disappearing. *See* disappearing deductible. **(G)**

deductible, franchise. *See* franchise deductible. **(G)**

deductible, per cause. A deductible that must be satisfied for each separate claim. **(H)**

deep pockets liability. A term used to describe the legal doctrine of joint-and-several liability, under which recovery can be sought from any of several co-defendants on the basis of ability to pay, rather than the degree of negligence. For example, A and B are jointly liable for an injury. A was 90% negligent and B was 10% negligent, but A has no assets; the claimant is permitted to reach into the deep pockets of B for the full amount of the award against A and B. **(LE)**

defamation. Under insurance law an unfair trade practice involving false, maliciously critical, or derogatory statement intended to injure a person engaged in the insurance business. **(G)**

defamation. Any derogatory statement that is designed to injure a person's business or reputation. Defamation can be accomplished as libel (written) or slander (spoken). *See also* **libel or slander. (LE)**

defendant. The person being sued in a court action. **(LE)**

deferred annuity. An annuity contract that provides for the initiation of payments at some designated future date, in contrast to one in which payment begins immediately on purchase. **(AN)**

deferred compensation. A plan that may be qualified or nonqualified and that allows a key person to defer receipt of current income in accordance with a written agreement with the employer. Deferral is usually until death, disability, or retirement. **(PE)**

deferred compensation administrator. This refers to a company that provides services under a deferred compensation plan. Services may include administration of self-insured plans, compensation planning, salary surveys, retirement planning, and so forth. **(H)**

deferred group annuity. A group annuity contract providing for the purchase each year of a paid-up deferred annuity for each person covered in the group. The total amount of the annuity payments starts at a deferred date, usually retirement, and is the sum of the individual paid-up annuities. **(AN)**

deferred premium. The unpaid and yet undue premiums on life insurance, paid on other than an annual premium basis. **(LI)**

deferred vesting. That form of vesting under which rights to vested benefits are acquired by a participant commencing upon a fulfillment of specified requirements, usually reaching a certain age or number of years of service or membership. *See also* **vesting. (LI)**

deficiency reserve. A supplemental reserve that life insurers are required to show in their balance sheet if the gross premium charged on a class of insureds is less than the net level premium reserve or modified reserve. **(LI)**

deficit. Any excess of debits over credits at the end of a given accounting period. **(G, R)**

deficit carried forward. The transfer of a debit balance from one accounting period to another. **(G)**

defined benefit pension plan. A qualified retirement plan in which the employer makes contributions on behalf of all eligible employees to provide a specific retirement benefit. The amount of the contribution is not specifically defined, but the amount of the retirement benefit is defined. **(PE)**

defined contribution pension plan. A type of pension plan under which contributions are fixed as flat amounts or flat percentages of an employee's salary. Benefits consist of whatever amounts the accumulated contributions will produce. **(PE)**

deflation. An economic period characterized by falling prices, high unemployment, and a generally sluggish or slow economy. **(G)**

degree of care. A duty owed to others that depends on circumstances. Persons who invite others on their premises, those who invite children on their premises, and those who sell what might be considered inherently dangerous products are all required to take different degrees of care to prevent harm to others. **(LE)**

degree of risk. The amount of uncertainty that exists in a given situation. For instance, if you've chosen heads in the flip of a coin, the degree of risk present is 50%, since there is a 50% chance any flip of the coin will come up tails. *See also* **law of large number, odds,** and **probability. (G)**

delay clause. (1) A contract provision permitting the insurer to defer granting a loan on the sole security of the policy for any other purpose than that of paying premiums on the policy for a stated interval of time, usually six months. **(LI)** (2) A contract provision that excludes liability as a result of damage or loss of market arising out of delayed voyages. **(OM)**

delayed payment clause. In life insurance, a clause deferring payment to the beneficiary for a specified period after the death of the insured, with proceeds to be paid to contingent beneficiaries or the estate if the primary beneficiary does not survive the delay. It is used as one method of handling common-disaster situations, such as the death of the insured and the death of the primary beneficiary occurring in the same accident. The clause usually states that the beneficiary has to survive the death of the insured by a certain period of time in order to collect. **(LI)**

delivered business. Contracts issued by an insurer and delivered to an insured but not yet paid for. *See also* **examined business, paid business,** and **written business. (LI)**

delivery. The actual placing of a life or health insurance policy in the hands of an insured. **(H, LI)**

demand loan. Any loan with an indefinite maturity. **(G)**

demolition clause. A provision that excludes liability for costs incurred in demolishing undamaged property, often necessitated by building ordinances requiring that structures must be demolished after a certain degree of damage has been sustained. **(PR)**

demolition insurance. Insurance written to cover the cost of demolition excluded by a demolition clause. It may be endorsed to property insurance for an additional premium. *See also* **demolition clause. (PR)**

demurrer. A formal statement in a court action stating that even if the other party's facts are true, there is no cause of action. **(LE)**

dental insurance. A group health insurance contract that provides payment for certain enumerated dental services. **(H)**

dental plan. A dental plan is any contractual arrangement for dental services provided or arranged for on a prepaid or postpaid individual or group service basis. **(H)**

dental plan organization (DPO). A dental plan organization refers to a direct provider of dental services, compensated on a prepaid or postpaid basis, to individuals or groups. An arrangement for providing dental services indirectly through independent contractors or on a fee-for-service basis is not a DPO. A DPO may be an arrangement for dental services to be provided through an agreement with providers, or by employing dentists, where the dentists agree to treat enrollees of the plan in their private offices or a central facility. **(H)**

dental plan, supplemental. A supplemental dental plan is an arrangement in which a dentist or group of dentists agrees to relieve patients of paying any patient charges or copayments associated with dental insurance or other dental coverage for a predetermined fee. Supplemental dental plan may also refer to an arrangement that covers less than 50% of an enrollee's dental expenses, regardless of whether the enrollee has other coverage. **(H)**

Department of Health and Human Services. A federal department whose responsibility is primarily dealing with social service functions, such as administration and supervision of the Medicare program. **(H)**

dependent. An individual who depends on another for support and maintenance. **(G)**

dependent care plan. An employee benefit whereby the employee is reimbursed for dependent care expenses or an actual day care program provided by the employer on business premises. **(H)**

dependent coverage. Insurance coverage on the head of a family that is extended to his or her dependents, including only the lawful spouse and unmarried children who are not yet employed on a full-time basis. Children may be step, foster, and adopted children, as well as natural children. Certain age restrictions on children usually apply. **(H, LI)**

dependent life insurance. A life insurance benefit that is part of a group life insurance contract that provides death protection to the eligible dependents of a covered employee. **(LI)**

dependent properties. Properties that an insured business does not own, operate, or control, but upon which the insured's income depends. Examples include major suppliers or customers. Previously known as contingent properties. **(PR)**

deposit. The contributions or payments made to a fund by the employer, or, sometimes by both the employer and employee if there are employee contributions in the plan. **(PE)**

deposit administration (DA). A group annuity providing for the accumulation of contributions in an undivided fund out of which annuities are purchased for each covered person in the group for retirement purposes. **(LI)**

deposit administration group annuity. A group contract providing a deposit fund before retirement, with annuities bought from the fund at retirement. **(PE)**

deposit (or provisional) premium. The premium paid at the inception of a contract that provides for future premium adjustments. It is based on an estimate of what the final premium will be. *See also* **basic premium. (G)**

deposition. A sworn statement of a witness or other party in a judicial proceeding, usually conducted in an oral question and answer format where attendance is compelled. **(LE)**

depositor's forgery insurance. A type of protection against the forgery or alteration of instruments, such as checks, drafts, and promissory notes purported to have been written by the insured. It is issued to individuals, firms, and corporations, but not to banks or building and loan associations. It can be written to cover incoming items, but this is seldom done. **(C)**

depository bond. A form of bond that guarantees to the government that its deposits with banks will not be subject to loss. **(S)**

depreciation. A decrease in the value of any type of tangible property over a period of time resulting from use, wear and tear, or obsolescence. **(G)**

depreciation insurance. *See* replacement cost insurance. **(PR)**

designated mental health provider. The organization hired by a health plan to provide mental health and substance abuse services. **(H)**

detoxification. The process an individual goes through when withdrawing from alcohol. Usually is done under guidance of medical personnel. **(H)**

deviated rate. Companies that adhere to rates promulgated by a bureau sometimes offer lower rates than those recommended in certain areas. The company is said to have deviated from the bureau rate for that area. **(G)**

deviation. (1) Voluntary departure, not brought about by necessity and not resulting from reasonable cause, from the customary, usual course between the port of shipment and the port of destination; or certain fundamental breaches of the carrier's obligations under the contract of carriage. There are various types of deviations, including geographical deviation, deviation by carriage on a vessel other than the one agreed upon, deviation by carriage by rail, deviation by dry-docking with cargo on board, deviation by unreasonable delay, and deviation by carriage on deck. There are conditions under which deviation is excused, such as when it is reasonably necessary for the safety of the ship and cargo or for humanitarian reasons, such as rescuing another ship in distress. **(OM)** (2) A rate that varies from the manual rate. **(G)**

deviation clause. An ocean marine insurance clause providing the insured with coverage in the event of a deviation en route beyond the insured's control. **(OM)**

devise. A gift of real property in accordance with a valid will. **(EP)**

diagnosis. The process of identifying a disease. **(H)**

diagnosis related groups (DRGs). A method of classifying inpatient hospital services. It is used as a method of determining financing to reimburse various providers for services performed. **(H)**

difference in conditions (DIC). A separate contract that expands or supplements insurance on property written on a named perils basis so as to cover on an open perils (all risk) basis, subject to certain exclusions. **(PR)**

direct loss (or damage). A loss that is a direct consequence of a particular peril. Fire damage to a refrigerator would be a direct loss. Spoiling of food in the refrigerator as a result of the fire damage would be an indirect loss. *See also* **indirect loss** and **consequential loss. (PR)**

direct selling system. A distribution system within which an insurer deals directly with its insureds through its own employees. This definition applies typically to property and liability insurance business. Included are mail-order insurance and the sale of insurance from vending machines at airport booths and elsewhere. *See also* **independent agency system. (G)**

direct writer. (1) An insurer whose distribution mechanism is either the direct selling system or the exclusive agency system. **(LA, PR)** (2) The insurer that negotiates with the insured, as distinguished from the reinsurer. **(R)**

direct written premium. The premiums collected, without any allowance for premiums ceded to reinsurers. **(LA, PR)**

directed verdict. A verdict for the defendant based on the court's decision that the plaintiff's case has not been proven. **(LE)**

Director of Insurance. A title used in some states for the head of the Department of Insurance. *See also* **Commissioner of Insurance. (G)**

directors and officers liability insurance. Insurance that protects directors and officers from liability claims arising out of alleged errors in judgment, breaches of duty, and wrongful acts related to their organizational activities. **(LA)**

disability. A condition that curtails to some degree a person's ability to carry on normal pursuits. A disability may be partial or total, and temporary or permanent. **(G)**

disability benefit. The benefit payable under a disability income policy or a provision of some other policy, such as a life insurance contract. **(H, LI)**

disability benefits law. A state law requiring an employer to provide disability benefits to covered employees for nonoccupational injuries, in contrast to workers' compensation, which pays for occupational injuries. These laws are currently in effect in New York, New Jersey, Rhode Island, California, and Hawaii. **(H)**

disability buy-sell. A disability income policy used to fund a disability buy-sell agreement whereby after the elimination period, policy benefits enable a firm's partners to purchase the business interest held by a disabled partner. The policy's benefits may be paid in a lump sum or in installments. **(H)**

disability income insurance. A form of health insurance that provides periodic payments to replace income, actually or presumptively lost, when the insured is unable to work as a result of sickness or injury. **(H)**

Disability Insurance Training Council, Inc. The educational arm of the National Association of Health Underwriters, the health insurance agents' professional society. It seeks to encourage agent educational projects by local health associations, conducts university seminars in advanced health underwriting areas, and conducts annual seminars for home office executives in sociological social insurance and demographic trends that may affect future application of policy forms and health insurance. **(H)**

disability insured. A Social Security insured status required to satisfy eligibility for disability income benefits. The status is based on having paid Social Security taxes in 20 of the 40 calendar quarters ending with the quarter in which a disability claim is submitted. **(H)**

disability, long-term. *See* long-term disability . **(H)**

disability pension. A pension paid to a disabled worker before the time of normal retirement. **(LI)**

disability, permanent partial. *See* permanent partial disability. **(H, WC)**

disability, permanent total. *See* permanent total disability. **(H, WC)**

disability, short-term. *See* short-term disability. **(H)**

disability, temporary partial. *See* temporary partial disability. **(H, WC)**

disability, temporary total. *See* temporary total disability. **(H, WC)**

disappearing deductible. A type of deductible that gradually disappears as the loss gets larger. If the deductible is $50, the insurer will pay 111% of that part of the loss that is in excess of $50. The deductible on losses between $50 and $500 is gradually reduced by this system, and if the loss reaches $500, the full amount is covered. **(PR)**

discharge planning. Determining what the patient's medical needs will be after discharge from a hospital or other inpatient treatment. **(H)**

disclosure authorization form. A form authorizing the disclosure of personal information obtained in connection with an insurance transaction. Insurers are required to give applicants advance notice of their information practices. Among other things, the form must state the kind of information collected and to whom information may be disclosed. **(G)**

discount. The difference between an amount due at a future date and its present value at a specified rate of interest. **(PE)**

discounted (commuted) value table. A table showing the discounted or present value, for several interest rates, of dollars payable at various times in the future. **(G)**

discovery cover. A reinsurance treaty covering losses that are discovered during the term of the treaty regardless of when they were sustained. **(R)**

discovery period. (1) The period of time allowed an insured who has canceled a bond to discover and report to the previous surety a loss that occurred during the term of that bond. Losses so reported are paid by the original surety even though another surety is on the risk at the time of the discovery. The usual discovery period is one year. (2) A condition found in commercial crime policies that provides a period of time following the termination of the policy during which losses that occurred during the policy period, but were discovered after termination, will be covered. **(C, S)**

discrimination. Refusal of an insurer to provide comparable insurance or use comparable rates for certain individuals or groups with basic characteristics the same as those to whom the coverage or rates are offered. Unfair discrimination is prohibited by law. **(G)**

dishonesty, disappearance, and destruction policy (3-D policy). A once-popular commercial crime insurance form used to protect money and securities against loss by employee dishonesty, robbery, depositor's forgery, and other causes of loss. The 3-D policy has been replaced by modern commercial crime coverage forms. **(C)**

dismemberment. The loss of, or loss of use of, specified members of the body resulting from accidental bodily injury. **(H)**

dismemberment benefit. The benefits payable for various types of dismemberment. *See also* **accidental death and dismemberment** and **multiple indemnity. (H)**

dissent. This occurs when one or more judges disagrees with the majority decision. **(LE)**

distribution clause. *See* **pro rata distribution clause. (PR)**

divided cover. The placing of insurance on a given subject or object with more than one insurer. **(G)**

dividend. (1) The return of part of the premium paid for a policy issued on a participating basis by either a mutual or a stock insurer. (2) A portion of the surplus paid to the stockholders of a corporation. **(G)**

dividend accumulation. One of the options in a life insurance policy that allows the policyholder to leave any premium dividends with the insurer to accumulate at compound interest. **(LI)**

dividend additions. An option whereby the insured can leave dividends with the insurer, and each dividend is used to buy a single premium life insurance policy for whatever amount it will purchase. Also called **paid-up additions. (LI)**

dividend option. Alternative ways in which insureds under participating life insurance policies may elect to receive their policyholder dividends. **(LI)**

divisible contract clause. A clause providing that a violation of the conditions of the policy at one insured location will not void the coverage at other locations. **(PR)**

domestic. *See* residence employee. **(WC)**

domestic insurer (or company). An insurer formed under the laws of the state in which the insurance is written. **(G)**

donee. The recipient of a gift. **(EP)**

donor. The individual who gives a gift. **(EP)**

double indemnity. Payment of twice the basic benefit in the event of loss resulting from specified causes or under specified circumstances. For example, a life insurance contract may provide for twice the basic benefit if death is due to an accident. Accident policies may provide double indemnity coverage for death due to an elevator accident. *See also* **multiple indemnity. (H, LI)**

double protection. A form of life insurance combining whole life and an equivalent amount of term, with the term expiring at a stated future date, usually at 65 years of age. For example, an individual may purchase $50,000 worth of life insurance protection, $25,000 of it being term insurance and the other $25,000 whole life. The provision would state that the $25,000 of term insurance ceases when the insured reaches age 65. **(LI)**

dram shop laws. Liquor liability laws are called dram shop laws. They provide that a person serving someone who is intoxicated or contributing to the intoxication of another person may be liable for injury or damage caused by the intoxicated person. **(LE)**

dram shop liability insurance. A form of insurance contract that protects the owners of an establishment in which alcoholic beverages are sold against liability arising out of accidents caused by intoxicated customers who have been served or sold the alcoholic beverages. **(LA)**

dread (or specified) disease policy. Coverage, usually with a high maximum limit, for all types of medical expenses arising out of diseases named in the contract. Common diseases covered are poliomyelitis, diphtheria, multiple sclerosis, spinal meningitis, and tetanus. Cancer is sometimes covered or may be added with some companies by a rider. **(H)**

drive-in claim service. A facility maintained by an automobile insurer in which the extent of damage to a claimant's automobile can be determined and, in many cases, a settlement made. **(G)**

drive-other-car endorsement (DOC). A coverage that may be added to an automobile policy affording auto coverage to the individuals named in the endorsement while they are driving cars not owned by the individuals and not named in the policy. **(AU)**

drug formulary. A schedule of prescription drugs approved for use that will be covered by the plan and dispensed through participating pharmacies. **(H)**

drug price review (DPR). A procedure used to determine drug price maximums. It involves determining wholesale drug prices on the basis of the *American Druggist Blue Book.* **(H)**

drug utilization review (DUR). A method for evaluating or reviewing the use of drugs in order to determine the appropriateness of the drug therapy. **(H)**

druggists liability insurance. A contract that protects a druggist in case of a suit arising out of filling prescriptions, missed delivery of drugs, and other operations normal to a drugstore. **(LA)**

dual choice. The federal requirement that employers with 25 or more employees who are within the service area of a federally qualified HMO, who are paying at least minimum wage, and offer a health plan to their employees must offer HMO coverage as well as an indemnity plan. **(H)**

dual life stock company. A stock life insurer issuing both participating and nonparticipating policy contracts. **(G)**

Dun and Bradstreet, Inc. (D&B). A corporation that furnishes insurance companies with financial reports that assist them in the underwriting of prospective policyholders. **(G)**

duplicate coverage inquiry (DCI). A request to determine whether other coverage exists. Used to apply the coordination of benefits provisions where two or more insurance companies are involved. **(H)**

duplication of benefits. A situation in which identical or overlapping coverage exists between two or more insurance companies or service organizations. **(H)**

dwelling forms. A policy form designed specifically to cover a dwelling building and the personal property in it plus other additional coverages. There are several forms available, depending on what coverage is to be provided. **(PR)**

dynamo clause. *See* electrical exemption clause. **(PR)**

E

EC. *See* Extended Coverage. **(PR)**

ERISA. *See* Employee Retirement Income Security Act. **(H, LI)**

PRESENTATION OF TERMS

earned income. The money individuals earn as a result of working at some job or occupation for which they are paid a salary. **(G)**

earned premium. The amount of the premium that has been used up during the term of a policy. For example, if a one-year policy has been in effect six months, half of the total premium has been earned. **(G)**

earnings insurance. A form of gross earnings business interruption insurance, whose principal feature is the lack of a coinsurance clause. It is designed for small risks, and the maximum amount of loss the insured can collect in any 30-day period is established when the policy is written. **(PR)**

earth movement. A peril including landslide, mudflow, earth sinking, rising or shifting, and earthquake. Usually excluded on homeowners' and commercial property policies. **(PR)**

earthquake insurance. Insurance covering damage caused by an earthquake as defined in the contract. **(PR)**

easement. An interest in land owned by another that entitles its holder to specific uses. **(PR)**

economic risk. A risk experienced by those who invest in securities identified as the uncertainty of the economy. **(PE)**

educational assistance plan. An employee benefit whereby certain educational expenses incurred by the employee are reimbursed on a tax-favorable basis by the employer. **(PE)**

educational fund. One of the uses of life insurance. It is designed to provide money for a child's education should the breadwinner of the family die. **(LI)**

effective date. The date on which the protection of an insurance policy or bond goes into effect. **(G)**

elective benefits. Lump sum payments that the insured may generally choose in lieu of periodic payments for certain injuries, such as fractures and dislocations. **(H)**

elective deferral plan. A type of qualified plan (401(k) or TSA) whereby participants voluntarily elect to defer current amounts of compensation and these amounts are placed in a retirement plan on a tax favorable basis. **(PE)**

elective indemnities. *See* elective benefits. **(H)**

electrical (or electrical apparatus) exemption clause. A clause providing that damage to electrical appliances caused by artificially generated electrical currents is recoverable only if fire ensues and then only for the damage caused by the fire. **(PR)**

electronic data processing (EDP) coverage. Specialized type of insurance designed to cover computer equipment, data systems, information storage media, and expenses or income loss related to EDP losses. **(PR)**

elevator collision coverage. Coverage for damage caused by collision of an elevator without regard to fault. This includes damage to personal property, the building, and thes elevator itself. Liability coverage is usually provided automatically by business liability policies. **(LA, PR)**

eligibility date. The date that a person is eligible for benefits. **(H)**

eligibility period. (1) The period during which potential members of a group life or health program may enroll without providing evidence of insurability. (2) The period under a major medical policy during which reimbursable expenses may be accrued. **(H)**

eligibility requirements. Requirements imposed for eligibility for coverage, usually in a group insurance or pension plan. **(H, LI)**

eligible dependent. A dependent of an insured person who is eligible for coverage according to the requirements set forth in the contract. **(H)**

eligible employee. An employee who is eligible on the basis of the requirements as indicated in the group contract. **(H)**

eligible expenses. Expenses as defined in the health plan as being eligible for coverage. This could involve specified health services fees or customary and reasonable charges. **(H)**

eligible person. Similar to eligible employee, except that it could be a contract covering people who are not employees of a specified employer. An example might be members of an association or union. **(H)**

elimination period. A loosely used term, sometimes designating the probationary period, but most often designating the waiting period in a health insurance policy. *See also* **probationary period** and **waiting period. (H)**

embezzlement. Fraudulent use of money or property that has been entrusted to one's care. **(S)**

emergency. An injury or disease that happens suddenly and requires treatment within 24 hours. **(H)**

emergency accident benefit. A group medical benefit that reimburses the insured for expenses incurred for emergency treatment of accidents. **(H)**

emergency fund. One of the uses of life insurance that provides money for the emergency expenses of a deceased's family before the final settlement of the estate. **(LI)**

emergi-center. *See* freestanding emergency medical services center. **(H)**

emotional distress. *See* mental distress. **(G)**

employee benefit program. Benefits offered an employee at work by the employer, covering such contingencies as medical expenses, disability, retirement, and death, usually paid for wholly or in part by the employer. These benefits are usually insured. **(H, LI)**

employee certificate of insurance. The employee's evidence of participation in a group insurance plan, consisting of a brief summary of plan benefits. The employee is provided with a certificate of insurance rather than the actual insurance policy. **(H, LI)**

employee contribution. The employee's share of the premium costs. **(H)**

employee contribution. Deduction from employee's pay to apply toward the cost of a retirement plan. **(PE)**

employee dishonesty. Any dishonest act of an employee that may contribute to a loss for the employer. **(C)**

employee dishonesty coverage form. A commercial crime coverage form, which is actually a fidelity bond, providing coverage for losses resulting from employee dishonesty. This form covers losses of money, securities, and property other than money and securities. Separate crime coverage forms have been largely replaced by newer crime policies that provide multiple coverage options in a single policy. **(C)**

employee pension benefit plan or pension plan. Any program established and maintained by an employer or an employee organization providing retirement benefits to employees or deferred income until employment is terminated. **(PE)**

Employee Retirement Income Security Act (ERISA). This act prescribes federal standards for funding, participation, vesting, termination, disclosure, fiduciary responsibility, and tax treatment of private pension plans. **(LI)**

employee stock ownership plan (ESOP). A qualified employee plan that provides eligible employees with part ownership in the corporation for which they work. Stock is issued and held in trust for the benefit of the employees. **(PE)**

employee welfare benefit plan. Any program established or maintained by an employer or an employee organization to provide its participants or their beneficiaries with medical, surgical, or hospital care, or benefits in the event of sickness, accident, disability, death or unemployment. **(PE)**

employees' trust. One way for a pension or profit-sharing plan to be financed and given effect. **(PE)**

employer contribution. The portion of the cost of a health insurance plan that is borne by the employer. **(H)**

employers liability coverage. This is coverage B of the standard workers' compensation policy. It provides coverage against the common law liability of an employer for injuries to employees, as distinguished from the liability imposed by a workers' compensation law. Employers liability applies in situations where a worker does not come under these laws. **(WC)**

employers nonownership liability insurance. Protects the employer for liability arising from the use by employees of their own cars on company business. **(AU)**

employment benefit plan. Any plan that is both an employee welfare plan and an employee pension plan. **(PE)**

employment practices liability insurance. Type of policy that covers a business's losses arising out of wrongful termination, discrimination, sexual harassment, and other employment-related practices. **(LA)**

encounter. Each time a person meets with a health care provider to receive services, it is a separate encounter. **(H)**

encumbrance. A claim on property, such as a mortgage, a lien for work and materials, or a right of dower. The interest of the property owner is reduced by the amount of the encumbrance. **(LE)**

endorsement. A written or printed form attached to the policy that alters provisions of the contract. **(G)**

endorsement extending period of indemnity. An endorsement attached to business interruption policies that extends coverage to the period during which a business has reopened for business but has not reached the level of business activity that existed before the business interruption loss. **(PR)**

endorsement split dollar. A split-dollar plan in which the employer owns and controls a life policy on the life of an employee. The employee's rights to certain policy benefits are protected by an employer endorsement. **(LI)**

endowment insurance. A form of life insurance in which the face amount is payable to the insured at the end of the contract period or to a beneficiary if the insured dies before that. An example would be an insured purchasing an endowment payable at age 65. Upon reaching that age, the proceeds would be payable to the insured. If the insured dies before reaching that age, the proceeds would be payable to the designated beneficiary as a life insurance benefit. **(LI)**

engineer (loss prevention engineer or safety consultant). An insurer's staff member who is charged with the responsibility of loss prevention and who assists in the securing of underwriting and rating information. **(LA, PR)**

enrollee. An eligible individual who is enrolled in a health plan; does not include an eligible dependent. **(H)**

enrolling unit. The organization (such as an employer) that contracts for participation in a health insurance plan. **(H)**

enrollment. Used to describe the total number of enrollees in a health plan. It may also be used to refer to the process of enrolling people in a health plan. **(H)**

enrollment period. The amount of time an employee has to sign up for a contributory health plan. **(H)**

entire contract clause. A provision in an insurance contract stating that the entire agreement between the insured and the insurer is contained in the contract, including the application if it is attached, declarations, insuring agreements, exclusions, conditions, and endorsements. **(H, LI)**

entity agreement. A buy-sell agreement usually used with a partnership in which the partnership agrees to purchase the interest of a deceased or disabled partner. **(LI)**

entry age. The age when an employee satisfies all the age, service, and other eligibility requirements for participation in a pension plan. **(PE)**

entry date into claims-made. Initial effective date of a claims-made liability policy. An entry date is used to determine extent of maturity for rating purposes. If claims-made coverage is interrupted and reestablished, or if a retroactive date is changed on renewal, the entry date will change. **(LA)**

environmental restoration. Restitution for the loss, damage, or destruction of natural resources arising out of the accidental discharge or escape of any commodity transported by a motor carrier, including the cost of removal and measures to minimize damage to human health, the natural environment, fish, shellfish, and wildlife. Federal regulations require common carriers of hazardous materials to maintain minimum liability coverages for bodily injury, property damage, and environmental restoration. **(AU, LE)**

equipment breakdown protection coverage. *See* boiler and machinery insurance. **(PR)**

equipment floater. A form that covers various types of equipment (e.g., construction equipment) against specified perils or occasionally on an all-risk basis subject to exclusions. **(IM)**

equity. The money value of an insurance company that is over and above its liabilities. Liabilities include almost all of its reserves. **(G)**

equity-indexed annuity. An annuity that provides a guarantee of principal and also has interest rates that are linked to growth in the equity (stock) markets as measured by a market index. The owner enjoys the upside potential of the equity markets but is not subject to downside risk. **(AN)**

ERISA liability. Liability imposed by law upon officers or other employees operating in a fiduciary capacity for the proper handling of pension funds and other employee benefits. It is excluded from most general liability policies. *See* **Employee Retirement Income Security Act (ERISA). (LA)**

errors and omissions clause. A clause usually found in an obligatory reinsurance treaty that provides that if an error is made or an omission takes place in describing a risk that falls within the automatic reinsurance coverage of the treaty, it shall not invalidate the liability of the reinsurer for the risk. **(R)**

errors and omissions insurance. (1) A form of insurance that indemnifies the insured for any loss sustained because of an error or oversight on his part. For instance, an insurance agency purchases this type of coverage to protect itself against losses from such things as failing to issue a policy. (2) A form of insurance that covers losses resulting from financial institutions failing to effect insurance coverage. **(LA)**

estate plan. A plan for the disposition of one's property at death, including the handling of property in the event of the incompetency or total disability of the estate owner. A will is part of an estate plan. **(G)**

estate planning. The process of accumulation, conservation, distribution, and administration of an estate in order to minimize the impact of taxation and estate shrinkage. **(EP)**

estate tax. A tax payable to the federal government. The amount is based on the value of the estate of the decedent. **(EP, LE)**

estimated premium. A provisional premium that is adjusted at the end of the year. For example, in workers' compensation insurance, an estimated premium is based on estimated payrolls for the coming year. At the end of the year, final payrolls are determined and the final premium is computed. **(G)**

estoppel. The legal principle whereby a person loses the right to deny that a certain condition exists by virtue of having acted in such a way as to persuade others that the condition does exist. For example, if an insurer allows an insured to violate one of the conditions of the policy, the insurer cannot at a later date void the policy because the condition was violated. The insurer has acted in such a way as to lead the insured to believe that the violation did not void the coverage. **(LE)**

evidence clause. A clause in a policy that requires the insured to cooperate in the investigation of a claim by producing records and submitting to examinations. This is required to help an adjuster establish the validity of a claim. An evidence clause in a health policy requires the insured to submit to physical examinations. **(G)**

evidence of coverage. *See* certificate of insurance. **(H)**

evidence of insurability. Any information concerning health status required for to satisfy underwriting standards, such as a medical examination or physician's statement. **(H, LI)**

ex gratia payment. Latin for "from favor." A payment by an insurer to an insured for which there is no liability under the contract. In some cases, an insurer may feel there has been a mistake or a misunderstanding, and it may pay a claim even though it does not appear to be liable. **(G)**

examination. An examination of an insurance company by the state insurance department. **(G)**

Examiner. An employee assigned by the state insurance department to audit insurers' records. **(G)**

examiner. A physician appointed by the medical director of a life or health insurer to examine applicants. **(H, LI)**

excepted period. *See* probationary period. **(H, LI)**

exception. A provision in an insurance policy that eliminates coverage. *See also* exclusion. **(H)**

excess insurance. A coverage that is designed to be in excess over one or more primary coverages and that does not pay a loss until the loss amount exceeds a certain sum. *See also* primary coverage. **(G)**

excess interest. Interest credited to an insured's contract in excess of the amount guaranteed by the terms of the contract. **(LI)**

excess limit. (1) The limit provided in a policy that is in excess of the basic limit. *See* basic limit. (2) A limit provided in a separate policy with another insurer that is in excess of the limit provided in the basic policy. **(LA)**

excess line broker. A person licensed to place insurance not available in his state through insurers not licensed to do business in the state. A person licensed to deal with nonadmitted insurers. **(G)**

excess loss premium factor. This expression is used in connection with retrospective rating plans. It is a factor that compensates the insurer for the fact that the insured has elected to limit the effects of any one large loss under the retrospective rating formula. For example, the insured might elect a loss limitation of $50,000, which would mean that would be the maximum amount of any one loss that would go into the retrospective calculation. **(WC)**

excess of loss ratio reinsurance. *See* aggregate excess of loss reinsurance. **(R)**

excess of loss reinsurance. (1) A generic term describing reinsurance that, subject to a specified limit, indemnifies the ceding company against the amount of loss in excess of the specified retention. It includes various types of reinsurance, such as catastrophe, per risk, per account, and aggregate excess of loss. *See also* **pro rata reinsurance.** (2) A form of reinsurance that indemnifies the ceding company for the portion of the loss that results from a single occurrence, however defined, that exceeds a predetermined amount, which is referred to as a first loss retention or deductible. **(R)**

excess per risk reinsurance. A form of excess of loss reinsurance that, subject to a specified limit, indemnifies the ceding company against the amount of loss in excess of a specified retention with respect to each risk involved in each occurrence. **(R)**

excess plan. A retirement plan designed around the benefits of Social Security. **(PE)**

excluded period. *See* probationary period. **(H)**

exclusion. A contractual provision that denies coverage for certain perils, persons, property, or locations. **(G)**

exclusion ratio. The relationship or ratio of cost basis to total expected return from an annuity; used to calculate the percentage of each annuity payment that is considered to be a return of cost basis. **(AN)**

exclusive agency system. An insurance distribution system within which agents sell and service insurance contracts that limit representation to one insurer and that reserve to the insurer the ownership, use, and control of policy records and expiration date. *See also* **captive agent, direct writer,** and **independent agency system. (G)**

exclusive provider organization (EPO). A type of preferred provider organization in which individual members use particular preferred providers rather than having a choice of a variety of preferred providers. EPOs are characterized by a primary physician who monitors care and makes referrals to a network of providers. **(H)**

exculpatory. The portion of a contract or agreement that relieves one party to the agreement of the consequences of his own acts. **(LE)**

executor. The person or entity specified by will who is responsible for the probating of an individual's will and the settlement of an estate. **(G)**

exemplary damages. *See* punitive damages. **(LE)**

exhibitions insurance. A type of policy designed for people who display their products through public exhibitions. Usually written on an all-risk basis with certain specified exclusions. **(IM)**

expectation of life. The average number of years of life remaining for persons of a given age according to a particular mortality table. Also called life expectancy. **(LI)**

expected claims. The estimated claims for a person or group for a contract year, usually based on actuarial statistics. **(H)**

expected morbidity. The expected incidence of sickness or injury within a given group during a given period of time as shown on a morbidity table. **(H)**

expected mortality. The expected incidence of death within a given group during a given period as shown on a mortality table. **(LI)**

expediting expenses. Expenses incurred in order to speed up repair or replacement so as to reduce the amount of loss by a peril covered in a policy. Most commonly used in connection with business interruption and boiler and machinery insurance. Expediting expenses are generally covered if they do reduce the amount of the loss that the insurer would otherwise have to pay. **(PR)**

expense. A policy's share of the company's operating costs, fees for medical examinations and inspection reports, underwriting, printing costs, commissions, advertising, agency expenses, premium taxes, salaries, rent, and so forth. Such costs are important in determining dividends and premium rates. **(H)**

expense allowance. A compensation paid to an insurance agent in excess of prescribed commissions. **(G)**

expense constant. A flat charge added to the premium of small accounts where the premium is so low that the cost of issuing and servicing the policy cannot be recovered. Most often used with workers' compensation policies. **(G)**

expense guarantee. One of the guarantees of all annuities—that is, the guarantee that expenses, such as the cost of doing business, will not be increased or exceed a certain percentage of the annuity contributions. **(AN)**

expense incurred. *See* incurred expense. **(G)**

expense loading. The amount added to the rate during the ratemaking process to cover expenses. **(G)**

expense ratio. The percentage of the premium dollar devoted to paying the expenses of an insurer, other than losses. **(G)**

expense reimbursement allowance. *See* expense allowance. **(G)**

expense reserve. A liability for incurred but unpaid expenses. **(G)**

expenses. The cost of conducting an insurance operation aside from the amount paid for losses. **(G)**

experience. (1) The loss record. It can be that of an insured, an agent, a territory, a type of insurance written, or any other category. (2) A statistical compilation relating losses to premiums. **(G)**

experience modification. The increase or decrease in premiums resulting from the application of an experience rating plan, usually expressed as a percentage. *See* experience rating. **(G)**

experience, policy year. *See* policy year experience. **(G)**

experience rating. A method of adjusting the premium for a risk on the basis of past loss experience for that risk, compared with loss experience for an average risk. *See also* prospective rating and retrospective rating. **(G)**

experience refund. In life reinsurance, a predetermined percentage of the net reinsurance profit that the reinsurer returns to the ceding company as a form of profit sharing at year's end. **(R)**

experienced mortality. The mortality that actually occurs to a group of insureds of a given insurance company, in contrast to expected mortality. *See* expected mortality. **(LI)**

experienced mortality or morbidity. The actual mortality or morbidity experienced in a group of insureds, compared with the expected mortality or morbidity. **(H, LI)**

experimental or unproven procedures. Any health care services, supplies, procedures, therapies, or devices that the health plan determines regarding coverage for a particular case to be either (1) not proven by scientific evidence to be effective, or (2) not accepted by health care professionals as being effective. **(H)**

expiration. The date indicated in an insurance contract as its termination date. **(G)**

expiration card. A way of recording the date on which a policy terminates. It is used to remind the agent or sales representative of a policy coming up for renewal. **(G)**

expiration file. A record kept by agents or insurers of the dates on which policies they have written or are servicing expire. **(G)**

expiration notice. Notification to the insured of the impending termination of the insurance contract. **(G)**

expiry. The termination of a term life insurance policy at the end of its period of coverage. **(LI)**

explanation of benefits (EOB). The statement sent to a participant in a health plan listing services, amounts paid by the plan, and total amount billed to the patient. **(H)**

explanation of Medicare benefits. A notice that is sent to the Medicare patient and that provides information designed to explain how the claim is to be paid. **(H)**

explosion, collapse, and underground Damage. *See* XCU. **(LA)**

explosion insurance. Insurance against loss of property due to explosion but not including explosion of steam boilers, pipes, and certain pressure instruments. Most commonly written as part of the extended coverage endorsement. **(PR)**

exports. Materials and goods shipped to other countries. **(G)**

exposure. (1) The state of being subject to the possibility of loss. (2) The extent of risk as measured by payroll, gate receipts, area, or other standards. (3) The possibility of loss to a risk being caused by its surroundings. This is used in property insurance rating. (4) Surroundings producing a loss to the insured property. An example of the last two definitions (3 and 4) would be an insured building suffering loss because a dynamite factory next to it exploded. **(G)**

exposure units. (1) These units refer to individuals or property that may be subject to loss or damage on which a monetary value may be placed. When these exposure units have similar characteristics they meet the requirement of insurability as homogeneous exposure units. (2) The term may also be used to refer to the premium base, in the sense that the exposure multiplied by the rate equals the premium. For example, in workers' compensation, each $100 of payroll is an exposure unit. **(G)**

express authority. Authority of an agent that is specifically granted by the insurer in the agency contract or agreement. **(G)**

extended care facility. A facility such as a nursing home that is licensed to provide 24-hour nursing care service in accordance with state and local laws. Three levels of care—skilled, intermediate, and custodial—or any combination of them may be provided. **(H)**

extended coverage (EC). A common extension of property insurance beyond coverage for fire and lightning. Extended coverage adds insurance against loss by the perils of windstorm, hail, explosion, riot and riot attending a strike, aircraft damage, vehicle damage, and smoke damage. At one time, EC was added by endorsement. In recent years, it has been included on many forms as either an optional coverage or as part of the minimum coverages provided. **(PR)**

extended death benefit. A group policy provision that will pay the life benefit when (1) the insured is totally and continuously disabled at the time the policyholder stops paying premium until the insured's death, and (2) if the insured dies within one year of the date the premium payments stopped, or prior to age 65. **(LI)**

extended nonowner liability. An endorsement attached to a personal auto policy to provide broader liability coverage only for specifically named individuals. When attached, it covers nonowned autos furnished for the regular use of an insured, use of vehicles to carry persons or property for a fee, and broader coverage for business use of vehicles. **(AU)**

extended period of indemnity. A business income coverage that continues coverage for income losses for a period of time after operations have resumed. **(PR)**

extended reporting period (ERP). A period allowing for making claims after expiration of a claims-made liability policy. Also known as a tail. *See also* **basic ERP, supplemental ERP, mini tail, midi tail,** and **maxi tail. (LA)**

extended term insurance. A provision in most policies that provides the option of continuing the existing amount of insurance as term insurance for as long a period as the contract's cash value will purchase. This is one of the nonforfeiture options available to the insured in case a premium is not paid within the grace period. *See also* **nonforfeiture values. (LI)**

extended wait. A form of reinsurance under which, after the ceding insurer has paid monthly benefits to the claimant for a given number of months under a disability insurance contract, further benefits will be paid by the reinsurer. **(R)**

extension of benefits. A condition in the insurance policy that allows coverage to continue beyond the expiration date of the policy in the case of employees who are not actively at work or dependents who are hospitalized on that date. The extended coverage applies only where the employee or dependent is disabled as of that date and continues only until the employee returns to work or the dependent leaves the hospital. **(H)**

extortion. The surrender of property away from an insured's premises as a result of a threat to do bodily harm to an insured or an employee, or to a relative or invitee of either, who is or allegedly is being held captive. **(C)**

extortion coverage form. A commercial crime coverage form that protects against loss of money, securities, and property other than money and securities, resulting from extortion. Separate crime coverage forms have been largely replaced by newer crime policies that provide multiple coverage options in a single policy. **(C)**

extra expense coverage form. A commercial property form designed to cover extra expenses incurred by a business so it can remain in operation following a property loss. *See* **extra expense insurance. (PR)**

extra expense insurance. A form that provides reimbursement to the insured for the extra expenses reasonably incurred to continue the operation of a business when the described property has been damaged by a peril covered by the contract. This insurance is normally used by businesses where continuity of operation, regardless of cost, is a necessity, such as any business that would permanently lose customers if there were any suspension of operations. The term **additional living expense insurance** is defined with regard to extra expenses incurred by individuals, and such coverage is a common feature of homeowner policies. **(PR)**

extra percentage tables. Mortality or morbidity tables showing the extra premium for certain impaired health conditions. Usually, this premium is shown as a percentage of the standard premium. A form of substandard rating. **(H, LI)**

extra premium. An added premium charge for extra hazardous exposures that is levied because the normal rate does not take these into account. **(G)**

extra premium removal. Removal of an extra premium when the cause for it ceases to exist. **(G)**

F

ABBREVIATIONS AND ACRONYMS

FAIR plan. Fair Access to Insurance Requirements. State-run pools that make insurance available to those in high-risk areas who cannot obtain insurance through normal channels. Coverages for fire and allied perils are available, with considerably high limits, after inspection of the premises. **(PR)**

FAS. *See* **free along side. (OM)**

FASB. *See* **Financial Accounting Standards Board. (H)**

FCAS. *See* **Fellow of the Casualty Actuarial Society. (G)**

FC&S. *See* **free-of-capture-and-seizure clause. (OM)**

FC&S Bulletins. *Fire, Casualty, and Surety Bulletins.* Bulletins published by the National Underwriter Company, explaining coverages, forms, underwriting, and rating procedures for the various property, casualty, and surety lines of insurance. **(G)**

FCII. Fellow of the Chartered Insurance Institute, whose designation is gained by the completion of examinations and other requisites. **(G)**

FDIC. *See* **Federal Deposit Insurance Corporation. (G)**

FEGLI. Federal Employees Group Life Insurance. **(LI)**

FEMA. *See* **Federal Emergency Management Agency. (PR)**

FICA. Federal Insurance Contributions Act. A law imposing a payroll tax to assist in funding Social Security benefits. **(G)**

FLMI. Fellow of the Life Management Institute. *See* **Life Office Management Association. (LI)**

FOB. *See* **free on board. (G)**

FPA. *See* **free of particular average. (OM)**

FSA. *See* **Fellow of the Society of Actuaries. (G)**

face. The first page of a life insurance policy. **(LI)**

PRESENTATION OF TERMS

face amount. The amount of insurance provided by the terms of an insurance contract, usually found on the face of the policy. In a life insurance policy, the death benefit. **(G)**

facility-of-payment clause. A contract provision found in industrial life policies that permits the insurer to pay a portion of the proceeds of the policy to any relative or person who has possession of the policy and who appears equitably entitled to such payment. This provision is designed to facilitate payment when some doubt may exist as to who the beneficiary is and to save legal expenses in the settling of an estate. **(LI)**

factored rating. *See* adjusted community rating. **(H)**

factory mutuals. Member insurers of the Factory Mutual System, which is a group of mutual coinsurers formed to provide member insurers with insurance and engineering services. **(PR)**

facultative certificate of reinsurance. A document formalizing a facultative reinsurance policy. **(R)**

facultative (or specific) reinsurance. Reinsurance by offer and acceptance of individual risks, wherein the reinsurer retains the faculty to accept or reject each risk offered by the ceding company. *See also* treaty reinsurance. **(R)**

Fair Credit Reporting Act. Public Law 91-508 requires that an applicant be advised if a consumer report may be requested and be told the scope of the possible investigation. Should the request for insurance be declined because of information contained in that report, the applicant must be given the name and address of the reporting agency. **(G)**

fair rental value coverage. Insurance that pays the loss of rental value, minus expenses that do not continue, when property rented to others or held for rental is damaged by a peril insured against. **(PR)**

family automobile policy. A form that was once widely used to write automobile insurance for individual car owners. It is a package policy that provides protection against legal liability for bodily injury and property damage to others, injury to the insured and other occupants of the vehicle, and damage to the vehicle itself. It has largely been replaced by the more modernized personal auto policy. **(AU)**

family dependent. A person entitled to coverage because he is (1) the enrollee's spouse, or (2) a single dependent child of either the enrollee or the enrollee's spouse (including stepchildren and legally adopted children), and (3) a resident of the enrollee's home. **(H)**

family expense policy. A policy that insures the medical expenses of all members of a family. **(H)**

family income policy. A policy that pays an income up to some future date designated in the policy to the beneficiary after the death of the insured. The period of payment is measured from the date of the inception of the contract, and at the end of the income period, the face amount of the policy is paid to the beneficiary. If the insured lives beyond the income period, only the face amount is payable in the event of the insured's death. **(LI)**

family maintenance policy. A policy that pays an income to the beneficiary starting after the death of the insured and continuing for a stated period. At the end of the income period, the face amount of the policy is paid to the beneficiary. **(LI)**

family policy. This policy typically consists of whole life insurance for the head of the household, with smaller amounts of term insurance on other family members. **(LI)**

family protection endorsement. *See* uninsured motorists endorsement. **(AU)**

farm coverage part. One of the coverage parts available under the commercial package policy program. Coverages may be included for farm property, agricultural equipment, livestock, and farm liability. **(LA, PR)**

farm liability coverage form. A commercial liability form attached to a farm coverage part to provide coverage for bodily injury, property damage, personal injury, advertising injury, and medical payments for farm exposures. **(LA)**

farm personal property. Scheduled or unscheduled classes of farm property that may be covered by the farm property coverage form. It may include grain, feed, supplies, livestock, farm machines, and farm vehicles. *See also* household personal property. **(PR)**

farm property coverage form. A farm coverage form that may be used to cover residential dwellings, other private structures, household personal property, farm personal property, and other farm structures. **(PR)**

farmers comprehensive personal liability. Similar to the comprehensive personal liability policy but adapted to cover farm hazards, such as damage caused by grazing animals. **(LA)**

farmowners-ranchowners policy. A package policy providing property coverage on farm dwelling buildings and contents, as well as barns, stables, and other farm outbuildings. Liability coverage is also included. It is similar to a homeowners policy adapted to cover farm properties. **(PR)**

Federal Crime Insurance Program. A federally administered program under which pooling companies write crime insurance for those unable to secure it in the open market. Available for residential and commercial risks in various states. **(C)**

Federal Crop Insurance Corporation. An agency within the US Department of Agriculture that provides insurance on growing crops. **(PR)**

Federal Deposit Insurance Corporation (FDIC). An agency of the federal government that insures bank deposits up to a stated maximum. **(G)**

Federal Emergency Management Agency (FEMA). A government agency that provides disaster relief during emergencies such as floods, fires, and earthquakes. **(PR)**

Federal Employees Compensation Act. Under this act, workers' compensation benefits are provided to civilian federal government employees. The US government administers and operates the system, as well as provides the benefits. Therefore, no private insurance is involved. **(WC)**

Federal Employers Liability Act (FELA). Passed by Congress in 1908 before there were workers' compensation statutes and benefits in this country, this act applies to railroad workers only. It puts injured workers in a favorable position in terms of liability claims, allowing them to sue the employer for negligence. Because railroad workers and their unions were unwilling to trade their favorable positions for statutory benefits, they remain exempt from compensation laws in many states. Cases are decided on the issue of employer liability. **(WC)**

federal estate tax. The federal tax imposed on the deceased's estate, which includes the total assets composing a person's estate at death. **(G)**

Federal Insurance Administration. A government office, part of the Department of Housing and Urban Development,, that oversees the handling of Fair Access to Insurance Requirements plans, Federal Crime Insurance plans, and the federal flood program. **(G)**

Federal Insurance Contributions Act (FICA). *See* FICA. **(G)**

federal officials bond. A bond that provides reimbursement to the federal government for loss occasioned by the dishonest acts of its employees or their lack of faithful performance. **(S)**

federal qualification. Approval of any HMO made by the **Centers for Medicare and Medicaid Services** after conducting their evaluation of methods of doing business, documents, contracts, facilities, and systems. **(H)**

Federal Terrorism Risk Insurance Act of 2002. Federal law designed to ensure that insurance coverage for terrorism losses under commercial lines policies will be available and affordable. It requires insurers to pay a specified amount for terrorism losses in a given calendar year; once that limit is reached, the federal government will reimburse insurers a specified percentage of insured losses that exceed the limit. **(G)**

fee-for-service equivalency. The difference between the amount a provider receives from a reimbursement system, such as capitation (e.g., a flat charge per month), compared with fee-for-service reimbursement. **(H)**

fee-for-service reimbursement. A health care system in which physicians and other providers receive payment on the basis of their billed charge for each service provided. **(H)**

fee maximum. The maximum amount available to a provider for specific health care services under a contract. **(H)**

fee schedule. A list of maximum fees for providers who are on a fee-for-service basis. **(H)**

fee simple. Complete ownership of property with the unconditional right to dispose of it. *See also* **joint tenancy** and **tenancy in common.** **(LE)**

Fellow, Life Management Institute (FLMI). *See* Life Office Management Association. **(LI)**

Fellow of the Casualty Actuarial Society (FCAS). This designation is gained by the completion of a series of examinations and other requirements. **(LA)**

Fellow of the Society of Actuaries (FSA). A designation gained by the completion of a series of examinations, as well as other experience requirements. **(LA, PR)**

fellow servant rule. A common-law defense used by employers before the passage of compensation laws. It held that if an employee was injured as a result of the carelessness of a fellow employee, the right of action was against the fellow worker and not against the employer. **(WC)**

fictitious groups. Groups formed primarily for the purpose of buying insurance. Under the law, such groups may not be underwritten. **(G)**

fidelity bond. A bond that will reimburse an employer, the insured, for loss due to the dishonest acts of a covered employee. **(S)**

fiduciary. A person holding the funds or property of another in a position of trust, who is obligated to act in a prudent and ethical manner. Examples would be an attorney, a bank trustee, and the executor of an estate. **(G)**

fiduciary bond. A bond that guarantees the faithful performance of a fiduciary. **(S)**

field. (1) *See* field force. (2) A type or line of insurance (e.g., the life insurance field). (3) An area or territory covered by an agent, agency, or insurer. **(G)**

field force. The agents and supervisory personnel of insurers who operate away from the home office in the branch offices and general agencies of the company. **(G)**

field representative. *See* special agent. **(G)**

field underwriting. The initial screening of prospective buyers of health insurance, performed by sales personnel in the field. May also include quoting of premium rates. **(H)**

file-and-use rating laws. State laws pertaining to insurance rates that permit insurers to adopt new rates without the prior approval of the insurance department. Usually, insurers submit their new rates along with supporting statistical evidence, but this is not necessary in all cases. **(LE)**

financed insurance. Payment of insurance premiums, in whole or in part, with funds derived from borrowing, usually from the cash value of the policy. Also known as minimum deposit insurance. **(LE)**

financed premium. The payment of insurance premiums with funds borrowed outside the contract itself. **(LI)**

Financial Accounting Standards Board (FASB). A nongovernmental group that sets standards for generally accepted accounting principles. **(H)**

financial guarantee bond. A guarantee that others will pay sums of money due. A sales tax bond, for example, guarantees the state that the merchant will pay sales taxes on time and in full. **(S)**

financial responsibility clause. A clause stating that a policy conforms to the financial responsibility laws of any state in which the insured is operating the insured vehicle. **(AU)**

financial responsibility law. A state law that requires the insured to furnish evidence of ability to pay for losses. Some laws require this evidence before an accident, whereas others require evidence after the first accident. Evidence of ability to pay most often takes the form of an insurance policy with certain minimum limits of coverage. **(AU)**

financial statement. The disclosure of the financial results of a firm's operations. It involves the balance sheet, profit and loss statement, and associated information. **(G)**

fine arts floater. Covers fine arts, such as antiques, leaded glass, and other art work of all types, usually on an open perils (all risk) basis. **(IM)**

fine print. A reference to imaginary small type in a policy contract supposedly containing exclusions, reductions, exemptions, and limitations of coverage. Most state laws include specifications for the minimum type size that can be used in a policy, and they also provide that exclusions cannot be printed in type smaller than that used to print the benefits. **(G)**

fire. Combustion that is rapid enough to produce a flame or glow. Property insurance only covers hostile fires, which means fires that have escaped their intended limits or that were not started intentionally. Fires in their proper contained area are called friendly fires and are not covered under most basic property insurance policies. **(PR)**

fire damage limit. A general liability limit that applies only to the coverage for fire legal liability. **(LA)**

fire department service clause. A provision in a fire insurance policy that provides the insured with indemnification for charges incurred as a result of action by a fire department to save the insured's property. It is useful for property located outside the jurisdiction of the nearest fire department and where the call will be answered only for a fee. **(PR)**

fire legal liability. An insurance policy that protects the insured against liability incurred when the insured's negligent actions result in the destruction of property that is in the insured's care, custody, or control. **(PR)**

fire maps. A visual record of the distribution of fire insurance written by all reporting insurers placed on sectional maps. The maps show graphically the distribution of the insureds' covered properties in a given area and make it possible to avoid catastrophic losses. **(PR)**

fire mark. An insignia, generally metal, once placed on buildings insured by the insurer represented by the mark. Because the insurers had their own fire brigades, they had to check the mark on a burning building to determine whether they should extinguish the fire. **(G)**

fire marshal. A public official responsible for the prevention and investigation of fires. The marshal and his office are usually financed by a tax on the premiums of property insurers. **(PR)**

fire-resistive construction. A building that has exterior walls, floors, and roof constructed of masonry or other fire-resistive materials. **(PR)**

fire wall. A structure (wall) designed to seal off fires within a building. **(PR)**

fireproof. A term used in describing building construction. It refers to buildings that are of such construction as to be practically undamageable by fire. However, the term is a misnomer because no building is completely undamageable by fire, and it is gradually being replaced by the words *fire resistive*. **(PR)**

first loss insurance. (1) Popularly used, an insurance policy that is called upon to pay a loss before others covering the same risk. (2) A contract written in such an amount as to cover only an insured's expected loss during the policy period with no other insurance in existence. **(G)**

first loss retention (or deductible). *See* excess of loss reinsurance. **(R)**

first named insured. The first named insured appearing on a commercial policy. The latest forms permit the insurer to satisfy contractual duties by giving notice to the first named insured rather than requiring notice to all named insureds. **(G)**

first offer plan. A provision in a buy-sell agreement specifying that an offer to sell common stock must first be made to current stockholders. **(PE)**

first-party insurance. Insurance that applies to coverage for the insured's own property or person. *See also* **third-party insurance. (G)**

first surplus reinsurance. The first amount allocated to reinsurance in excess of the original insurer's net retention. *See also* **surplus reinsurance** and **lines. (R)**

first surplus treaty. A contract under which the reinsurer shares the risk with the ceding company on a pro rata basis. Under this form of insurance, the reinsurer would pay a proportion of each loss. **(R)**

first year. The term used to refer to various matters during the first year a policy is in force, such as first-year premiums and first-year claims. **(G)**

first-year commission. The commission paid to an insurance agent on the first year's premium as compensation for a newly sold policy. **(LI)**

fiscal intermediary. A commercial insurer contracted by the Department of Health and Human Services for the purpose of processing and administering Part A Medicare claims. **(H)**

501(C)(9) trust. A voluntary employee beneficiary association. **(H)**

five-year income averaging. A tax device for lump-sum distributions from a qualified plan that enables the individual to pay a lesser amount of income tax on the distribution. **(PE)**

fixed-amount installments. A settlement option under which fixed, periodic benefits payments are made until the principal and interest are exhausted. **(LI)**

fixed annuity. An annuity that provides that the annuitant will receive a fixed payment during the period of the annuity. **(AN)**

fixed-base liability. The liability coverage needed by fixed-base operators (i.e., those who operate commercial enterprises and operate out of one airport). Aircraft dealers, charterers, and instructors are examples. **(AV)**

fixed benefit. A benefit, the dollar amount of which does not vary. **(LI)**

fixed-benefit retirement plan. A plan providing retirement benefits only on a fixed amount or at a fixed percentage, such as 1% of monthly salary times the number of years of credited employment, or 25% of the employee's average pay over the last few years before retirement. **(PE)**

fixed-dollar annuity. Guarantees a fixed, minimum dollar payout during each payout period. **(AN)**

fixed-period installments. A settlement option under which the proceeds are guaranteed to be paid in equal installments for a specified period. **(LI)**

flat. Without interest or service charges. *See also* **flat cancellation. (G)**

flat cancellation. A policy that is canceled upon its effective date. Usually under a flat cancellation, no premium charge is made. **(G)**

flat commission. A standard scale commission paid to an agent regardless of the type of exposure or the type of policy. *See also* **graded commission. (G)**

flat deductible. A deductible that is not one of the disappearing or franchise type. A specific amount deducted from each loss or claim. **(PR)**

flat maternity benefit. A stipulated benefit in a hospital reimbursement policy that is paid for maternity confinement, regardless of the actual cost of the confinement. **(H)**

flat rate. A reinsurance premium rate based on the entire premium income received by the ceding company from business ceded to the reinsurer, as distinguished from a rate applicable only to the excess limits premium. **(R)**

fleet (or group) of companies. A number of insurance organizations under common ownership and often common management. **(G)**

fleet policy. An insurance contract that applies to a number of vehicles. Usually, five or more self-propelled vehicles constitute a fleet. **(AU)**

Flesch test. A method for determining the degree of ease or difficulty for reading material. This method counts not only the number of words in a sentence, but also the number of syllables in each word. It has come into popular use because of state laws requiring that contracts of insurance be easily understandable by someone who reads at the eighth grade level. **(G)**

flexible benefit plan. A type of program in which employees can tailor their benefits to meet their specific needs. **(H)**

flexible-premium adjustable life insurance policy. This is another term used to describe universal life-type policies. **(LI)**

flexible-premium annuity. An annuity that allows the contract holder to vary the amount of the premium payment or to stop payments and resume payments at will. A flexible-premium annuity is used to fund individual retirement account and Keogh retirement plans because it allows the amount of premium to change as wages change. **(AN)**

flexible-premium policy. A life insurance policy under which the policyholder may vary the amount or timing of premium payments. **(LI)**

flexible-premium variable life. A whole life contract and a security that features flexible premium payments, nonguaranteed cash values, and either a minimum guaranteed death benefit or no guaranteed death benefit. Policy values are dependent on the performance of a separate account. **(LI)**

flexible spending account (FSA). A salary reduction cafeteria plan whereby employee funds are used to provide various types of health care benefits. **(H)**

floater. A form of insurance that applies to movable property, whatever its location, if it is within the territorial limits imposed by the contract. The coverage floats with the property. **(IM)**

flood. A general and temporary condition of partial or complete inundation of normally dry land areas from (1) overflow of inland or tidal waters, (2) the unusual accumulation and runoff of surface waters from any source, or (3) abnormal, flood-related erosion and undermining of shorelines. *Flood* also means inundation from mud flows caused by accumulations of water on or under the ground, as long as the mud flow and not a landslide is the proximate cause of loss. **(PR)**

flood insurance. A form of insurance designed to reimburse property owners from loss due to the defined peril of flood. Usually sold in connection with a government flood insurance plan. **(PR)**

floor plan insurance. A form of insurance covering merchandise held for sale by a retailer that has been used as collateral for a loan. The lending institution, in effect, is insuring its collateral, the merchandise on the floor of the retailer. **(PR)**

following form. A term for a fire or other form written exactly under the same terms and coverages as other insurance on the same property. **(PR)**

foreign insurer. An insurer domiciled in a state of the United States other than the one where the insured's insurance is written. **(G)**

forfeitures. The nonvested remainders in pension plans left by terminated employees. Forfeitures must be used to reduce employer contributions in subsequent years. In profit-sharing plans, forfeitures may be allocated among remaining participants. **(PE)**

forgery. The false and fraudulent making or altering of a written instrument. **(C)**

forgery bond. *See* depositor's forgery insurance. **(C)**

forgery or alteration coverage form. A commercial crime coverage form that protects the insured against losses resulting from forgery or alteration of outgoing checks, drafts, promissory notes, and similar instruments drawn against the insured's accounts. Separate crime coverage forms have been largely replaced by newer crime policies that provide multiple coverage options in a single policy. **(C)**

form. (1) An insurance document used to complete or create an insurance policy. (2) Any rider or endorsement, such as a deductible endorsement form. **(G)**

formal plan. A retirement plan set forth in writing under which contractual and legally enforceable rights pass on to the participating employees. **(PE)**

formula. How the amount of pension to be received, or contribution to be made, under a retirement plan is determined. **(PE)**

formulary. *See* drug formulary. **(H)**

fortuitous event. *See* accident. **(G)**

foundation exclusion clause. A provision in a fire insurance contract that provides that the value of the foundation is not to be included when determining the value of property at the time of a loss. **(PR)**

foundering. This term refers to a ship that is sinking. **(OM)**

401(h) trust. Governed by IRS Codes, these accounts have limited use for tax-free funding of postretirement benefits. An employer's 401(h) contribution is limited to no more than 25% of total contributions to all retiree benefits, including pension benefits. Because the health liabilities for most employers are so large, a 401(h) could provide only incidental funding. **(H)**

401(k) plan. A qualified elective deferral plan in which employee contributions are made by means of a salary reduction agreement, with or without matching employer contributions. Authorized by section 401(k) of the Internal Revenue Code. **(PE)**

403(b). A section of the Internal Revenue Code authorizing tax-sheltered annuities as qualified pension plans for employees of non-profit organizations. **(PE)**

fractional premium. A proportionate amount of the annual premium, such as semiannual, quarterly, or other fraction. **(G)**

frame. A type of construction. A frame building is primarily made with wood frames and joists. **(PR)**

franchise clause. *See* franchise deductible. **(G)**

franchise deductible. A type of deductible that originated with marine insurance. It states that no claim is payable unless it exceeds a stated amount or a stated percentage of the amount of insurance. Once the claim exceeds that amount or percentage, the entire amount of the claim is payable. **(G)**

franchise insurance. A plan for covering groups of persons with individual policies that have uniform provisions, although they may differ in benefits. Individual contracts are issued to each person, with individual underwriting. It is usually applied to groups too small to qualify for true group coverage, and the solicitation of cases usually takes place among an employer's workforce with employer consent. In life insurance, it is sometimes called wholesale insurance. *See also* **true group insurance. (H)**

fraternal insurance. Insurance offered to a special group of people, namely members of a lodge or a fraternal order. Such insurance may be written on an assessment basis or on a legal reserve basis. **(H, LI)**

fraud. Deceit, trickery, or misrepresentation with the intent to induce another to part with something of value or surrender a legal right. **(LE)**

fraudulent delivery. In connection with transportation floaters, when a shipper surrenders goods to someone posing as an agent for the carrier, it is held that the goods did not come into the custody of the carrier. If the carrier delivers goods to someone posing as an agent for the receiver, it is held that no valid delivery is made and the carrier is liable for the loss. **(IM)**

free along side (FAS). A marine shipping agreement that requires the seller to place the goods alongside a named vessel or a designated dock. The seller is responsible for insuring goods up to the time they are alongside. **(OM)**

free look. A period of time (usually 10, 20, or 30 days) during which a policyholder may examine a newly issued individual policy of life or health insurance and surrender it in exchange for a full refund of premium if not satisfied for any reason. **(H, LI)**

free-of-capture-and-seizure clause. An insurance contract provision that excludes losses due to war, capture, and seizure. **(OM)**

free of particular average (FPA). A contract provision that excuses the insurer from liability for losses below a certain percentage or fixed amount. Similar to a deductible. **(OM)**

free on board (FOB). The term has special significance in marine insurance, where it is vital to determine when title passes from the seller to the buyer. If the materials are shipped FOB point of destination, the seller is liable for damage caused during the course of transportation. If the material is shipped FOB point of departure, the buyer becomes liable for it. **(G)**

free-standing emergency medical service center. A facility whose primary purpose is the provision of care for emergency medical conditions. Also called emergi-center or urgi-center. **(H)**

free-standing outpatient surgical center. A facility that only provides outpatient surgical services. Also called surgi-center. **(H)**

freight. A charge for the transportation of goods. **(IM, OM)**

frequency. The number of times a service is provided over a given period. **(H)**

friendly fire. *See* fire. **(PR)**

fringe benefits. *See* employee benefit program. **(H, LA)**

fronting. A situation in which the ceding company retains a very small part of a risk and reinsures the large majority of it with one or more reinsurers. **(R)**

full coverage. Insurance that provides for the payment of all insured losses in full. For example, some health insurance policies provide for full coverage without a deductible, participation, or a coinsurance clause. **(G)**

full preliminary term reserve valuation. A method for determining reserves on life insurance contracts, whereby no reserve is required for the first year of a contract's life, with an appropriate adjustment in subsequent years' reserves to make up the difference. This method of valuation makes it possible for an insured to have more funds available for the high first-year expenses incurred in the writing of life insurance. **(LI)**

full reporting clause. Under this clause, an insured is required to report values periodically. The clause provides for a penalty to the insured if true values are not reported. **(PR)**

fully insured plan. A qualified plan whereby contributions are made to an insurer, and benefits and plan administration are provided by the insurance company on behalf of plan participants. **(PE)**

fully insured status. A provision of Old Age, Survivors, Disability, and Health Insurance that sets forth the qualifications a person must have before being eligible for retirement benefits under the Social Security system. For most people, this means having worked 40 calendar quarters (usually 10 years) at covered employment, though there are some exceptions. *See also* **currently insured status. (G)**

fully paid policy. A limited payment life insurance contract on which all required payments have been made. For instance, a 20-pay life policy would be fully paid after the insured has paid premiums for 20 years. **(LI)**

fund. (1) Money and investments held in trust in order to pay pension benefits. (2) To accumulate money necessary to pay pension benefits; to pay into the fund each year enough to cover the pension plan's obligations for that year. **(PE)**

funded. Having sufficient funds to meet future liabilities. This term is most often used with a pension plan's outstanding claims account. **(G)**

funding level. The dollar amount required to purchase a particular medical care program. Usually measured by the premium rate for an insured program, or an amount assessed for expected claim loss and related fees under a self-funded program. **(H)**

funding medium/funding vehicle. The arrangement through which funding methods operate (i.e., a trust agreement, a custodial account, a deposit administration contract, or a group annuity contract). **(PE)**

funding method. How money is accumulated for future payment of pension benefits. **(PE)**

funding methods. The agreed means by which an employer pays for health coverage. **(H)**

funding, advance. When predetermined sums are set aside to provide for the payment of future retirement benefits. **(PE)**

funding, disbursement. Also known as the pay-as-you-go method, this type of funding requires no funds to be set aside to provide retirement benefits. All benefits paid to retired employees are paid from the company's gross income and are deducted as a normal business expense. **(PE)**

funding, terminal. This type of funding also requires no funds to be set aside for retirement benefits; however, as each employee retires, an immediate lifetime annuity is purchased for him. **(PE)**

fur and jewelry floater. Usually an open perils (all risk) form that applies to the furs and jewelry scheduled in the policy whatever their location worldwide. **(IM)**

furriers customers insurance. An inland marine form purchased by a furrier to protect furs in storage belonging to customers. **(IM)**

future increase option. An option that allows the insured to increase disability income benefits at predetermined times, specified in the policy, without evidence of insurability. **(H)**

future interest. Generally means the future interest and enjoyment of personal property provided for an individual by means of a gift. **(EP, LE)**

G

GA. *See* general agent. **(G)**

GAAP. *See* generally accepted accounting principles. **(G)**

GAB. *See* General Adjustment Bureau, Inc. **(G)**

GAMC. *See* General Agents and Managers Conference. **(H, LI)**

PRESENTATION OF TERMS

GI Insurance. *See* United States Government Life Insurance **(G, LI)**

gain and loss exhibit. The portion of the convention blank that represents an analysis of gains, losses, and surplus during an accounting period. **(G)**

gambling. The creation of a situation where there is a chance of either loss or gain. This is the opposite of insurance, which either eliminates or reduces the risk of loss and presents no chance of gain. **(G)**

garage coverage form. A commercial automobile insurance coverage form used to insure automobile dealers. Garage liability, garagekeepers coverage, and physical damage coverages may be included. **(AU)**

garagekeepers legal liability insurance. An insurance contract that protects a garagekeeper against liability for damage to vehicles in the keeper's care, custody, or control caused by specific perils. **(LA)**

garage liability insurance. Insurance to protect automobile dealers for liabilities arising out of their business operations. **(LA)**

gatekeeper model. Under this model of HMO and PPO organizations, the primary care physician (the gatekeeper) is the initial contact for the patient for medical care and for referrals. This is also called a closed access or closed panel. **(H)**

gender rule. One method of determining which parent's medical coverage will be primary for dependent children: the father's coverage will automatically be considered primary and will pay first. **(H)**

general account. An investment portfolio used by the insurer for investment of premium income. This portfolio generally consists of safe, conservative, guaranteed investments, such as real estate and mortgages. **(AN)**

General Adjustment Bureau, Inc. (GAB). An independent company which adjusts claims of all types for insurance companies. GAB also provides training programs for adjusters. **(G)**

general agency system. The marketing of life insurance through general agents. **(LI)**

general agent (GA). An individual appointed by a life or health insurer to administer its business in a given territory. General agents are responsible for building their own agency and service force and are compensated on a commission basis, with possibly some additional expense allowances. **(H, LI)**

General Agents and Managers Conference. An association of insurance general agents and managers affiliated with the National Association of Life Underwriters. **(H, LI)**

general aggregate limit. A commercial general liability limit that applies to all damages paid for bodily injury, property damage, personal and advertising injury, and medical expenses, except damages included in the products-completed operations hazard. **(LA)**

general and insurance expense. *See* general operating expense. **(G)**

general average. A partial loss incurred to save the total venture from destruction. Any such losses are prorated among all parties to the venture, including the parties whose interests first suffered such loss. An example would be throwing cargo overboard in order to save a ship from a particular peril. **(OM)**

general cover form. An old term for reporting form policy. *See* **reporting form. (PR)**

general liability insurance. A form of insurance designed to protect owners and operators of businesses from a wide variety of liability exposures. These exposures could include liability arising from accidents resulting from the premises or the operations of an insured, products sold by the insured, operations completed by the insured, and contractual liability. **(LA)**

general LTC rider. An LTC rider that is attached to a life insurance policy but stands alone or is independent of the life policy. Any LTC benefits paid do not reduce any of the life insurance benefits. **(H)**

general operating expense. The expense of an insurer other than commissions and taxes. Called "general and insurance expense" in the convention statement blank. **(G)**

general partnership. A business enterprise owned and operated by two or more persons for the purpose of generating business income and profits. **(G)**

general power of appointment. A donee is given the authority to pass on a property interest to whomever he pleases. **(EP)**

generally accepted accounting principles (GAAP). These principles have substantial authoritative support for use in the insurance business. They are intended to produce financial results consistent with those of other industries and to assure consistency in financial reporting. *See also* **statutory accounting principles. (G)**

generation-skipping transfer. A transfer of property, through death or by gift, to a person who is two or more generations younger than the grantor. **(EP)**

generic drug. A drug that is exactly the same as a brand name drug and that is allowed to be produced after the brand name drug's patent has expired. It is also called a generic equivalent. **(H)**

generic equivalence. *See* generic drug. **(H)**

geographical Limitation. A contractual provision that specifically names geographical areas outside of which the insurance is not effective. *See also* **territorial limitation. (G)**

gift. A sale, exchange, or transfer of property without adequate consideration. **(EP)**

gift tax. Both federal and state governments have gift tax laws that tax gifts made by one person to another. **(EP, G)**

glass coverage form. A commercial property form used to insure plate glass, lettering, frames, and ornamentation. This form has been largely replaced by newer commercial property forms that cover glass. **(PR)**

good driver discount. A system that entitles good drivers (as defined by driving safety record, number of miles driven annually, number of years of driving experience, and other factors related to the risk of loss) to discounts on automobile insurance rates and premiums. *See also* **safe driver plan. (AU)**

good student discount. A discount granted to students with high scholastic ratings. There is a proven relationship between good grades and safe driving. **(AU)**

goodwill. An intangible business asset. It refers to the value of a business that has been built up through the reputation of the business concern and its owners. **(G)**

governing classification. The classification assigned to the operations of an insured that carries the largest amount of payroll. **(WC)**

grace period. A prescribed period, usually 30 to 31 days from the premium due date, during which an insurance contract is in force and the premium may be paid. **(H, LI)**

graded commission. A compensation scale for agents that provides for varying commission rates depending on the class, type, or volume of insurance written. *See also* **flat commission. (G)**

graded death benefits. A provision in life insurance contracts for death benefits that, in the early years of the contract, are less than the face amount of the policy but that increase with the passage of time. Most commonly found in juvenile policies issued at or near age zero. **(LI)**

graded premium. A modified life insurance policy for which the initial premium is low and then increases in steps over a period of time (usually five years), after which it becomes a level premium. **(LI)**

grading schedule for cities and towns. A schedule prepared by the National Board of Fire Underwriters for the purpose of determining which of eleven grades to assign to a city for fire rating purposes, on the basis of such factors of fire protection as water supply. **(PR)**

graduated life table. A mortality table in which the experience has been smoothed out by formula. **(LI)**

grantee. The buyer of real estate. **(G)**

grantor. The seller of real estate. **(G)**

grantor retained annuity trust (GRAT). A trust in which the grantor substitutes retention of a right to payment of a fixed income in exchange for a fixed period of time. **(EP)**

grantor retained interest trust (GRIT). An irrevocable trust in which the grantor of the trust property receives an income for a fixed period of time. Usually, a personal residence is used as the trust property. **(EP)**

grantor retained unitrust trust (GRUT). A trust in which a grantor substitutes retention of a right to a fixed percentage of the trust value in exchange for a fixed period of time. **(EP)**

grievance procedure. A procedure that allows a member of a health plan or a provider of benefits to express complaints and seek remedies. **(H)**

gross earnings. An accounting term that is arrived at by subtracting the cost of goods sold from the total sales. Traditionally, the term was used primarily in business interruption insurance as the basis for determining how much insurance a policyholder should carry. The latest business income insurance forms have dropped this term. **(PR)**

gross earnings form. A form once used widely in the writing of business interruption insurance. Coverage was written on either the gross earnings form or the earnings form. The latest business income coverage forms no longer refer to gross earnings. **(PR)**

gross line. The total limit accepted by an insurer on an individual risk, including the amount to be reinsured. **(G)**

gross negligence. Willful and wanton negligence or misconduct. *See also* negligence. **(LE)**

gross premium. The net premium plus operating expenses, commissions and other expenses. **(G)**

gross premium. The premium for participating life insurance. If an insured elects to use dividends to pay premiums, this becomes the net premium when dividends are subtracted from it. *See also* **net premium. (LI)**

ground coverage. Insurance for specified perils applicable to the hull when a plane is not flying. Similar to collision and comprehensive coverage in an automobile policy. There are different forms of ground coverage: *Not in Flight* covers the plane on the ground only but includes taxiing, whereas *Not in Motion* covers the plane on the ground and not in motion. **(AV)**

group. Coverage of a number of individuals under one contract. The most common group is employees of the same employer. **(H)**

group I rates. Under the latest commercial lines program, this term replaces the term *fire rates* for property coverages. Rates are included in group I for fire, lightning, explosion, sprinkler leakage, and vandalism. **(PR)**

group II rates. Under the latest commercial lines program, this term replaces the term *extended coverage rates* for property coverages. Rates are included in group II for windstorm, hail, smoke, riot or civil commotion, aircraft, vehicles, sinkhole collapse, and volcanic action. **(PR)**

group annuity. A retirement plan designed for a group of persons (usually employees of a single employer) funded by a single annuity contract, which is written on a group basis. **(AN, PE)**

group certificate. The document provided to each member of a group plan. It shows the benefits provided under the group contract issued to the employer or other insured. **(H, LI)**

group contract. A contract of insurance made with an employer or other entity that covers a group of persons identified by reference to their relationship to the entity buying the contract. The group contractual arrangement is generally used to cover employees of a common employer, members of a trade association or trusteeship, members of a welfare or employee benefit association, members of a labor union, or members of a professional or other association not formed only for the purpose of obtaining insurance. **(H, LI)**

group credit insurance. Insurance on the life or health of debtors of a creditor, payable for reduction or extinguishment of the debts in case of the disability or death of the debtor. **(H, LI)**

group deposit administration contract. A funding contract for a qualified plan whereby contributions are accounted for on an unallocated basis for the benefit of all plan participants. **(PE)**

group disability insurance. Coverage provided for a group of individuals for loss of compensation due to accident or sickness. **(H)**

group health insurance. The same definition as life insurance but with the application to health insurance coverages. *See* **group life insurance. (H)**

group life insurance. Life insurance provided for members of a group. It is most often issued to a group of employees but may be issued to any group provided it is not formed for the purpose of buying insurance. The cost is lower than for individual policies because administrative expenses per life are decreased, there are certain tax advantages, and measures taken against adverse selection are effective. *See also* **franchise insurance, true group** and **master policy. (LI)**

group model HMO. A health plan where a group of physicians is reimbursed for services they provide at a negotiated rate. The HMO also contracts with hospitals for the care of the patients of the physicians who belong to the group. **(H)**

group of companies. *See* fleet of companies. **(G)**

group ordinary life insurance. Level premium ordinary life insurance issued on a group basis. **(PE)**

group permanent insurance. A retirement plan that combines life insurance with retirement benefits. It uses the level premium method under a group contract. **(PE)**

group permanent life insurance. A form of life insurance under which members of a group are provided one of several plans of permanent life insurance on a group basis instead of the more usual plan of term life insurance. **(LI)**

group property and liability insurance. The same definition as group life insurance but applied to property and liability coverages. *See* group life insurance. **(LA, PR)**

group renewable term insurance. Yearly renewable term insurance on a group basis; often called group life insurance. **(PE)**

group retirement income insurance. Level premium retirement income insurance issued on a group basis. **(PE)**

guaranteed cash value. In whole life insurance, the policy's cash value increases over the life of the policy until the insured reaches age 100, when the cash value is equal to the policy's face amount. **(LI)**

guaranteed continuable. *See* guaranteed renewable. **(G)**

guaranteed cost. A premium charged on a prospective basis, fixed or adjustable, or on a specified rating basis, but never on the basis of loss experience. In other words, the cost is guaranteed to the extent that it will not be adjusted on the basis of the loss experience of the insured during the period of coverage. **(LA, WC)**

guaranteed insurability. An option in life and health insurance contracts that permits the insured to buy additional prescribed amounts of insurance at prescribed future time intervals without evidence of insurability. **(H, LI)**

guaranteed renewable. A contract that the insured has the right to continue in force by the timely payment of premiums for a substantial period as set forth in the contract. During that period, the insurer has no right to make any change in any provision of the contract other than a change in the premium rate for all insureds in the same class. *See also* **noncancelable. (H, LI)**

guaranteed standard issue (GSI). An underwriting term used to describe the fact that a group insurance contract was issued without reference to any medical underwriting. All group participants are covered regardless of health history. **(H)**

guarantor. One who guarantees or promises to back up another's actions or debts. It is a term used in surety bonds; usually the surety company is the guarantor. **(S)**

guaranty funds. Funds created by state law from contributions by insurance companies operating in the state that are used to make good any unpaid claims or otherwise to make money available to insolvent companies. Each state which has a fund has a different plan. *See* **Insurance Guaranty Act** and **insolvency funds. (G)**

guardian. A person appointed by the court to take care of affairs of another. A common example would be a guardian to take care of the affairs of a minor or a mentally incompetent. **(LE)**

Guertin laws. The valuation and nonforfeiture laws that have been standard in all states since 1947, named for Alfred Guertin, then actuary of the New Jersey Insurance Department and head of the NAIC committee that developed the model bill for these laws. *See also* **nonforfeiture values. (LI)**

guest law. Some states have legislation that restricts the rights of a guest to collect from the driver of an automobile in which he is riding on the grounds of ordinary negligence. Usually such cases require proof of willful and wanton negligence on the part of the driver before the guest can collect. *See also* **assumption of risk. (LE)**

guest property coverage. Two commercial crime coverage forms are available for hotels, motels, inns, and other lodging facilities to protect the property of guests against loss or damage. One form covers guests' property while it is in a safe deposit box on the insured's premises. The other form covers an insured's legal liability for loss or damage to guests' property while in the insured's premises or in the insured's possession. Separate crime coverage forms have been largely replaced by newer crime policies that provide multiple coverage options in a single policy. **(C)**

guideline premium. A universal life insurance term used to describe the maximum premium that may be paid while still qualifying as life insurance under the federal Internal Revenue Code. **(LI)**

guiding principles. Rules established by major property and liability trade associations for the adjustment of losses, particularly with respect to how losses should be apportioned between insurance companies under certain circumstances. **(G)**

H

ABBREVIATIONS AND ACRONYMS

HHS. The United States Department of Health and Human Services, which administers the OASDHI, Medicare, and Public Assistance programs. **(G)**

HIAA. *See* **Health Insurance Association of America. (H)**

HIQA. Health Insurance Quality Award. An award granted annually by the International Association of Health Underwriters or the National Association of Life Underwriters for high persistency of health insurance policies written by agents. *See also* **persistency. (H)**

HIV. *See* **human immunodeficiency virus. (H, LI)**

HMO. *See* **health maintenance organization. (H)**

HPR. *See* **highly protected risk. (PR)**

HR-10 plan. *See* **Keogh Act plan. (LI)**

HUD. United States Department of Housing and Urban Development. **(G)**

PRESENTATION OF TERMS

hail insurance. Insurance against loss of crops caused by hail. **(PR)**

hangarkeepers legal liability insurance. Insurance that the owner of an airplane hanger buys to protect against liability for damage or injury to others arising out of the ownership, maintenance, or use of the premises for an aircraft hanger. **(G)**

hazard. A specific situation that increases the probability of the occurrence of loss arising from a peril or that may influence the extent of the loss. For example, accident, sickness, fire, flood, liability, burglary, and explosion are perils. Slippery floors, unsanitary conditions, shingled roofs, congested traffic, unguarded premises, and uninspected boilers are hazards. **(G)**

hazard, legal. *See* **legal hazard. (LE)**

hazard, moral. *See* moral hazard. **(G)**

hazard, morale. *See* morale hazard. **(G)**

hazard, physical. *See* physical hazard. **(G)**

head office. *See* home office. The term *head office* is primarily used in British insurance operations, whereas *home office* is used for American operations. **(G)**

health benefits package. The coverages offered by a health plan to an individual or group. **(H)**

health history. A form used by underwriters to assist in evaluating groups or individuals to determine whether they are acceptable risks. **(H)**

health plan. Any kind of plan that covers health care services, such as HMOs, insured plans, and preferred provider organizations. **(H)**

health insurance. Insurance against loss by sickness or bodily injury. The generic form for forms of insurance that provide lump-sum or periodic payments in the event of loss occasioned by bodily injury, sickness or disease, and medical expense. The term *health insurance* is now used to replace such terms as accident insurance, sickness insurance, medical expense insurance, accidental death insurance, and dismemberment insurance. The form is sometimes called accident and health, accident and sickness, accident, or disability income insurance. **(H)**

Health Insurance Association of America (HIAA). An association supported by life and health insurers to provide the research, public relations, education, and legislative base for the promotion of voluntary private health insurance. **(H)**

health maintenance organization (HMO). An HMO is a prepaid medical service plan that provides services to plan members. Medical providers contract with the HMO to provide medical services to plan members. Members must use contracted providers. The emphasis is on preventive medicine, and it is an alternative to employee benefit plans. Employers of more than 25 persons are required to offer the alternative of HMO to employees, but not if the cost exceeds that of present employee benefit plans. **(H)**

health service agreement (HSA). The agreement between employer and the health plan that outlines a description of benefits, enrollment procedures, eligibility standards, and so forth. **(H)**

health services. The benefits covered under a health contract. **(H)**

hearsay. Testimony based on what someone else has said or told a witness. **(LE)**

high-pressure tactics. An illegal method of marketing insurance policies (often associated with Medicare supplement policies) through the use of tactics that have the tendency to induce the purchase or to recommend the purchase of coverage through force, fright, explicit or implied threat, or undue pressure. **(H)**

highly protected risk (HPR). Refers to property risks that meet the standards required for lower rates. Risks of this type are usually protected by sprinklers and have better-than-average construction and occupancy. The term is most often used in connection with the factory mutuals, factory insurance association, and the improved risk mutuals. **(PR)**

hired automobile. Autos the insured leases, hires, rents, or borrows, but not autos owned by employees or members of their households. **(AU)**

hold harmless agreement. A contractual arrangement whereby one party assumes the liability inherent in a situation, thereby relieving the other party of responsibility. Such agreements are typically found in contracts like leases, sidetrack agreements, and easements. For example, a typical lease may provide that the lessee must hold harmless the lessor for any liability from accidents arising out of the premises. The effect of such an agreement is that the lessee must provide a defense for the lessor, and if any judgment is rendered against the lessor, the lessee would have to pay. **(LA)**

holdup. A form of robbery. *See* **robbery. (C)**

holographic will. A valid will that is completely handwritten and signed by the testator. **(EP)**

home health agency. A certified facility approved by a health plan to provide services under contract. **(H)**

home health care. Care received at home as part-time skilled nursing care, speech therapy, physical or occupational therapy, part-time services of home health aides, or help from homemakers or choreworkers. **(H)**

home health services. Health care services provided by a licensed home health agency in the patient's home; a covered expense under Part A of Medicare. **(H)**

home office. Generally, the corporate headquarters of insurers and the location where the chief officers of the organization are housed. **(G)**

Home Office Life Underwriters Association. An organization offering a course of study for home office life underwriters. **(LI)**

home service insurance. A variation in the industrial life concept, home service life insurance policies are usually modest in size, ranging from $10,000 to $15,000 in face value, and are typically sold on a monthly debit plan (automatic bank draft) or through payments by mail. **(LI)**

homeowners policy. A property and liability insurance contract that provides insurance against various property and liability perils to which a homeowner or renter is exposed. **(LA, PR)**

honesty clause. *See* full reporting clause. **(PR)**

honorable undertaking. This is stated in the reinsurance contract: "This agreement is considered by the parties hereto as an honorable undertaking, the purpose of which is not to be defeated by a strict or narrow interaction of the language thereof." **(R)**

hospice. An organization that is primarily designed to provide pain relief, symptom management, and supportive services for terminally ill patients and their families. Hospice care is covered under Part A of Medicare. **(H)**

hospital affiliation. A contract whereby one or more hospitals agree to provide benefits to members of a specific health plan. **(H)**

hospital alliances. A group of hospitals that work together to share common services and thereby reduce health costs. By grouping together, they are better able to compete with other alliances or chains. **(H)**

hospital benefits. Benefits payable for hospital room and board, plus miscellaneous charges resulting from hospitalization. **(H)**

hospital confinement rider. An optional disability income rider that results in the elimination period being waived when the insured is hospitalized as an inpatient. **(H)**

hospital expense insurance. *See* hospitalization insurance. **(H)**

hospital income insurance. A form of insurance that provides a stated weekly or monthly payment while the insured is hospitalized, regardless of expenses incurred and regardless of whether other insurance is in force. The insured can use the weekly or monthly benefit as he chooses, for hospital or other expenses. **(H)**

hospital indemnity. Coverage that pays on the basis of daily, weekly, or monthly limits regardless of the amount of actual hospital expenses. **(H)**

hospital insurance (HI). Also identified as Part A of Medicare. HI provides inpatient hospital care, skilled nursing care, home health care, and hospice care subject to a benefit period deductible and copayments for certain services. **(H)**

hospital tax. A Social Security tax of 1.45% on an unlimited amount of income, paid by both the employee and employer to prepay for Part A of Medicare. **(H)**

hospitalization expense policy. A policy that covers daily hospital room and board charges and also miscellaneous hospital expenses (e.g., x-rays). It also often covers emergency treatment charges and many times will also include a surgical benefit. **(H)**

hospitalization insurance. A form of insurance that provides reimbursement within contractual limits for hospital and specific related expenses arising from hospitalization caused by injury or sickness. **(H)**

hostile fire. *See* fire. **(PR)**

house confinement. A provision in some health insurance contracts that requires an insured to be confined to the house to be eligible for benefits. This provision is most commonly found in policies providing loss of income benefits. **(H)**

household personal property. The term given to household goods, furniture, and personal belongings of residents of a farm dwelling. The Farm Property Coverage Form uses the term *household* to distinguish it from the separate coverage for farm property. *See also* **farm personal property. (PR)**

housekeeping. The general care, cleanliness, and maintenance of an insured's property. It is an important underwriting consideration in many forms of insurance, such as workers' compensation and property. **(G)**

HR-10. A qualified retirement plan for the self-employed. Also known as a Keogh plan. **(PE)**

hull policy. A contract that provides indemnification for damage sustained to or loss of an insured vessel or airplane. **(AV, OM)**

hull syndicates. A group of companies that agree to share or prorate insurance on oceangoing vessels or aircraft. Coverage on the ship or plane itself is called hull insurance. **(AV, OM)**

human immunodeficiency virus (HIV). The virus that causes acquired immunodeficiency syndrome (AIDS), an infectious and incurable disease. **(G)**

human life value. A method of determining life insurance needs by considering a person's income, expenses, remaining years of earning capacity, and depreciation in the value of the dollar over time. **(LI)**

I

IASA. Insurance Accounting Statistical Association. **(G)**

IASS. Insurance Accounting and Statistical Society. **(G)**

IBNR. *See* **incurred but not reported (G)**

ICA. International Claim Association. **(G)**

ICC. Interstate Commerce Commission. **(G)**

ICEDS. Insurance Company Education Directors Society. **(G)**

ICPI. Insurance Crime Prevention Institute. **(G)**

IHOU. Institute of Home Office Underwriters. **(G)**

IIA. *See* **Insurance Institute of America, Inc (G)**.

IIAA. *See* **Independent Insurance Agents of America (G)**.

IIC. Independent Insurance Conference or Insurance Institute of Canada. **(G)**

III. *See* **Insurance Information Institute (G)**.

IIS. International Insurance Seminars, Inc **(G)**.

IRA. *See* **individual retirement account (G)**.

IRIS. *See* **Insurance Regulatory Information System (G)**.

ISO. *See* **Insurance Services Office (G)**.

PRESENTATION OF TERMS

identification card. A card given to each person covered under the plan that identifies the person as being eligible for benefits. **(H)**

identification of benefits. A provision that the cost of putting a disabled insured in touch with and in the care of relatives will be reimbursed, usually up to a maximum amount. **(H)**

if clauses. Clauses that terminate coverage if certain conditions are created or discovered. An example is the concealment or misrepresentation provision, which states that if this is discovered, the coverage is void. *See also* **while clauses (PR).**

illegal occupation provision. A health insurance policy provision that voids liability if the loss results from the insured's committing or attempting to commit a felony or from the insured's engaging in an illegal occupation. **(H)**

illness. A loss that is sustained as a result of sickness or disease, usually due to an organic cause. **(H)**

immature policies. Claims-made coverage that has not been in effect, on an uninterrupted basis, for at least five years. For rating purposes, a discount applies to manual rates for immature policies. **(LA)**

immediate annuity. An annuity that commences payment to the annuitant at the end of the first prescribed payment period. If an insured buys an immediate annuity with monthly payments, he will start receiving benefits at the end of the first month after the purchase. **(AN, LI)**

immediate vesting. A term used in pension or retirement plans. With immediate vesting, an employee's right to benefits begin as soon as he enters the plan. *See also* **vesting (LI, PE).**

impaired insurer. An insurer that is in financial difficulty to the point where its ability to meet financial obligations or regulatory requirements is in question. **(G)**

impaired property. Tangible property that cannot be used or has become less useful because it incorporates the insured's product or work, which is defective or inadequate, or because the insured has failed to fulfill a contractual obligation. **(LA)**

impaired risk. A risk, or subject of insurance, with insurable qualifications below the standard of risks on which the premium for the coverage was based. For example, a life insurance prospect with heart disease would be an impaired risk. *See* **substandard risk.** *See also* **standard risk (H, LI).**

impairment of capital. A condition in which the surplus account of a stock insurer has been exhausted so that it must invade the capital account (amounts contributed by stockholders) to meet liabilities. Some jurisdictions allow a percentage invasion of capital; some do not. **(G)**

impeach. Evidence that tends to detract from the credibility of the witness. **(LE)**

implied authority. Authority of an agent that the public may reasonably believe the agent to have. If the authority to collect and remit premiums is not expressly granted in the agency contract, but the agent does so on a regular basis and the insurer accepts, the agent has implied authority to do so. **(G)**

implied seaworthiness. Seaworthiness of a vessel insured in an ocean marine contract is an implied warranty. The assumption is that the vessel, its equipment, and its crew are in good condition and prepared to make the voyage. **(OM)**

implied warranty. In certain cases, the law says that one has given a warranty to another even though the warranty is not in writing. An example would be in sales: a seller implies that the product is fit for the purpose it purports to serve. **(LE)**

import. Goods or services purchased from another country and brought into one's own country. **(G)**

improvements and betterments. Additions or changes made by a lessee at his own cost to a building that he is occupying and that enhance its value. These become part of the realty and require special insurance consideration. **(PR)**

imputed. Occurs when actions of one party, usually the agent, are deemed to be actions of the other party, usually the principal. **(LE)**

in-area services. Services that are provided within the authorized service area as designated in the plan. **(H)**

in kind. An expression relating to the insurer's right in many property contracts to replace damaged objects with new or equivalent (in kind) material, rather than to pay a cash benefit. **(PR)**

incentive stock option (ISO) plans. A type of stock plan whereby executives are granted options to purchase company stock without incurring a tax liability at the time the option is granted or subsequently exercised. **(PE)**

Inchmaree clause. A provision that provides reimbursement to an insured in the event of a loss due to the negligence of the master or crew of a vessel. **(OM)**

incidents of ownership. Various rights that may be exercised under the policy contract by the policyowner. Some of the incidents of ownership would be: (1) the right to cash in the policy, (2) to receive a loan on the cash value of the policy, and (3) to change the beneficiary. **(LI)**

income policy. A life insurance contract that provides income on a monthly basis, as opposed to a policy that pays proceeds in a lump sum. **(LI)**

incompetent. A person who cannot manage his own affairs. One who is legally declared insane would be an example of an incompetent. Children under a certain age are also considered to be incompetent for some purposes. **(LE)**

incontestable clause. A clause in a policy providing that after a policy has been in effect for a given length of time (two or three years), the insurer shall not be able to contest the statements contained in the application. A health insurance provision also states that after that time no claim shall be denied or reduced on the grounds that a condition not excluded by name at the time of issue existed before the effective date. In life policies, if an insured lied as to the condition of his health at the time the policy was taken out, that lie could not be used to contest payment under the policy if death occurred after the time limit stated in the incontestable clause. **(H, LI)**

increased cost of construction insurance. Insurance that covers the additional cost of reconstructing a damaged or destroyed building where ordinances require rebuilding with more expensive materials, services, or techniques. **(PR)**

increased hazard. Property insurance policies provide that coverage shall be suspended when the hazard in a risk is increased beyond that contemplated when the insurance was written. For example, if a dwelling owner commences manufacturing dynamite in his home, the hazard is extremely increased, and coverage could be denied by the insurer if there were a loss. **(PR)**

increasing term insurance. A term life insurance policy for which the death benefit increases but the premium remains level for the policy term. *See also* **decreasing term insurance, level term insurance,** and **term insurance (LI)**.

incurred but not reported. This refers to losses that have occurred during a stated period, usually a calendar year, but have not yet been reported to the insurer as of the date under consideration. For instance, insurance company statements prepared after the end of the calendar year would have to include an estimate of losses that occurred during that year but have not yet been reported. **(G)**

incurred expense. Expenses not yet paid. Can also include paid expenses in some accounting systems. **(G)**

incurred loss ratio. The percentage of losses incurred to premiums earned. **(G)**

incurred losses. The losses occurring within a fixed period, whether or not adjusted or paid during the same period. As an example, in workers' compensation claims, losses occur during a given policy period, but benefits may continue to be paid for many years. The estimated value of the total claim would be an incurred loss for the policy period during which the loss occurred. **(G)**

indemnify. To restore the victim of a loss to the same position as before the loss occurred. **(G)**

indemnitor. An entity or person who enters into an agreement with a surety to hold the surety harmless from loss incurred as a result of issuing a contract bond to an applicant who falls just short of acceptability. If the principal defaults, the indemnitor, rather than the surety, assumes the obligation. **(S)**

indemnity. Restoration to the victim of a loss by payment, repair, or replacement. **(G)**

indemnity bond. A bond that indemnifies an obligee against loss that may arise as the result of failure to perform on the part of the principal. **(S)**

independent adjuster. An adjuster who works as an independent contractor, hiring out to insurance companies or other organizations for the investigation and settlement of claims. Independent adjusters represent the interests of insurance companies. *See also* **public adjuster (G)**.

independent agency system. An insurance distribution system within which independent contractors, known as agents, sell and service insurance solely on a commission or fee basis under contract with one or more insurers that recognize the agent's ownership, use, and control of policy records and expiration data. **(G)**

independent agent. An agent operating as an independent contractor under the independent agency system. **(G)**

independent contractor. One who agrees to perform according to a contract and who is not an employee. **(G)**

independent contractors insurance. *See* owners and contractors protective liability policy. **(LA)**

Independent Insurance Agents of America (IIAA). An association of independent insurance agents historically known to represent stock insurance companies more than mutual companies. Members are also members of their state associations. **(G)**

index bureau experience. A measure of losses related to claims reported through a claim office during a 12-month period. **(G)**

indexing year. The second year prior to attainment of age 62, death, or disability, whichever occurs first, used for purposes of adjusting wages to allow for inflation when calculating Social Security benefits. **(H)**

indirect loss (or damage). Loss resulting from a peril but not caused directly and immediately by that peril. For example, loss of property due to fire is a direct loss, whereas the loss of rental income as the result of the fire would be an indirect loss. *See also* **consequential loss (PR)**.

individual account plan. A defined contribution plan or a profit-sharing plan that provides an individual account for each participant and whose benefits are based solely on the amount contributed to the participant's account and any income, expenses, gains, and losses, as well as forfeitures that may be allocated to the remaining participant's account. **(PE)**

individual contract. A contract made with an individual that covers that individual and perhaps also specified members of his family for benefits as described in the policy. **(H)**

individual contract pension trust. A pension plan under which a trust holds title to individual insurance or annuity contracts for employees covered by the plan. **(PE)**

individual life insurance. (1) The type of life insurance that covers in one contract usually only one insured. (2) The term used to distinguish this type of life insurance from group life insurance. **(LI)**

individual practice association (IPA) model HMO. A situation in which an individual practice association is contracted with to provide health care services. The individual practice association contracts with individual physicians or groups of physicians for their services. **(H)**

individual retirement account (IRA). A qualified retirement plan established by ERISA for anyone under age 70½ with earned income, allowing them to set aside a specified amount each year on a tax-favorable basis for retirement purposes. **(PE)**

individual risk premium modification rating plan. A plan that modifies the premium on large package policies by considering such factors as reduced expenses for handling costs (expense modification) and special characteristics of the risk not contemplated by the basic rate (risk modification). **(G)**

industrial life insurance. One of the major classes of insurance. It is generally sold in amounts of less than $1,000 by agents who service insureds on debits. The premiums are collected weekly or monthly at the address of the insured. *See also* debit **(LI)**.

industrial risk insurers. A consortium of major stock property and casualty insurers formed to write large, highly protected risks. The organization was formed in 1975 by the merger of the Factory Insurance Association and the Oil Insurance Association. **(G)**

inevitable accident. *See* accident **(G)**.

inflation. An economic period characterized by rising prices, low unemployment, an expanding economy, and erosion of consumer's purchasing power due to the higher cost of living. **(G)**

inflation factor. A premium loading to provide for future increases in medical costs and loss payments resulting from inflation. **(H)**

inflation guard coverage. Coverage that provides for automatic periodic increases in the amount of insurance on buildings to keep an appropriate limit to value, considering the effect of inflation on building replacement costs. An endorsement is usually used to add this coverage to a homeowners policy. On the latest commercial property forms, inflation guard coverage is an option that may be activated by an entry in the declarations. **(PR)**

inflation protection. Provisions in a health insurance policy that increase benefit levels to account for anticipated increases in the cost of covered services. **(H)**

in-force business. Life or health insurance for which premiums are being paid or for which premiums have been fully paid. The term refers to the total face amount of a life insurer's portfolio of business. In health insurance, it refers to the total premium volume of an insurer's portfolio of business. **(H, LI)**

informal plan. A retirement system under which the employer has no legal obligation and the employee has no legal rights. These plans have no standard of benefits to be paid and have no special method of funding. **(PE)**

inherent explosion. An explosion caused by some condition existing in and natural to an insured's premises. An example would be a dust explosion in a grain elevator. **(PR)**

inherent vice. A fault in property that leads to its self-destruction. Insurance contracts usually exclude such damage. **(IM, PR)**

initial eligibility period. The period during which prospective members can apply for coverage without providing evidence of insurability. **(H)**

initial premium. An amount paid at the inception of an insurance contract, usually subject to adjustment at the end of the policy period. **(G)**

injunction. A court order intended to prevent a person from doing something that might later be termed to be wrongful or illegal. **(LE)**

inland marine insurance. A branch of the insurance business that developed from the insuring of shipments that did not involve ocean voyages. The inland marine forms borrowed their language from fire, ocean marine, theft, and other contracts. Exposures eligible for this form of protection are described in the nationwide definition of marine insurance. Such diverse properties as bridges, tunnels, jewelry, and furs can now be written under inland marine forms. **(IM)**

in-patient. A patient admitted to a hospital or other similar medical facility as a resident patient. **(G)**

inside limits. Limits placed on hospital expense benefits that modify benefits from the overall maximums listed in the policy. When applied to room and board, an inside limit limits the benefit to not only a maximum amount payable, but also limits the number of days the benefit will be paid. **(H)**

insolvency clause. A clause that holds a reinsurer liable for the reinsurer's share of a loss assumed under a treaty even though the primary insurer has become insolvent. *See also* **strike-through clause. (R)**

insolvency funds. *See* guarantee funds. **(G)**

insolvent. Where a person's or business's liabilities exceed their assets. **(LE)**

insolvent insurer. An insurer that is unable to meet its financial obligations. **(G)**

inspection. Independent checking on facts about an applicant, policyholder, or claimant, usually by a commercial inspection agency. **(G)**

inspection bureau. An organization created by property and liability insurers to investigate exposures and to establish rates. Many bureaus that establish fire and related perils rates for property contracts are called inspection bureaus. **(LA, PR)**

inspection report. A summary statement of the physical, financial, and moral attributes of an insured or an applicant for insurance on the insured's property. Such reports are prepared by inspection bureaus, specialized organizations, and insurers. **(G)**

installment refund annuity. An annuity that promises to continue the periodic payments after the death of the annuitant, until the combined benefits paid to the annuitant and to the beneficiary have equaled the purchase price of the annuity. **(AN)**

installment refund option. An annuity option that provides for continued annuity payments after the death of the annuitant until the total benefits paid have equaled the purchase price of the annuity. **(AN)**

installment sales floater. *See* conditional sales floater. **(IM)**

installment settlement. Payment of the proceeds of a life insurance policy or its cash value in installments rather than in a lump sum. The term refers to any one of the options in a life insurance policy that has this result. **(LI)**

installments certain. A settlement option under which the proceeds are guaranteed to be paid in equal installments for a specified period. **(LI)**

Institute of Life Insurance. Formerly an agency of the life insurance business responsible for building the image of life insurance through a variety of programs. It is now a division of the American Council of Life Insurance. **(LI)**

institutional property. Property eligible for special treatment under package policies. Essentially, these are properties occupied by sanitariums and educational, religious, charitable, government, and nonprofit organizations. **(PR)**

insurability. Acceptability to the insurer of an applicant for insurance. **(G)**

insurable interest. Any interest a person has in a possible subject of insurance, such as a car or home, of such a nature that a certain happening might cause that person financial loss. **(G)**

insurable risk. A risk that meets most of the following requisites: (1) The loss insured against must be capable of being defined. (2) It must be accidental. (3) It must be large enough to cause a hardship to the insured. (4) It must belong to a homogeneous group of risks large enough to make losses predictable. (5) It must not be subject to the same loss at the same time as a large number of other risks. (6) The insurance company must be able to determine a reasonable cost for the insurance. (7) The insurance company must be able to calculate the chance of loss. **(G)**

insurance. A formal social device for reducing risk by transferring the risks of several individual entities to an insurer. The insurer agrees, for a consideration, to assume, to a specified extent, the losses suffered by the insured. **(G)**

insurance carrier. *See* insurer **(G)**

Insurance Commissioner. The head of a state's insurance regulatory agency in most jurisdictions. In some states, the title of Director or Superintendent is used. **(G)**

insurance company. *See* insurer. **(G)**

Insurance Company Education Directors Society (ICEDS). An organization of insurance company educators whose primary purposes are to promote insurance education and exchange information on the subject. **(G)**

insurance department. A governmental bureau in each state and the federal government in Canada charged with the administration of insurance laws, including the licensing of agents and insurers and their regulation and examination. In some jurisdictions, the department is a division of another state department or bureau. **(G)**

insurance examiner. The representative of a state insurance department assigned to participate in the official audit and examination of an insurer. **(G)**

Insurance Guaranty Act. The legislation enacted in many states providing for guaranty funds for the policyholders of insolvent insurers. *See* guaranty funds. **(G)**

Insurance Hall of Fame. An institution created to honor those who have made outstanding contributions to insurance thought and practice. Selections are made on an international basis. **(G)**

insurance in force. (1) The face amounts of contracts still to be paid out to insureds. **(LI)** (2) The annual premium payable on current contracts of insurance. **(H)**

Insurance Information Institute (III). The agency of the property and liability business designed to deal with the public relations programs of various segments of the business. **(LA, PR)**

Insurance Institute of America, Inc. (IIA). An organization that develops programs and conducts national examinations in general insurance, risk management, management, adjusting, underwriting, auditing, and loss control management. Diplomas are given to recognize achievement in these areas. **(G)**

insurance policy. The printed form that serves as the contract between an insurer and an insured. **(G)**

insurance, quota share. *See* quota share insurance. **(G)**

Insurance Regulatory Examiners Society (IRES). An organization made up of the state regulatory examiners who conduct financial and market conduct examinations of insurance companies, and whose purpose it is to foster educational programs, cooperation, and support between state examiners. **(G)**

Insurance Regulatory Information System (IRIS). Information and early-warning system used by the National Association of Insurance Commissioners (NAIC) to keep track of the financial soundness of insurers. **(G)**

Insurance Services Office (ISO). An organization of the property and liability insurance business designed to gather statistics, promulgate rates, and develop policy forms. **(LA, PR)**

insurance to value. Insurance written in an amount approximating the value of the property insured. **(G)**

insured. The party to an insurance arrangement whom the insurer agrees to indemnify for losses, provide benefits for, or render services to. This term is preferred to such terms as policyholder, policyowner, and assured. *See also* **named insured. (G)**

insured contract. A definition that shapes the extent of contractual liability coverage by describing the types of contracts that are insured. On modern liability forms, insured contract includes leases of premises, sidetrack agreements, elevator maintenance agreements, easement agreements, and other agreements related to the insured's business. **(LA)**

insured, named. *See* named insured. **(G)**

insured plan. A retirement plan under which some kind of benefits are guaranteed by an insurance carrier. It does not imply that there is an element of life insurance connected with the plan. **(PE)**

insurer. The party to an insurance arrangement who undertakes to indemnify for losses, provide pecuniary benefits, or render services. It is desirable to use the word *insurer* in preference to *carrier* or *company* since it is a functional word applicable without ambiguity to all types of individuals or organizations performing the insurance function. The word insurer is generally used in statutory law. **(G)**

insuring agreement (or clause). The portion of an insurance contract that states the perils insured against, the persons and/or property covered, their locations, and the period of the contract. **(G)**

integrated long-term care rider. A long-term care rider that is added to a life insurance policy whereby long-term care benefits paid will reduce the life insurance policy's benefits. Long-term care benefits are dependent on the life insurance benefits available. **(H)**

integrated plan. A pension plan that builds benefits according to an approved Treasury Department formula. **(PE)**

intentional injury. An injury resulting from an act intended to inflict injury. In an accident insurance contract, an intentionally self-inflicted injury is not covered (because it is not an accident). In general, intentional injuries inflicted on the insured are covered (assuming no collusion). **(H)**

inter vivos transfer. Transfer of all or a portion of the assets of a person's estate while that person is still alive. *See also* **testamentary transfer. (LE)**

inter vivos trust. A trust that is created and takes effect during the lifetime of the grantor. *See also* **testamentary trust. (LE)**

interest. In the calculation of premium, it is the rate of return on the company's investment of premium dollars over the lifetime of the policy. Insurance company investment experience will affect life insurance cost. **(LI)**

interest-adjusted cost. A method of determining the cost of life insurance that takes into account the interest that might have been earned on premium money if it had been invested rather than put into premiums. **(LI)**

interest, postjudgment. Money the plaintiff would have earned if the favorable judgment had been paid at the time of the first judgment, instead of at a later date, because of an appeal. **(LA)**

interest, prejudgment. Money the plaintiff would have earned if the favorable judgment had been paid at the time of injury or damage, instead of at a later date when a judgment is made. **(LA)**

interest rate risk. A risk faced by investors who invest in bonds; the risk is characterized by an individual being locked into a lower interest rate when interest rates are generally increasing in the economy. **(G)**

interest-sensitive provision. Provisions in variable and flexible premium policies that guarantee certain interest earnings plus an additional interest percentage should the current interest rate rise above a specified percentage. **(LI)**

interinsurance exchange. *See* reciprocal insurance exchange. **(G)**

interline endorsement. Commercial endorsements that apply, or could apply, to more than one coverage part of a package policy. **(G)**

intermediary. A reinsurance broker who negotiates contracts of reinsurance on behalf of the insured. These transactions normally take place with those reinsurers that recognize brokers and pay them commissions on reinsurance premiums ceded. **(R)**

intermediate care. A level of care associated with a skilled nursing facility that provides nursing care under the supervision of physicians or a registered nurse. The care provided is a step down from the degree of care described as skilled nursing care. **(H)**

intermediate care facility. A facility licensed by the state that provides nursing care to persons who do not require the degree of care that a hospital or skilled nursing facility provides. **(H)**

intermediate disability. *See* temporary partial disability and **permanent partial disability. (H, WC)**

intermediate report. A claim report on the condition of a continuing disability. **(H, WC)**

International Association of Health Underwriters. An association of agents and related personnel in the health insurance business. **(H)**

International Insurance Seminars, Inc. (IIS). An institution established to promote worldwide exchanges of ideas and techniques between insurance people. The major focus of IIS is its annual seminar, which brings together academicians and insurance practitioners. **(G)**

interrogatories. A procedure for gaining evidence that involves one party submitting questions to the other party in order to gather facts and information to prepare for a trial. **(LE)**

interstate carrier. A transportation company that does business across state lines. **(G)**

Interstate Commerce Commission endorsement. An endorsement required on all policies issued to interstate motor carriers who haul goods for hire. This endorsement guarantees that all losses to cargo will be paid by the insurer, up to specified minimum limits, regardless of the perils specified in the policy. The common carrier, however, agrees to repay the insurer for any loss it has to pay that is not covered by the ordinary policy. **(IM)**

intervening cause. A possible defense against negligence. Negligence may be avoided or reduced if it can be shown that an intervening cause broke the uninterrupted chain of events required to establish a proximate cause. *See also* **proximate cause (LE)**

intestate. Dying without a will, thus permitting the probate court to appoint an administrator to settle the estate. **(LE)**

intoxicants and narcotics provision. A health insurance policy provision that voids liability if the loss results from the insured's being intoxicated or under the influence of any narcotic unless administered on the advice of a physician. **(H)**

intrastate carrier. A transportation company whose business is confined to one state. **(IM)**

invalidity. Sickness. **(H)**

investigative consumer report. A report ordered on an insured or applicant under which information about the person's character, reputation, or lifestyle is obtained through personal interviews with the person's neighbors, friends, associates or acquaintances. *See also* **consumer report (G)**

Investment Company Act of 1940. A federal law that regulates the organization and activities of investment companies and requires the registration of investment companies with the federal government. **(G)**

investment income. The return received by insurers from their investment portfolios, including interest, dividends, and realized capital gains on stocks. Realized capital gains means the profit realized on stocks that have actually been sold for more than their purchase price. **(G)**

investment manager. A fiduciary (other than a trustee or a plan's named fiduciary) who manages, acquires, or disposes of a pension plan's assets. **(PE)**

investment reserve. An item in the balance sheet of an insurance company that represents a setting aside of assets to compensate for a possible reduction in the market value of securities owned by the company. **(G)**

invitee. One who has been either expressly or implicitly invited onto the premises of another. The most common example would be customers invited to a store to purchase goods or services. **(LE)**

involuntary unemployment insurance. Insurance providing coverage for consumer credit repayment obligations when an insured is involuntarily unemployed because of individual or mass layoff, general strike, termination by employer, unionized labor dispute, or lockout. Usually sold to borrowers under a master group policy issued to a creditor (e.g., bank, association, or other financial institution). Also called **job loss insurance.** Can be classified as either property/casualty or life/health insurance. **(G)**

iron safe clause. A provision in a property insurance policy that requires the insured to keep records in a safe when they are not used. **(PR)**

irrevocable beneficiary. A beneficiary designation that cannot be changed without the beneficiary's consent. **(LI)**

irrevocable trust. A type of trust instrument that cannot be revoked by the person who created it. *See also* **revocable trust (LE)**

issued business. Contracts actually written by an insurer and paid for but not yet delivered to or accepted by the insured. **(LI)**

item. (1) A term used to identify a statement in a policy as to what is insured. In a fire policy, one might refer to the contents item, meaning the coverage in the policy that applies to the contents. (2) An individual entry, such as a piece of jewelry, listed with its description and valuation on a schedule by a policy showing items covered. **(G)**

J

JUA. *See* joint underwriting association. **(G)**

PRESENTATION OF TERMS

jettison. The act of throwing overboard part of a vessel's cargo or hull in hopes of saving the ship from sinking. **(OM)**

jewelers block insurance. An open perils (all risk) insurance contract that provides jewelers with coverage on most types of losses to which they are exposed. A contract covering both owned property and property in their care, custody, and control. **(IM)**

jewelry floater. An all-risk policy covering listed jewelry. Usually, each item is described and insured for a specific amount. **(IM)**

joint and several liability. A legal doctrine permitting recovery from any of several codefendants on the basis of ability to pay, rather than the degree of negligence. *See* **deep pockets liability. (LE)**

joint and survivorship annuity. An annuity that is payable to the named annuitants during the period of their joint lives and that will continue to the survivor when the first annuitant dies. **(LI)**

joint and survivorship option. An option in a life insurance contract that permits the cash value of the policy to be paid out as a joint and survivorship annuity. *See also* **joint and survivorship annuity. (LI)**

joint annuity. An annuity that is paid to the two named persons until the first one dies, at which time the annuity ceases. An example might be an annuity payable to a husband and wife that would cease upon the death of the first spouse. **(LI)**

Joint Committee on Interpretation and Complaint. A committee formed to rule on what types of insurance can be included in the standard definition of marine insurance. *See* **nationwide definition of marine insurance. (IM, OM)**

joint control. Control of the handling of an estate by both the surety (bonding company) and the fiduciary (e.g., administrator or executor). Funds are kept in joint accounts, and disbursements are made only with both signatures so the surety can assure itself that the affairs of the estate are being handled properly. **(S)**

joint insurance. Insurance written on two or more persons, with benefits usually payable only at the first death. **(LI)**

joint insured. One whose life is insured by a joint insurance contract. *See* joint insurance. **(LI)**

joint liability. Liability that rests upon more than one person. **(LA)**

joint life and survivorship annuity. A contract that provides income to two or more people and continues in force as long as any one of them survives. **(LI)**

joint life annuity. This policy pays a benefit that continues throughout the joint lifetime of two people but terminates at the first death. **(LI)**

joint life insurance. *See* joint insurance. **(LI)**

joint-survivor option. An annuity option that provides for a guaranteed income to the annuitant and, upon death of the annuitant, a continued income to the annuitant's survivor. **(AN)**

joint tenancy. Ownership of property shared equally by two or more parties under which the survivor assumes complete ownership. This is different from a tenancy in common where the heirs of a deceased party to the tenancy inherit his share. *See also* **fee simple** and **tenants in common. (LE)**

joint underwriting association (JUA). An unincorporated association of insurance companies formed to provide a particular form of insurance to the public. Those who insure with a JUA pay assessments in addition to their premiums, which provide monies for the operation of the association. JUAs are usually free to set their own rate levels and use whatever coverage forms are deemed proper, subject to approval by state authorities. **(G)**

joint venture. This expression is applied most often to construction ventures for which several contractors agree to combine together on a construction project rather than to act as separate contractors. Under the joint venture agreement, they share profits and losses in some agreed-upon proportion. **(G)**

joisted masonry construction. A building that has exterior walls constructed of masonry materials, such as adobe, brick, concrete, gypsum block, hollow concrete block, stone, tile, or other similar materials and a roof and floor constructed of combustible materials. A floor that rests directly on the ground is an exception and may be disregarded. **(PR)**

Jones Act. The federal act that provides for the covering of ships' crews under workers' compensation plans. **(WC)**

judicial bond. A bond required in civil and criminal court actions. **(LE)**

judgment or decree. The formal decision by a judge or court. **(LE)**

judgment rates. *See* A rates. **(G)**

jumping juvenile. A popular name for a life insurance contract written on the life of a child, usually in units of $1,000. When the child reaches a prescribed age, generally 21, the face of the policy is increased automatically without the imposition of either an additional premium charge or a medical examination, hence the term *jumping* juvenile. **(LI)**

jurisdiction. Authority of the court to decide cases of a particular type or in a particular area. **(LE)**

juvenile insurance. Life insurance written on a child. **(LI)**

K

Keogh Act (HR-10) plan. A plan under the Self-Employed Individual's Tax Retirement Act that permits a self-employed individual to establish a formal retirement plan and to obtain tax advantages similar to those available in qualified corporate pension plans. **(LI)**

key employee insurance. (1) Insurance on the life or health of a key employee, the loss of whose services would cause an employer financial loss. The policy is owned by and payable to the employer.
(2) In health insurance, the term is also used to designate salary continuation insurance or a medical benefit plan payable to the key employee for which the employer pays all or part of the premium. **(H, LI)**

key person (key employee) insurance policy. An insurance policy on the life of a key employee whose death would cause the employer financial loss, owned by and payable to the employer. In health insurance, the term is also used to designate salary continuation insurance payable to a key employee or to a medical benefits plan, payable to that employee paying all or part of the premium. **(LI)**

kidnap-ransom insurance. This insurance is written primarily for financial institutions and covers named employees for individual or aggregate amounts paid as ransom, with deductible requiring the insured to participate in about 10% of any loss. There are few markets for this coverage and no standardization of rates. *See also* **extortion coverage form. (C)**

kidnapping coverage. Insurance against the hazard of a person being seized outside the insured premises and forced to return and open the premises of a safe therein or to give information that will enable the criminal to do so. This has frequently been one of the perils covered under a package crime policy. *See also* **extortion coverage form. (C)**

L

ABBREVIATIONS AND ACRONYMS

LIFO. Last in, first out. Refers to a method of keeping inventory records for accounting purposes where the last item purchased for inventory is the first item used. **(G)**

LIMRA International. An organization that, through research, seeks solutions to the problems of administering the agency costs of a life insurer. **(LI)**

LOMA. *See* Life Office Management Association. **(LI)**

LUTC. *See* Life Underwriting Training Council. **(LI)**

PRESENTATION OF TERMS

labor and material bond. *See* payment bond. **(S)**

lag coverage. *See* endorsement extending period of indemnity. **(PR)**

land contract. A type of instrument used in connection with the sale of real estate. It differs from a mortgage in that title to the land remains with the seller until the buyer has completed the payments, though possession rests with the buyer. Specifically, a land contract is the instrument that conveys the deed of land from one person to another upon full payment of the stated purchase price. **(G)**

landlords protective liability. Coverage provided to the owner of property who leases the entire premises to another. This coverage is very reasonable because the full control of the premises rests with the lease. **(LA)**

lapse. Termination of a policy because of failure to pay the premium. In life insurance, the term refers to nonpayment before the policy has developed any nonforfeiture values. If it has, and the premium is not paid, it is said to have lapsed except as to any nonforfeiture benefits that may apply. **(G)**

lapse ratio. The ratio of the number of life insurance contracts lapsed within a given period to the number in force at the beginning of that period. **(LI)**

lapsed policy. A policy that has been allowed to expire because of nonpayment of premiums. **(G)**

larceny. The unlawful taking of the personal property of another without the person's consent and with intent to deprive him of ownership or use thereof. It is a broader term than burglary or robbery and is largely synonymous with theft. **(C)**

large claim pooling. A system designed to help stabilize premium fluctuations in smaller groups. Large claims (those over a stated amount) are charged to a pool contributed to by many small groups who belong and share in that pool. The smaller the group of groups, the lower the pooling level. Larger groups will have a larger pooling level. **(H)**

laser beam endorsement. An endorsement to a claims-made liability form used to exclude specific accidents, products, work, or locations. It earned its nickname because it allows an insurer to zero in with a sharp focus to exclude specific exposures. **(LA)**

last clear chance. A doctrine that liability may attach to a person who, immediately before an accident, had a last clear chance to avoid it and did not. **(LE)**

last in, first out. *See* LIFO. **(G)**

latent defect. A defect that is not immediately apparent. **(G)**

law of large numbers. This law states that the larger the number of exposures considered, the more closely the losses reported will match the underlying probability of loss. The simplest example of this law is the flipping of a coin. The more times the coin is flipped, the closer it will come to actually reaching the underlying probability of 50% heads and 50% tails. *See also* **degree of risk, odds,** and **probability. (G)**

leader location. A location that attracts customers to the insured's business. One of the four types of dependent properties for which business income coverage may be written. **(PR)**

lease. Contract whereby the owner or user of property (the lessor) agrees to let another party (the lessee) use the property for a consideration (money or rent). **(LE)**

leasehold. An agreement that gives a person the right to use and occupy property. **(G)**

leasehold interest coverage form. Commercial property coverage form used to insure an insured tenant's interest in a favorable lease under which the rent paid is less than the rental value of alternative premises. Pays the difference between rent paid and the rental value for remainder of the lease if the lease is canceled because of property damage caused by a peril insured against. **(PR)**

leasehold interest insurance. A form of property insurance that provides protection against the loss of a favorable lease if it should be terminated as a result of damage to the property by a peril covered by the contract. A leasehold value is determined by finding the difference between the rental value of the property at current rates and the rent payable under the terms of the lease. This amount is multiplied by the remaining term of the lease. **(PR)**

ledger cost. The net cost of a life insurance contract; it is found by subtracting the cash value of the contract at the end of a given year from the premiums paid, less all dividends. **(LI)**

legacy. A gift of personal property in accordance with the provisions of a will. **(EP)**

legal expense insurance. A group form of insurance that provides members with legal services paid for on a schedule basis. Similar to dental insurance. **(LA)**

legal hazard. An increase in the likelihood that a loss will occur because of court actions. **(LE)**

legal liability. Liability under the law as opposed to liability arising from contracts or agreements. In insurance, it is most often used to refer to the liability that an individual has if he should negligently injure another party. For example, an owner of an automobile may be held legally liable if he is negligent in the operation of the automobile and injures another person or damages another person's property as a result of that negligence. **(LE)**

legal reserve. The minimum reserves required to be established for a life insurance contract under the laws of the jurisdiction within which an insurer operates. **(LI)**

legal reserve life insurance company. A life insurer that maintains the reserves required by the jurisdiction within which it operates. **(LI)**

legend drug. A drug that has the following phrase on its label: "Caution: federal law prohibits dispensing without a prescription." **(H)**

legislated coverages. Coverages provided through creation of facilities legislated into existence by federal or state law. FAIR plans, the Flood Insurance Program, and the assigned risk pools are examples. **(G)**

legislative risk. A risk faced by investors whereby changes in tax laws can result in adverse effects on the individual's investment results. **(G)**

length of stay (LOS). The total number of days a participant stays in a facility such as a hospital. **(H)**

lessee. The person to whom a lease is granted. Commonly called the tenant. **(LE)**

lessee's safe deposit box coverage form. A commercial crime coverage form that protects against loss of property other than money while it is in the insured's safe deposit box inside a depository premises. Separate crime coverage forms have been largely replaced by newer crime policies that provide multiple coverage options in a single policy. **(C)**

lessor. The person granting a lease. Also known as the landlord. **(LE)**

level annual premium funding method. A method of accumulating money for payment of future pensions under which the level annual charge is payable each year until retirement so that the benefit is fully funded. **(PE)**

level commission system. A system of commissions in which the first year and all renewal commissions are the same percentage of the premium. **(G)**

level death benefit option. Under universal life insurance, the level death benefit option provides the greater of (1) the face amount of the policy at the time of death, or (2) a stipulated percentage of the accumulation value. **(LI)**

level premium insurance. The form of insurance for which the premium remains the same throughout the life of the contract. Most whole life insurance is paid for in this way. The amount of a level premium is higher than needed for the protection afforded during the early years of the contract but less than needed for protection during the later years. It is a method of leveling off the cost of insurance so as not to have it increase each year until it becomes unaffordable. *See also* **net level premium. (LI)**

level term insurance. (1) A term life insurance policy for which the death benefit and premium remain level for the policy term. *See also* **decreasing term insurance, increasing term insurance,** and **term insurance. (LI)**. (2) A type of term policy for which the face value remains the same from the effective date until the expiration date. *See also* **term insurance. (LI)**

liabilities. Money owed or expected to be owed. Insurance company financial statements, for example, show assets and liabilities. **(G)**

liability. *See* **legal liability. (LE)**

liability insurance. Insurance that pays and renders service on behalf of an insured for loss arising out of his responsibility to others imposed by law or assumed by contract. **(LA)**

liability limits. The maximum amount for which a liability insurance company provides protection in a particular policy. **(LA)**

libel. A written statement about someone that is personally injurious to that individual. In maritime law, it means legal action brought against the owner of another ship. *See also* **defamation** and **slander. (LE)**

libel insurance. A form of liability insurance that protects the insured against legal liability for libelous statements he may write. **(LA)**

liberalization clause. A clause in property insurance contracts that provides that if policy or endorsement forms are broadened by legislation or ruling from rating authorities and no additional premium is required, all existing similar policies will be construed to include the broadened coverage. **(PR)**

license. A certification of authority for an agent or insurer to operate, given by the appropriate jurisdiction. **(G)**

license and permit bonds. Bonds often required by jurisdictions to be posted by persons performing certain services, such as security dealers and plumbers. It provides indemnification in the event that the licensee fails to conform to pertinent regulations of the jurisdiction. **(S)**

licensee. (1) One who is licensed. (2) A person who goes on the premises of another for his own interests. The owner of the premises must use ordinary care not to injure a licensee. A person using another's land for a shortcut, as long as he had the permission of the owner, would be an example. *See also* **degree of care. (LE)**

lien. A claim against property that then serves as security for the payment of that claim. **(LE)**

lien plan. (1) A plan for issuing coverage on substandard risks under which a standard premium is paid but less than the full face amount of the policy is payable if death occurs within a certain number of years. It is rarely used and is even illegal in some states. (2) A plan under which an impairment of the insurer's assets if offset by pro rata liens against policies to be deducted from the face amount when paid as a claim. **(LI)**

life annuity. A contract that provides a stated income for life, payable annually or more frequently. **(AN)**

life conservation. The administration of efforts to preserve human life through research, legislation, and appeals to society. **(LI)**

life estate. Ownership of land for an individual's lifetime. **(EP, LE)**

life expectancy. The average number of years remaining for a person of a given age to live as shown on the mortality or annuity table used as a reference. **(LI)**

life expectancy term insurance. A form of term life insurance that provides protection for a person's expectation of life. This becomes the term of the policy, as opposed to the ordinary term policies, which are for a given number of years or to a stated age, such as 65. **(LI)**

life income. A settlement option under which equal installments are paid as long as the beneficiary lives, even if the principal has been exhausted. **(LI)**

life insurance (generic). A contractual system of risk sharing under which contributions are accumulated and redistributed to meet the economic consequences of the uncertain duration of life. **(LI)**

life insurance (narrow). An agreement that guarantees the payment of a stated amount of monetary benefits upon the death of the insured or under other circumstances specified in the contract, such as total disability. **(LI)**

life insurance cost surrender index. The guaranteed cash surrender value of a life insurance policy is often required to be calculated into an index for presentation to prospective life insurance buyers. Such an index determines the guaranteed cash surrender value, if any, available at the end of the 10th and 20th policy years according to the accumulation of the annual cash dividends at 5% interest compounded annually to the end of a selected period, if the policy is a participating policy. **(LI)**

life insurance, ordinary. *See* ordinary life insurance. **(LI)**

life insurance, straight. *See* ordinary life insurance. **(LI)**

life insurance trust. A type of life insurance policy where a trust company is named as the beneficiary and distributes the proceeds of the policy under the terms of the trust agreement. **(LI)**

life insurance, whole life. *See* whole life insurance. **(LI)**

Life Insurers Conference. An organization that provides for exchange of information on management problems among the member insurers. **(LI)**

Life Office Management Association (LOMA). An organization serving a large proportion of the life insurance business by providing educational programs related to administrative and technical procedures within the industry. It confers the designation of Fellow, Life Management Institute (FLMI) upon those who complete a prescribed course of study. **(LI)**

life paid up at age. A form of limited payment life insurance that provides protection for the whole of life but with payment of premiums to stop at a particular age, thus paying up the policy. A common form would be life paid up at age 65. **(LI)**

life underwriter. Usually, a life insurance agent. It can be more narrowly defined as a risk appraiser. *See also* risk appraiser. **(LI)**

Life Underwriting Training Council (LUTC). An organization that prepares and administers training programs for life insurance agents. **(LI)**

life with period certain. An annuity option that provides a lifetime income to the annuitant plus an extra guarantee of income for a specified period, such as 5 or 10 years. The period certain provides income to the annuitant or the annuitant's survivor. **(AN)**

lifetime policy. (1) A policy guaranteed renewable or noncancelable to age 65 or some later date. (2) A policy paying disability benefits for life. **(LI)**

limit, aggregate. *See* aggregate limit. **(G)**

limit, basic. *See* basic limit. **(G)**

limit, excess. *See* excess limit. **(LA)**

limit of liability. The maximum amount for which an insurer is liable as set forth in the contract. **(LA)**

limit of liability rule. A prescribed procedure for allocating property insurance losses among insurers that provide protection on a given piece of property. It is called the pro rata liability rule in a standard fire policy. **(PR)**

limit, standard. *See* basic limit. **(G)**

limitations. Exceptions to coverage and limitations of coverage as contained in an insurance contract. For example, a limit of liability would be one limitation on an automobile policy. Another example would be policies written to cover only certain described automobiles, or, in the case of general liability insurance, certain described premises. **(G)**

limited agent. An agent authorized to transact only a limited form of insurance, such as travel-accident or credit insurance. In many states, limited agents are exempt from licensing examination and education requirements. **(G)**

limited health insurance. Special health insurance policies that provide limited coverage for specific injuries or illnesses, such as travel accident, hospital income, and specified disease coverage. **(H)**

limited partnership. An association of two or more persons who operate and manage a business for profit; at least one of the partners does not work in the business but does have some management voice and financial investment. The limited partner has limited liability. **(G)**

limited payment life. A life insurance contract that provides protection for the whole of life, with premiums paid for an indicated number of years. *See also* **life paid up at age. (LI)**

limited payment whole life. A whole life policy that allows the policyholder to pay the entire premium in a shorter period (such as a 20-year period or to age 65). *See also* **continuous premium whole life** and **single premium whole life. (LI)**

limited policies. (1) Health insurance contracts, such as those offered by newspapers to their customers, with low limits and somewhat restricted forms. (2) Policies paid only upon the occurrence of certain contingencies, such as cancer, in contrast to policies covering all contingencies other than those excluded. **(H, LI)**

limited pollution liability coverage form. Commercial form providing pollution liability coverage on a claims-made basis, but not providing any coverage for cleanup costs. **(LA)**

limited theft coverage endorsement. This form may be attached to a dwelling policy to provide theft coverage for a named insured who is not an owner occupant. **(PR)**

limits. (1) Ages below or above which the insurer will not issue a policy or above which it will not continue a policy presently in force. (2) The maximum amount of benefits payable for a given situation or occurrence (e.g., a limit of $50,000 on the contents of a home, or a $40,000 per accident limit for property damage liability). *See also* **limit of liability. (G)**

line. A colloquial term with several meanings. It may be used to mean a particular type of insurance, such as the liability line. It may be used to describe all the various types of insurance written for a property owner (e.g., carrying all lines of the XYZ Company). It is also used to describe the amount of insurance on a given property (e.g., a $250,000 line on buildings of the XYZ Company). **(G)**

line card. A record kept by a property insurer of the insurance sold to any one particular insured. **(PR)**

line of business. The general classification of business as used in the insurance industry (e.g., fire, allied lines, and homeowners). **(G)**

line sheet. A schedule showing the limits of liability to be written by an insurer for different classes of risks. This kind of guide is also used by a ceding company to define the limits of liability it will assume on various types of exposures. **(G)**

line slip. A document (most commonly used at Lloyd's) that describes a risk to be insured. It is circulated by brokers, and underwriters subscribe to it by indicating what percentage of the risk they are willing to take. **(H)**

lines. The amount a reinsurer accepts, usually in multiples of a net retention, under a surplus treaty. If a given treaty specifies a retention of $10,000 and a risk is written for $50,000, four lines ($40,000) would be reinsured. *See also* **surplus reinsurance. (R)**

liquidated damages. Damages that are agreed to either by the court or by the parties to a suit or action. **(LE)**

liquidation of insurer. Action undertaken by a state insurance department to dissolve an impaired or insolvent insurer that cannot be restored to sound financial standing. *See also* **rehabilitation of insurer. (G)**

liquidity. The ability of an insurer to convert its assets into cash to pay claims if necessary. **(G)**

liquor control laws. *See* dram shop laws. **(LE)**

liquor liability insurance. *See* dram shop liability insurance. **(LA)**

litigant. One who is engaged in a lawsuit. **(LE)**

litigation bond. *See* court bond. **(S)**

livery use. Use of a vehicle for hire to carry persons. Livery use is excluded in automobile insurance contracts unless coverage for it is stated in the policy. **(AU)**

livestock coverage form. A commercial property form that may be attached to a farm coverage part to insure livestock. This form replaced various inland marine forms that were commonly used to insure farm property and livestock. **(PR)**

livestock insurance. A named-perils contract that provides a prescribed lump-sum payment to an insured upon the death of any animal covered by the policy. **(PR)**

livestock mortality insurance. The equivalent of life insurance for livestock. **(PR)**

livestock transit insurance. Insurance against accidents causing death or crippling on shipments of livestock while in transit by rail, truck, or other similar means of transportation. **(PR)**

living benefits rider. A rider attached to a life insurance policy that provides long-term care benefits or benefits for terminally ill patients. The benefits provided are derived from the available life insurance benefits. **(H)**

living need benefits. A combination of life insurance and long-term care insurance that allows life insurance benefits to generate long-term care benefits. Up to a certain percentage of the life insurance policy's death benefit may be used in advance to offset nursing home or medical expenses, reducing the face amount of the life policy. **(H)**

living trust. A trust created by a person during his lifetime. Also referred to as an inter vivos trust. **(EP)**

Lloyd's. Generally refers to Lloyd's of London, England, an institution within which individual underwriters accept or reject the risks offered to them. The Lloyd's Corporation provides the support facility for their activities. **(G)**

Lloyd's association. A group of individuals who band together to assume risks are sometimes called a Lloyd's association. They are organized along the same lines as, though not connected with, Lloyd's of London. Each person is responsible only for the share of the risk that he assumes. There are a limited number of these associations in the United States. **(G)**

Lloyd's broker. A person who has the authority to negotiate insurance contracts with the underwriters on the floor at Lloyd's. *See also* Lloyd's. **(G)**

Lloyd's syndicate. A consortium of individual Lloyd's or London underwriters. Usually, one person acts for the syndicate in accepting risks or rejecting them. **(G)**

Lloyd's underwriter. An individual who underwrites risks through the facility of Lloyd's. These individuals are liable only for their own assumptions of risk and not those assumed by others in the same syndicate or in the overall Lloyd's organization. **(G)**

loading. The amount added to the pure insurance cost to cover the cost of the operations of an insurer, the possibility that losses will be greater than statistically expected, and fluctuating interest rates on the insurer's investments. The pure insurance cost is the portion of the premium estimated to be necessary for losses. **(G)**

loan value. A term that refers to the amount of money an insured can borrow using the cash value of his life insurance policy as security. **(LI)**

local agent. An agent representing companies in a sales and service capacity as an independent contractor on a commission basis. A local agent usually has a small territory, and agent powers are limited by contract. **(G)**

long-term care (LTC). Care that is provided for persons with chronic diseases or disabilities. The term includes a wide range of health and social services provided under the supervision of medical professionals. **(H)**

long-term care facility. Usually a state-licensed facility that provides skilled nursing services, intermediate care, and custodial care. **(H)**

long-term care (LTC) insurance. A health insurance policy that provides daily benefits when the insured is confined to a nursing home. **(H)**

long-term disability insurance. A group or individual policy that provides coverage for longer than a short-term policy, often until the insured reaches age 65 in the case of illness and for life in the case of accident. *See also* **short-term disability insurance. (H)**

Longshoremen's and Harbor Workers' Act. A federal act that stipulates compensation levels for injured longshoremen and harbor workers. **(WC)**

loss. Generally refers to (1) the amount of reduction in the value of an insured's property caused by an insured peril, (2) the amount sought through an insured's claim, or (3) the amount paid on behalf of an insured under an insurance contract. **(G)**

loss adjustment expense. The cost of adjusting losses, excluding the amount of the loss itself. **(G)**

loss assessment charge. An insured's share of a loss assessment for property damage or liability that is charged by a corporation or association of property owners. Homeowners policies provide some coverage for loss assessments charged against the insured as owner or tenant of a residence premises. **(LA, PR)**

loss clause. *See* automatic reinstatement clause. **(PR)**

loss constant. A flat amount included in the premium for small workers' compensation policies, for dwellings in some jurisdictions, and for some prescribed inland marine insurance lines. The purpose of the loss constant is to offset the greater-than-average loss experience that most small risks have, compared with all other risks in a given classification. **(G)**

loss control. Any combination of actions taken to reduce the frequency or severity of losses. Installing locks, burglar or fire alarms, and sprinkler systems are loss control techniques. **(G)**

loss conversion factor. A term used in a retrospective rating plan. It is a factor applied to the losses in the formula to give the insurer the funds needed to handle the investigation of claims. **(LA, WC)**

loss costs. Factor used in figuring insurance rates that represents how much an insurance company needs to collect to cover expected losses. Individual insurers develop their own rating factors to reflect their own underwriting expenses and profit/contingencies. **(G)**

loss development. The difference between the amount of losses initially estimated by the insurer and the amount reported in an evaluation at a later date. **(G)**

loss development factor. This is a recent development under retrospective rating plans. It was designed to give the insurer additional money to allow for the subsequent development of losses and to reimburse for claims that are late in being reported. The factor was introduced primarily because of the effect of inflation on losses that take a long time to settle. *See also* IBNR. **(WC)**

loss expectancy. An underwriter's estimate of the probable maximum loss to be suffered on an exposure being considered, with attention given to the expected level of loss prevention activities on the part of the insured. **(G)**

loss frequency. The number of times a loss occurs over a specific period. **(G)**

loss limitation. Another term used in retrospective rating formulas. It is designed to limit the effect of catastrophic losses that would otherwise be considered in full in figuring the final retrospective premium. **(WC)**

loss loading. A factor applied to the pure loss cost to produce a reinsurance rate or premium. **(R)**

loss of income benefits. Benefits paid for the inability to work for remuneration because of disability resulting from accidental bodily injury or sickness. The loss of income may be real or presumptive. **(H)**

loss of income insurance. Insurance that pays loss of income benefits. **(H)**

loss of market. A term found in ocean and inland marine contracts as part of the delay and loss of market exclusion. Loss of market is the inability to sell a product to prospective buyers. This is considered a normal business risk and is not coverable under insurance contracts except in some cases, such as meats, where spoilage can result in loss of market. If the spoilage is the result of some event such as a storm at sea or a derailing, coverage can be purchased for an additional premium. **(IM, OM)**

loss of time benefits. *See* loss of income benefits. **(H)**

loss of time insurance. *See* loss of income insurance. **(H)**

loss of use insurance. Coverage to compensate an insured for the loss of use of property if it cannot be used because of a peril covered by the policy. *See also* **additional living expenses. (PR)**

loss payable clause. A provision in property insurance contracts that authorizes payment to persons other than the insured to the extent that they have an insurable interest in the property. This clause may be used when there is a lien or loan on the property being insured, and it protects the lender. **(PR)**

loss payee. The party to whom money or insurance proceeds are to be paid in the event of loss, such as the lienholder on an automobile or the mortgagee on real property. **(G)**

loss prevention engineer. *See* engineer. **(LA, PR)**

loss prevention service. Engineering and inspection work done by an insurance company or independent organization with the aim of removing or reducing dangerous conditions in order to prevent losses. **(G)**

loss ratio. The losses divided by the premiums paid. The numerator (losses) can be losses incurred or losses paid, and the denominator (premium) can be earned premiums or written premiums, depending on what use is going to be made of the loss ratio. **(G)**

loss report. *See* **claim report. (G)**

loss reserve. The estimated liability for unpaid insurance claims or losses that have occurred as of a given evaluation date. Usually includes losses incurred but not reported (IBNR), losses due but not yet paid, and amount not yet due. The above describes a loss reserve as it would appear in an insurer's financial statement. As to individual claims, the loss reserve is the estimate of what will ultimately be paid out on that case. **(G)**

loss severity. The amount of a loss expressed in financial terms. **(G)**

losses incurred. The total losses, whether paid or not, sustained by an insurer during a given period (e.g., 12 months). **(G)**

losses outstanding. A summary statement prepared by property, life, and liability insurers showing claims not yet settled. **(G)**

losses paid. A summary of claims paid. **(G)**

lost instrument bond. When the owner of a stock certificate loses it, the insurer of the certificate will not issue a duplicate until the owner furnishes an indemnity bond guaranteeing that, if he finds the original, he will turn it over to the surety company. **(S)**

lost policy release. A statement signed by an insured releasing the insurer from all liability for a lost or mislaid contract of insurance. It is usually signed after the company has issued a replacement policy. **(G)**

lost-or-not-lost clause. (1) A provision in an ocean marine contract that ensures coverage whether the property is in existence at the time the contract is written or has already been destroyed. (2) Coverage of a ship at sea afloat or sunk. The reason for such a clause is that many times the owners of cargoes or ships would insure them after the ship had left the port, and before modern methods of communication were available, there was no way of knowing whether the venture had been lost at the time the insurance was taken out. **(OM)**

lump sum. A method of settlement whereby the beneficiary receives the entire proceeds of a policy at once rather than in installments. **(LI)**

M

M&C. *See* manufacturers and contractors liability insurance. **(LA)**

MDO. *See* monthly debit ordinary. **(LI)**

MDRT. *See* Million Dollar Round Table. **(LI)**

MERP. *See* medical expense reimbursement plan. **(H)**

MIB. *See* Medical Information Bureau. **(LI)**

MLIRB. *See* Multiline Insurance Rating Bureau. **(G)**

MPIC. Multiple Peril Insurance Conference. **(PR)**

MVR. Motor vehicle record. **(AU)**

PRESENTATION OF TERMS

machinery breakdown insurance. *See* boiler and machinery insurance. **(PR)**

maintenance bond. A bond guaranteeing against defects in workmanship or materials for a stated time after the acceptance of completed work. Two years is a common term for a construction bond. **(S)**

maintenance, care, and wages. An admiralty law provision for coverage for injured seamen. Maintenance refers to providing food, shelter, and rehabilitation while the seaman is injured. Care refers to the medical treatment necessary for recovery. Wages, of course, refers to the usual seaman's wages, which under this law, must be paid even during an illness or after an accident. **(OM)**

major hospitalization policy. The same as major medical insurance, except that it applies to expenses incurred only when the insured is hospitalized. *See also* **major medical insurance. (H)**

major medical insurance. A type of health insurance that provides benefits up to a high limit for most types of medical expenses incurred, subject to a large deductible. Such contracts may contain limits on specific types of charges, such as room and board, and a percentage participation clause sometimes called a coinsurance clause. These policies usually pay covered expenses whether an individual is in or out of the hospital. **(H)**

malicious mischief. Similar to vandalism. Purposely damaging the rights or property of another. *See also* **V&MM. (G)**

malinger. To feign a disability for the purpose of continuing to collect benefits longer than actually necessary. **(G)**

Maloney Act. A 1938 amendment to the Securities Exchange Act of 1934. The Maloney Act established National Association of Security Dealers (NASD) as a self-regulatory organization (SRO) for those involved in the sale of securities. **(G)**

malpractice. Professional misconduct or lack of ordinary skill in the performance of a professional act that renders the practitioner liable to suit for damages. **(LA)**

malpractice insurance. Insurance on a professional practitioner that will (1) defend suits instituted against the insured professional for malpractice, and/or (2) pay any damages set by a court, subject to policy limits. **(LA)**

managed care. A system of health care where the goal is a system that delivers quality, cost-effective health care through monitoring and recommending utilization of services and cost of services. **(H)**

managed health care plan. A plan that involves financing, managing, and delivery of health care services. Typically, it involves a group of providers who share the financial risk of the plan or who have an incentive to deliver cost-effective, but quality, service. **(H)**

management expense. A charge deducted in a contingent commission formula to cover the reinsurer's overhead expenses. **(R)**

manager. A common title for the head of an agency that is operated as a branch office, as opposed to being operated as a general agency. The manager is a salaried employee, usually with an incentive bonus based on the agency's volume. **(G)**

mandated benefits. Benefits required by state or federal law. **(H)**

mandated providers. Types of providers of medical care whose services must be included by state or federal law. **(H)**

mandatory retirement. A specified age in a pension plan when the member must retire even if he does not wish to do so. **(PE)**

mandatory valuation reserve. A reserve required by a state law to offset any declines in the valuation of securities listed as admitted assets. **(G)**

manual. A book giving rates, classifications, and underwriting rules for some line of insurance. An example would be the Automobile Manual, which gives such information for automobile insurance. **(G)**

manual excess. The premium for an amount of insurance in excess of the basic limit of liability. This premium is determined by referring to a table of rate factors, which are then multiplied by the manual rate to arrive at a premium for the higher limit selected. **(LA)**

manual rates. (1) Rates based on average claims data for a large number of groups. These rates are then adjusted for specific groups on the basis of that group's characteristics, such as the type of industry and changes in benefits from the standard. **(H)**. (2) Usually the published rate for some unit of insurance. An example is in the Workers' Compensation Manual, where the rates shown apply to each $100 of the payroll of the insured, and $100 is the unit. **(G)**

manufacturers and contractors liability insurance (M&C). A form of premises and operations liability insurance designed to cover manufacturing or contracting risks. The basis of premiums for this coverage is the payroll. **(LA)**

manufacturers output policy. A policy covering the personal property of a manufacturer on an open-perils (all risk) basis. Coverage is usually restricted to property away from the premises. Its original use was for manufacturers who send some of their products out to be processed by other companies. **(PR)**

manufacturer's selling price clause. Values unsold finished goods at the price at which they could have been sold at the time of a loss. **(PR)**

manufacturing location. A location that manufactures products for delivery to the insured's customers under a sales contract. One of the four types of dependent properties for which business income coverage may be written. **(PR)**

manuscript policy. A policy written to include specific coverages or conditions not provided in a standard policy. It is often prepared by a large brokerage house for a large account, and it must conform to state laws. In the event of a dispute over policy language, the contract of adhesion doctrine is modified. **(G)**

map. A geographical map is used by a property insurance underwriter to locate the area and character of a risk, especially in a large city. Maps may also be used to keep track of the number of insureds in a particular area so that an insurer does not subject itself to a possible catastrophic loss. **(PR)**

map clerk. A junior underwriter who enters such essential data as policy numbers, amounts of coverage, and property covered on maps to enable an insurer to determine its liability or exposure in a given area. **(PR)**

marine definition. *See* nationwide definition of marine insurance. **(IM, OM)**

marine insurance. A form of insurance primarily concerned with means of transportation and goods in transit. *Marine* alone refers to ocean transportation, and *inland marine* refers to transportation and goods in transit by land. *See also* **inland marine insurance** and **ocean marine insurance. (IM, OM)**

marital deduction. An unlimited amount of qualifying property that can be passed or transferred upon the death of one spouse to the surviving spouse. **(EP)**

marital deduction trust. An arrangement whereby the surviving spouse is provided with full use of the family's wealth while minimizing the impact of federal estate taxes. **(EP)**

market assistance plan (MAP). A plan promulgated by the Department of Insurance to assist buyers to obtain certain types of insurance when they are limited in availability. **(H)**

market conduct. Used to measure how insurance companies and insurance agents comply with state laws regulating the sales and marketing, underwriting, and issuance of insurance products. Proper market conduct means conducting insurance business fairly and responsibly. **(G)**

market conduct examination. When state insurance department investigators examine the business practices and operations of an insurer and its agents to determine their authority to conduct insurance business in the state. **(G)**

market risk. A risk experienced by those who invest in securities, which is the risk of possible loss of investment, since there are no guarantees associated with such investments. **(G)**

market value. The price for which something would sell, especially the value of certain types of assets, such as stocks and bonds. It is based on what they would sell for under current market conditions. For example, common stock market value would be the price of the stock as of a specified date. *See also* **actual cash value. (G)**

market value clause. A provision that may be used in certain property insurance forms and that obligates an insurer to pay the established market price of destroyed or damaged stock rather than its cost to the insured, as is usually provided in the standard fire policy. This coverage is only available to manufacturers with finished products, not to wholesalers or retailers. **(PR)**

marketing representative. *See* special agent. **(G)**

masonry noncombustible construction. A building that has exterior walls constructed of masonry materials, such as adobe, brick, concrete, gypsum block, hollow concrete block, stone, tile, or other similar materials, with floors and roof constructed of metal or other noncombustible materials. **(PR)**

mass merchandising. A technique whereby a group of people, usually employees or members of a union or trade association, insure with one company. Premiums are collected and remitted to the insurer in a lump sum. **(G)**

master. The admiralty law term for the captain of a ship. **(OM)**

master contract. In group insurance, the master contract is given to the employer. Individuals insured under the plan receive certificates to evidence their coverage under the plan. **(PE)**

master policy. (1) The policy contract issued to an employer or other entity authorized by state law for a group insurance plan. *See also* **certificate of insurance.** (2) A property insurance policy issued to an insured who can issue certificates of coverage to cover the property of others. **(G)**

master-servant rule. The rule that all employers are obligated to protect the public from the acts of their employees. Courts hold employers liable for torts committed by employees during the course of their employment. **(LE)**

material fact. In insurance, it refers to a fact that is so important that the disclosure of it would change the decision of an insurance company, either with respect to writing coverage, settling a loss, or determining a premium. Usually, the misrepresentation of a material fact will void a policy. **(LE)**

mature. In insurance, a policy matures when its face amount becomes payable. This could occur upon the death of the insured, or in some forms of insurance such as endowments, as of a specified date. **(LI)**

mature policies. Uninterrupted claims-made coverage continuously in effect for at least five years and no longer eligible for rating credits given on immature policies. **(LA)**

maturity date. The date at which the face amount of a life insurance policy becomes payable by reason of either death or endowment. **(LI)**

maturity value. The amount payable to a living insured at the end of an endowment period or to the owner of a whole life policy if he lives past a certain age. **(LI)**

maxi tail, or full tail. Unlimited extended reporting period allowing for making claims after expiration of a claims-made liability policy. *See also* **supplemental extended reporting period**. **(LA)**

maximum allowable costs (MAC) list. A list of prescriptions where the reimbursement will be based on the cost of the generic product. **(H)**

maximum disability policy. A form of noncancellable disability income insurance that limits an insurer's liability for any one claim but not the aggregate amount of all claims. In other words, for any one claim there is a maximum amount payable, but there could be any number of separate claims for different disabilities. **(H)**

maximum foreseeable loss. *See* amount subject. **(PR)**

maximum out-of-pocket costs. The most a member will pay considering copayments, coinsurance, and deductibles. **(H)**

maximum possible loss. *See* amount subject. **(PR)**

maximum retrospective premium. The most an insured will be required to pay under a retrospective rating plan, regardless of the amount of losses incurred. **(LA, WC)**

McCarran-Ferguson Act. *See* Public Law 15. **(G)**

mediation. An informal means of trying to promote settlement of a dispute. It involves a third-party mediator who meets the parties to the dispute and tries to get them to agree on a settlement. **(LE)**

Medicaid. A medical benefits program administered by states and subsidized by the federal government. Under this plan, various medical expenses will be paid to those who qualify. It is technically referred to as Title XIX Benefits. **(H)**

medical care insurance. *See* medical expense insurance. **(H)**

medical examination. The examination of an applicant for insurance or a claimant by a physician who acts in the capacity of the insurer's agent. **(H, LI)**

medical examiner. The physician who examines an applicant or claimant on behalf of the insurer and as an agent of the insurer. **(H, LI)**

medical expense insurance. A form of health insurance that provides benefits for medical, surgical, and hospital expenses. This term is used to include coverage under the names hospital-surgical expense insurance and medical care insurance. **(H)**

medical expense reimbursement plan (MERP). A plan that provides for corporate reimbursement of specific health care expenses to employees. **(H)**

Medical Information Bureau (MIB). A data pool service that stores coded information on the health histories of persons who have applied for insurance from subscribing companies in the past. Most life and health insurers subscribe to this bureau to get more complete underwriting information. **(H, LI)**

medical loss ratio. Total health benefits divided by total premium. **(H)**

medical payments insurance. A form of coverage, optional in automobile and other public liability policies, that provides for the payment of medical and similar expenses without regard for liability. **(AU, LA)**

medical supplies. Any items that are essential in treating a patient's illness or injury. **(H)**

medically necessary. A service or treatment that is absolutely necessary in treating a patient and that could adversely affect the patient's condition if it were omitted. **(H)**

Medicare. The United States federal government plan for paying certain hospital and medical expenses for persons qualifying under the plan, usually those over age 65. The hospital benefits are Part A, and the medical expense portion is Part B. Part A is compulsory social insurance; Part B is voluntary government-subsidized, government-operated insurance. Part D provides prescription drug coverage. **(H)**

Medicare beneficiary. Anyone entitled to Medicare benefits on the basis of the designation by the Social Security Administration. **(H)**

Medicare Select policy. A Medicare supplement policy or certificate that contains restricted network provisions conditioning the payment of benefits on the use of network providers. **(H)**

Medicare supplement insurance. Insurance coverage sold on an individual or group basis that helps to fill the gaps in the protection provided by the Medicare program. Medicare supplements cannot duplicate any benefits provided by Medicare, but may pay part or all of Medicare's deductibles and copayments, and may cover some services and expenses not covered by Medicare. **(H)**

member. (1) Anyone covered under a health plan (enrollee or eligible dependent). **(H)**. (2) An employee who is qualified for coverage under a pension plan. Also referred to as a participant. **(PE)**

member certificate. Another term for certificate of coverage. **(H)**

member month. The total number of participants who are members for each month. **(H)**

members per year. The total number of member months divided by 12. **(H)**

mental (or emotional) distress. Usually not covered if a claimant was a bystander to an accident, but usually covered if he was physically involved. **(G)**

mental health provider. Individuals who are qualified to provide mental health services in accordance with the state or federal law that applies. Includes psychiatrists, social workers, and psychologists. **(H)**

mental health services and supplies. Items required for treatment of mental illness, including substance abuse and alcoholism. **(H)**

mercantile open stock policy. A once popular crime insurance form used by retail establishments to cover merchandise, furniture, and equipment after hours while the insured business was closed. It covered losses by burglary or robbery of a watchperson. This has been replaced by modern commercial crime coverage forms. **(C)**

mercantile risk. A term most often used in property insurance meaning a retail or wholesale risk, as contrasted with a service risk, a manufacturing risk, or a habitational risk. **(PR)**

mercantile robbery and safe burglary policy. A once-popular crime insurance form used by retail establishments to insure money and securities. This has been replaced by modern commercial crime coverage forms. **(C)**

merit rating. A type of rating plan used in several forms of insurance but most commonly in personal auto. It is a method whereby the insured's premium will vary depending on the insured's own past loss record. **(G)**

messenger. Under commercial crime insurance coverages, the named insured or any of the insured's partners or employees while having care and custody of property outside the insured's premises. **(C)**

messenger robbery insurance. Coverage on money and other property in the possession of persons who are away from the premises. An example would be an employee taking a deposit to the bank. **(C)**

midi tail. Automatic five-year extended reporting period allowing for the making of claims after expiration of a claims-made liability policy, but only applies to claims arising from occurrences that were reported no later than 60 days after the end of the policy. *See also* **extended reporting period. (LA)**

mill (or slow-burning) construction. Construction meeting certain high specifications and standards. Factories and warehouses constructed to meet these specifications qualify for reduced fire insurance rates. **(PR)**

Million Dollar Round Table (MDRT). An association of life insurance agents who qualify by selling $1 million worth or more of life insurance coverage. The policies must meet certain qualification standards, and applicants must be members of the National Association of Life Underwriters. **(LI)**

mini tail. Automatic 60-day extended reporting period allowing for the making of claims after expiration of a claims-made liability policy. *See also* **extended reporting period. (LA)**

minimum amount policy. A life insurance policy that is sold only with a minimum face amount. It can have a reduction in the rate over the same form of coverage written at lower amounts because certain insurance company expenses, like those of policywriting, do not increase proportionately with the face amount of the policy sold. **(LI)**

minimum compensation level. The amount of compensation an employee must earn before being eligible to participate in a pension or profit-sharing plan. **(PE)**

minimum deposit insurance. *See* financed insurance and minimum deposit policy. **(LI)**

minimum deposit policy. A cash value life insurance policy with a first-year loan value that is available to borrow against immediately upon payment of the first-year premium. This is not the case with most life insurance policies, the main reason being high first-year expenses. **(LI)**

minimum premium. (1) A cost plus arrangement whereby the employer pays the insurer only a portion of the premium that is to be used for administration costs. The remainder is placed in a bank account, which is then used by the insurer to pay claims. **(H)**. (2) The smallest amount of premium for which an insurer will issue coverage under a given policy. **(G)**

minimum rate. A rate for low hazard risks. **(PR)**

minimum retrospective premium. Used in a retrospective rating plan and defined as the lowest amount the insured can pay under the plan, regardless of the losses incurred. **(LA, WC)**

miscellaneous benefits. Benefits provided by a group medical policy that cover most inpatient medical expenses except room and board charges and surgical fees. **(H)**

miscellaneous expenses. Ancillary expenses, usually hospital charges other than daily room and board. Examples would be x-rays, drugs, and laboratory fees. The total amount of such charges that will be reimbursed is limited in most basic hospitalization policies. **(H)**

misrepresentation. The use of oral or written statements that do not truly reflect the facts either by an insured on an application for insurance or by an insurer concerning the terms or benefits of an insurance policy. **(LE)**

misstatement of age. (1) Giving the wrong age for oneself on an application for life and health insurance or for a beneficiary who is to receive benefits on the basis of his life contingency. (2) A provision in most life and health policies setting forth the action to be taken if a misstatement of age is discovered after the policy is issued.

This is one of the uniform provisions for individual health insurance policies. **(H, LI)**

mixed insurer (or company). An insurance company in which the ownership is split among stockholders and policyowners. The term can also be used to indicate an insurer issuing both life and health insurance policies. It is often erroneously used to describe an insurer offering both participating (dividend paying) and nonparticipating plans. **(G)**

mobile agricultural machinery and equipment coverage form. A commercial property form specifically designed to insure farm machinery and equipment when it is the only exposure, or when the coverage must be written separately. Similar coverage may also be included in the farm property coverage form. **(PR)**

mobile equipment. A term defined in general liability policies as land vehicles, including machinery and apparatus attached thereto, whether or not self-propelled, and (1) not subject to motor vehicle registration or financial responsibility laws, or (2) used exclusively on the insured's premises, or (3) designed principally for use off public roads, or (4) designed or maintained for the sole purpose of providing mobility for permanently attached equipment, such as cranes, loaders, pumps, generators, or welding equipment. **(LA)**

mobile home policy. A homeowners policy written on a mobile home that is permanently situated. **(PR)**

mode of premium payment. The method of premium payment (mode) elected by the policyowner. Modes generally available are monthly, quarterly, semiannually, and annually. **(G)**

modified. This term has several meanings, only a few of which will be mentioned here. (1) Under a modified coinsurance provision in life reinsurance, the ceding insurer retains and maintains the entire reserve, with the annual increase in reserve being transferred to the ceding insurer by the reinsurer at the end of the year. (2) Under preliminary term insurance, a modified reserving system permits at least part, if not all, of the first year's net premium on a life insurance policy to be used to meet first-year acquisition costs and claim expenses and requires that part of the renewal loading be added to the policy reserve accumulation. (3) Any premium that is altered from the regular premium for similar life policies, such as the premium for a modified life policy. **(LI)**

modified adjusted gross income. A worker's adjusted gross income plus tax-exempt interest received during a tax year. **(PE)**

modified community rating. A method of determining rates for medical services on the basis of data from a given geographic area. **(H)**

modified endowment contract. An endowment contract where the amount payable upon survival of the endowment period is greater than the face amount and the amount payable at death is the greater of the face amount or cash value. Modified endowment contracts are subject to taxation and subsequent penalties. **(LI)**

modified fee-for-service. A situation where reimbursement is made on the basis of the actual fees subject to maximums for each procedure. **(H)**

modified fire-resistive construction. A building that has exterior walls, floors, and roof constructed of masonry or fire-resistive materials. **(PR)**

modified life policy. An ordinary life contract under which the premiums are modified so as to be lower than normal for the first three to five years and higher than normal after that. A special case is a level term policy, under which no part of the premium goes toward savings and that is automatically converted to a whole life policy at a designated time. **(LI)**

money and securities broad form. A once-popular crime insurance form used by businesses to protect money and securities against many types of losses. This has been replaced by modern commercial crime coverage forms. *See* **theft, disappearance, and destruction coverage form. (C)**

money-purchase benefit formula. A type of pension plan under which contributions of both the employer and the employee are fixed as flat amounts or flat percentages of the employee's salary. *See* **defined contribution pension plan. (PE)**

money purchase plan. A term usually used to describe a pension or retirement plan. It refers to a plan in which a specified amount of money is used periodically to purchase an annuity for each employee covered by the plan. The total of these annuities is then paid to the employee at retirement. **(PE)**

monoline policy. Any insurance coverage written as a single line policy. *See also* **multiple line** or **package policy. (G)**

monopolistic state fund. The state-operated company in those states with laws requiring that all businesses buy workers' compensation insurance from the state. Private insurers cannot compete in these states. **(WC)**

monthly administration fee. In universal life insurance, an administrative fee is charged each month to cover administrative expenses. **(LI)**

monthly debit ordinary (MDO). Ordinary insurances the premiums for which are collected at the door monthly in the same fashion as industrial policies. **(LI)**

monthly debit ordinary status card. An IBM card showing the status of MDO business in force and lapsed. **(LI)**

moral hazard. A condition of morals or habits that increases the probability of loss from a peril. An extreme example would be an individual who previously burned his own property to collect the insurance. **(G)**

morale hazard. Hazard arising out of an insured's indifference to loss because of the existence of insurance. The attitude, "It's insured, so why worry," is an example of a morale hazard. **(G)**

morbidity. The relative incidence of disease. **(H)**

morbidity rate. The ratio of the incidence of sickness to the number of well persons in a given group of people over a given period of time. It may be the incidence of the number of new cases in the given time or the total number of cases of a given disease or disorder. **(H)**

morbidity table. A table showing the incidence of sickness at specified ages in the same fashion that a mortality table shows the incidence of death at specified ages. **(H)**

mortality charge. The charge for the element of pure insurance protection in a life insurance policy. **(LI)**

mortality cost. The first factor considered in life insurance premium rates. Insurers have an idea of the probability that any person will die at any particular age; this is the information shown on a mortality table. The pure mortality cost is the face amount of the policy multiplied by the probability that it will have to be paid out as a claim. **(LI)**

mortality, experienced. *See* experienced mortality. **(LI)**

mortality guarantee. The provision that an annuitant is guaranteed an income for life regardless of changes in the mortality of the population. **(AN)**

mortality rate. The number of deaths in a group of people, usually expressed as deaths per thousand. It can be the rate for the total population, called the crude mortality rate, or it can be refined by factors such as age groupings or causes of deaths. *See also* **death rate. (LI)**

mortality savings. The remainder, if any, after subtracting experienced mortality from expected mortality. **(LI)**

mortality table. A table showing the incidence of death at specified ages. It shows the number of persons in each age group who die, expressed in terms of deaths per thousand, and based on the deaths in a population of a million persons. **(LI)**

mortgage. Interest in real property conveyed to mortgagee as security for the loan of money by the mortgagee to the mortgagor, often the money being used by the mortgagor for the purchase of the real property from its seller (this is known as a purchase money mortgage). **(LE)**

mortgage (or mortgagee) clause. A provision attached to a fire or other direct damage policy that covers mortgaged property, specifying that the loss reimbursement shall be paid to the mortgagee as the mortgagee's interest may appear, that the mortgagee's rights of recovery shall not be defeated by any act or neglect of the insured, and giving the mortgagee other rights, privileges, and duties. For instance, one duty is that the mortgagee must report to the insurer any change in hazards of which he becomes aware. **(PR)**

mortgage holders errors and omissions coverage form. A commercial property form that protects the interests of mortgage holders from losses resulting from errors and omissions. **(PR)**

mortgage insurance. In life and health insurance, a policy covering a mortgagor from which the benefits are intended (1) to pay off the balance due on a mortgage upon the death of the insured, or (2) to meet the payments on a mortgage as they fall due in the case of the insured's death or disability. *See also* **mortgage redemption Insurance. (H, LI)**

mortgage redemption insurance. (1) *See* **mortgage insurance.** (2) A monthly reducing term policy used for mortgage insurance. **(H, LI)**

mortgagee. The creditor to whom a mortgage is given and who lends money on the security of the value of the property mortgaged. **(PR)**

mortgagor. The debtor who receives money and, in turn, grants a mortgage on his property as security for a loan. **(PR)**

Motor Carrier Act of 1980. Federal regulation that requires truckers and other commercial carriers to certify they are able to meet financial obligations if they become liable for injury or damage arising from their trucking operations. **(AU)**

motor carrier coverage form. Commercial auto coverage form used to cover anyone who transports property by auto in a commercial enterprise. **(AU)**

motor truck cargo policy—carrier's form. This form indemnifies the policyholder, a trucker, for loss or damage resulting from legal liability as a carrier while transporting the property of others. It does not insure against any loss for which he is not legally liable. Statutory law requires a trucker to carry a minimum amount of coverage. **(IM)**

motor truck cargo policy—owner's form. This form insures the owner of a truck against loss to his own property while being transported. It pays for the loss or damage of cargo for the perils insured against, regardless of the legal liability. **(IM)**

motor vehicle record (MVR). The record of an automobile driver's accidents and/or traffic violations. **(AU)**

multidisciplinary. Treatment that involves care provided by a wide range of specialists. **(H)**

multiemployer plan. A plan to which more than one employer contributes, or a plan mandated by a collective bargaining agreement. **(PE)**

multi-peril crop insurance (MPCI). Crop insurance usually providing coverage against crop losses by adverse weather (e.g., hail or wind), fire, flood, insects, plant disease, and other perils. **(PR)**

multi-peril policies. Policies that cover a number of perils, such as fire, burglary, and liability, in a single contract. **(G)**

multiple employer trust (MET). A trust consisting of multiple small employers in the same industry that is formed for the purpose of purchasing group health insurance or establishing a self-funded plan at a lower cost than would be available to the employers individually. **(H)**

multiple employer welfare arrangements (MEWA). Employer funds and trusts providing health care benefits to individuals. **(H)**

multiple funding. Providing retirement benefits through the use of a separate fund in addition to insurance cash values. **(PE)**

multiple indemnity. A provision that some or all of the benefits under a policy will be increased by a stated multiple, such as 100% or 200%, in the event that a peril occurs in a specified way (e.g., double indemnity on life insurance for accidental death). **(LI)**

multiple line law. A law passed by a state that allows an insurance company to write both property and casualty insurance. Before these laws were enacted, it was common for a state to allow some companies to write only property insurance and other companies to write only casualty insurance, depending on which type of insurance the company applied for in its license. **(G)**

multiple line policy. A policy that includes several different coverages, such as property, liability, and crime. Any personal or commercial package policy. **(G)**

multiple location policy. Protection of property in more than one location that is owned or controlled by one person. **(PR)**

multiple location rating plan. *See* **premium and dispersion credit plan. (PR)**

multiple option plan. Under this plan, employees can optionally choose from an HMO to a PPO to a major medical plan. **(H)**

multiple protection insurance. A combination of term and whole life insurance that pays some multiple of the face during the period of the term policy, becoming a regular whole life policy after the term policy expires. The multiple protection period is thus the period during which both the term and the whole life coverages are in effect. **(LI)**

mutual atomic energy reinsurance pool. A group of mutual insurance companies that reinsure liability policies written on private nuclear energy reactors. Most insurance contracts exclude this coverage, and it can usually only be provided by a pool. *See also* **radioactive contamination insurance. (LA)**

mutual benefit association. An organization offering benefits to members on a plan under which no fixed premiums are paid in advance but assessments are levied on members to meet specific losses as they occur. *See also* **assessment company, society,** or **insurer. (G)**

mutual fund. An investment company that raises money by selling its own stock to the public. It then invests the proceeds in other securities, and the value of its own stock fluctuates with its experience with the securities in its portfolio. Mutual funds are of two types: (1) open-end, in which capitalization is not fixed and more shares may be sold at any time; and (2) closed-end, in which capitalization is fixed and only the number of shares originally authorized may be sold. **(G)**

mutual insurer. An incorporated insurer without incorporated capital owned by its policyholders. Although mutual insurers do distribute their earnings to their policyholders in the form of dividends, the term should not be used in a sense that makes it synonymous with participating. In most jurisdictions, a mutual insurer is free to issue nonparticipating insurance if it chooses and a stock insurer is free to issue participating insurance. *See also* **stock insurer. (G)**

mutual insurer policy. Insurance issued by a mutual insurer. **(G)**

mutual investment trust. *See* **mutual fund. (G)**

mutualization. The process of converting a stock insurer to a mutual insurer, accomplished by having the insurer buy stock and retire it. **(G)**

mysterious disappearance. A disappearance of property that cannot be explained. Crime insurance policies use this term to give very broad coverage, as opposed to policies that narrow definitions to specific perils such as robbery and burglary. **(C)**

N

NAIB. *See* National Association of Insurance Brokers, Inc. **(G)**

NAIC. *See* National Association of Insurance Commissioners. **(G)**

NAII. *See* National Association of Independent Insurers. **(G)**

NAIW. National Association of Insurance Women. **(G)**

NALC. *See* National Association of Life Companies. **(H, LI)**

NAMIC. *See* National Association of Mutual Insurance Companies. **(G)**

NAPIA. National Association of Professional Insurance Agents. **(G)**

NASD. *See* National Association of Securities Dealers. **(G)**

NCCI. *See* National Council on Compensation Insurance. **(WC)**

NFIA. National Flood Insurers Association. **(G)**

NFPA. National Fire Protection Association. **(G)**

NOC. Not otherwise classified. A term often found in the classification section of liability or workers' compensation rating manuals. If a listing is followed by *NOC*, it means to use this classification if an insured cannot be classified more specifically. **(LA, WC)**

NPD. No payroll division. **(WC)**

NSLI. *See* National Service Life Insurance. **(LI)**

PRESENTATION OF TERMS

name position bond. A type of fidelity bond that covers losses caused by the dishonesty of only those employees holding positions specifically named in the bond. *See also* **name schedule bond** and **blanket bond. (C)**

name schedule bond. A type of fidelity bond that covers losses caused by the dishonesty of only those employees specifically named in the bond. *See also* **name position** and **blanket bond. (C)**

named insured. Any person, firm, or corporation, or any member thereof, specifically designated by name as the insured(s) in a policy. Others may be protected as insureds even though their names do not appear on the policy. A common application of this latter principle is in automobile policies where, under the definition of insured, protection is extended to cover other drivers using the car with the permission of the named insured. **(G)**

named nonowner policy. An automobile insurance policy issued to someone who does not own an automobile, but who drives borrowed or rented autos. **(AU)**

named perils. Perils specifically listed in an insurance policy as covered perils. *See also* **open-perils (all risk) insurance**, which covers all losses not specifically excluded. **(PR)**

National Association of Independent Insurers (NAII). An association composed of fire, casualty, and surety insurers that do not belong to large rating bureaus. The association distributes considerable information about legislation and litigation. **(G)**

National Association of Insurance Brokers, Inc. (NAIB). A voluntary association of insurance brokers that exists to exchange information and make recommendations to state legislatures. **(G)**

National Association of Insurance Commissioners (NAIC). Originally National Convention of Insurance Commissioners. An association of state insurance commissioners formed for the purpose of exchanging information and of developing uniformity in the regulatory practices of the several states through drafting model legislation and regulations. The NAIC has no official power to enforce compliance with its recommendations. **(G)**

National Association of Life Companies (NALC). A voluntary association of smaller and newer companies for exchange of information and ideas. **(H, LI)**

National Association of Life Underwriters (NALU). An association of life insurance agents, the activities of which center on the welfare and education of agents and legislation affecting agents. **(H, LI)**

National Association of Mutual Insurance Companies (NAMIC). A voluntary intercompany organization of mutual property and liability insurers formed for the exchange of information and discussion. **(G)**

National Association of Securities Dealers (NASD). A voluntary association of brokers and securities dealers handling over-the-counter securities. It serves a quasi-official function in the regulation of licensing and also acts as a bureau that formulates rates, rating plans, and policy wording for about half of the states. Many other states subscribe to the various services it provides. It is supported by the insurance companies which belong to it. **(G)**

National Auto Theft Bureau. An organization engaged in the prevention and reduction of motor vehicle fire and theft losses. **(G)**

National Council on Compensation Insurance (NCCI). An association of insurers selling compensation coverage and operating as a rating organization. NCCI collects statistics, develops rates and policy forms, and makes state filings for its members. **(WC)**

National Crop Insurance Association. A sister organization to the Crop Hail Insurance Actuarial Association (CHIAA). In 1989 these two organizations were consolidated to become National Crop Insurance Services (NCIS). **(PR)**

National Crop Insurance Services (NCIS). A voluntary, nonprofit organization made up of more than 140 member companies that compiles research and statistics in order to develop crop insurance rates and forms. **(PR)**

National Drug Code (NDC). A system for identifying drugs. **(H)**

National Flood Insurance Program (NFIP). Federal program providing flood insurance for fixed property. Under a dual program, coverage may be written directly by the NFIP or by private carriers whose losses may be reimbursed by the NFIP. **(PR)**

National Fraternal Congress of America. A federation of fraternal benefit societies. **(H, LI)**

national health insurance. Any system of socialized insurance benefits covering all or nearly all of the citizens of a country, established by its federal law, administered by its federal government, and supported or subsidized by taxation. **(H)**

National Insurance Association, Inc. An intercompany association of insurers formed to exchange information and ideas on common problems unique to the black community. **(G)**

National Safety Council. A nonprofit organization chartered by Congress in 1913. It is made up of approximately 12,000 industry members nationwide. The purpose of the council is the dissemination of safety education material. **(G)**

National Service Life Insurance (NSLI). Life insurance made available by the federal government for members of the United States armed forces from 1940 to 1951. **(LI)**

nationwide definition of marine insurance. A statement recommended by the National Association of Insurance Commissioners that indicates the types of insurance that are to be written under ocean or inland marine policies. Most states use this definition, subject to some individual exceptions. *See also* **ocean marine insurance** and **inland marine insurance. (IM, OM)**

natural death. Death by means other than accident or homicide. **(G)**

natural premium. The pure mortality cost of life insurance for one year at any given age. *See also* **pure premium. (LI)**

negligence. Failure to use the degree of care that an ordinary person of reasonable prudence would use under the given or similar circumstances. A person may be negligent by acts of omission or commission or both. **(G, LE)**

negligence, comparative. *See* comparative negligence. **(LE)**

negligence, contributory. *See* contributory negligence. **(LE)**

negligence, gross. *See* gross negligence. **(LE)**

negligence, presumed. *See res ipsa loquitor.* **(LE)**

net amount at risk. A term that refers to the differences between the face amount of a policy and the reserve or cash value that has been built up under that policy. **(LI)**

net cost. Premiums paid minus cash value and any policy dividends paid as of the date the calculation is being made. In the life business, it is common to draw up net cost comparisons at the end of ten and twenty years. **(G)**

net increase. The increase in the total amount of business an insurer has to force over a given period. It is figured as the total of new policies issued plus those renewed less policies lapsed and canceled. **(LI)**

net interest earned. The average interest earned by an insurer on its investments after investment expense but before federal income taxes. **(G)**

net level premium. The pure mortality cost of a life insurance policy from its inception to its maturity date, divided by the number of years the policy is to be in force. *See also* **level premium insurance. (LI)**

net level premium reserve. The reserve needed by an insurer to cover net level policies that are in their later years. Loosely speaking, the level premium system of paying for a long-term life or health policy involves overpayment during the early years and underpayment during the later years. **(H, LI)**

net line. The amount of coverage retained by the ceding company on an individual risk in a surplus reinsurance treaty. This term can also be used to mean the maximum amount of loss on a particular risk to which an insurer will expose itself without reinsurance. *See also* **lines** and **retention. (G, R)**

net loss. The amount of loss sustained by an insurer after giving effect to all applicable reinsurance, salvage, and subrogation recoveries. **(G)**

net premium. (1) The amount of premium minus the agent's commission. (2) The premium necessary to cover only anticipated losses, before loading to cover other expenses. (3) The original premium minus dividends paid or anticipated in participating life insurance when the insured elects to use dividends toward payment of the premiums. *See also* **gross premium. (G)**

net quick assets. The difference between allowable current assets and changeable current liabilities. This figure is referred to as the working capital. A contractor must have adequate working capital in order to be bonded. **(S)**

net rate. (1) See the third definition of **net premium** for the definition applicable to participating life insurance policies. (2) In a nonparticipating policy, the rate book rate. **(LI)**

net retained line. *See* **net line. (G)**

net retention. The amount of insurance that a ceding company keeps for its own account and does not reinsure. **(G)**

net worth. The amount by which assets exceed liabilities. It is of concern to bond indemnifiers in determining the size of a job a contractor can handle. **(S)**

network model HMO. Under this model, an HMO contracts with several physician groups. Physicians may share in savings, but may provide care for other than HMO members. **(H)**

new for old. Replacing old damaged parts or equipment with new ones rather than repairing them. **(G)**

New York Standard Fire Policy. The basic fire insurance contract that was used in nearly every state with only a handful of exceptions. It provided coverage against loss by fire, lightning, and removal, and established policy provisions that became the foundation for property insurance contracts. EC and V&MM coverage could be added by endorsement. With the introduction of modern policy forms, the standard fire policy has become obsolete, except in a few states where its use continues to be required by law. **(PR)**

newly acquired autos. Auto that the named insured obtains during the policy period. Coverage for newly acquired autos is contingent on several factors, such as the type of coverage, whether the auto is a replacement or additional vehicle, and when the insured notifies the insurer of the acquisition. **(AU)**

newspaper policy. A form of limited health insurance often sold by newspapers to build or conserve circulation. **(H)**

no benefit to bailee. A provision in an inland marine form stating that any insurance a person has on property in the possession of a bailee will not be for the benefit of the bailee. For example, if a suit is lost or destroyed at the cleaners, the cleaner cannot deny coverage on the basis that other insurance exists. **(IM)**

no-fault insurance. Many states have passed laws permitting the individual automobile accident victim to collect directly from his own insurance company for medical and hospital expenses regardless of who was at fault in the accident. There are many variations in the laws of those states that have no-fault statutes. Most states do allow the individual to sue the negligent party if the amount of damages exceeds a certain stated limit. **(AU)**

nominal damages. A small amount of money awarded to a plaintiff to verify his legal rights, even though no actual damages have been proven. **(LE)**

nonadmitted assets. Assets that do not qualify under state law for insurance statement purposes. Examples would be furniture, fixtures, agents' debit balances, and accounts receivable that are over ninety days old. **(G)**

nonadmitted insurer. An insurer not licensed to do business in the jurisdiction in question. *See also* **unauthorized insurer** and **unlicensed insurer. (G)**

nonadmitted reinsurance. Reinsurance for which no credit is given in a ceding company's annual statement because the reinsurer is not licensed or authorized to transact that particular line of business in the jurisdiction in question. **(R)**

nonassessable policy. A policy for which the policyowner pays a set premium. No additional premiums or amounts can be assessed. These are issued primarily by stock insurers, but can also be issued by mutual insurers who qualify to do so by meeting certain standards under state laws. **(G)**

nonassignable. A policy that the owner cannot assign to a third party. Most policies are nonassignable unless approval is given by the insurer. **(G)**

noncancelable (non-can). A contract of health insurance that the insured has a right to continue in force by payment of premiums, as set forth in the contract, for a substantial period, also as set forth in the contract. During that period, the insurer has no right to make any change in any provision of the contract. The NAIC recommends that the term *noncancelable* not be permitted to be used to designate any form that is not renewable to at least age 50 or for at least five years if issued after age 44. Note that this is in contrast to guaranteed renewable, on which the premium may be increased by classes. The premium for noncancelable policies must remain as stated in the policy at the time of issue. *See also* **guaranteed renewable. (H)**

nonconcurrency. The situation that exists when a number of insurance policies intended to cover the same property against the same hazards are not identical as to the extent of coverage. Nonconcurrency usually results in an insured not being fully covered for a loss. Modern forms have minimized the problem of nonconcurrency. **(PR)**

nonconfining sickness. Sickness that does not confine the insured indoors. **(H)**

noncontributory. A plan or program of insurance, usually group, for which the employer pays the entire premium and the employee contributes no part of the premium. **(H, LI)**

noncontributory retirement plan. A retirement plan funded entirely by the employer. **(PE)**

noncupative will. An oral will given in the presence of witnesses, usually at the time when the testator is very near death. **(EP)**

nondisabling injury. An injury that does not qualify the insured for total or partial disability benefits. A disability income policy may contain a provision for a small benefit in the case of such an injury, including medical costs of up to 25% or 50% of one month's disability benefit payment. **(H)**

nondisabling injury rider. An optional disability income policy rider that does not pay a disability benefit but rather provides for the payment of medical expenses incurred due to injury that does not result in total disability. **(H)**

nonduplication of benefits. A provision in some health insurance policies specifying that benefits will not be paid for amounts reimbursed by others. In group insurance, this is usually called coordination of benefits (COB). **(H)**

nonforfeitable benefit. A benefit payable under a pension plan that unconditionally belongs to a participant of the plan. **(PE)**

nonforfeiture values. Those values in a life insurance policy that by law the policyowner cannot forfeit even if he ceases to pay the premiums. These benefits are the cash surrender value, the loan value, the paid-up insurance value, and the extended term insurance value. The policyowner may choose one of these nonforfeiture options, but even if he fails to do so, the one specified in the contract for such a case automatically goes into effect. **(LI)**

noninsurable risk. A risk that cannot be measured actuarially or in which the chance of loss is so high that insurance cannot be written against it. **(G)**

noninsurance. Making no financial preparation for meeting losses. **(G)**

nonmedical (non-med). A contract of life or health insurance underwritten on the basis of an insured's statement of health with no medical examination required. **(H, LI)**

nonoccupational insurance. *See* unemployment compensation disability insurance. **(H)**

nonoccupational policy. A policy or provision of a policy that excludes accidents occurring on the job, when such employment is covered by workers' compensation. **(H)**

nonowned auto. (1) In personal auto insurance, an auto that is not furnished or available for the regular use of the insured or any family member. (2) In commercial auto insurance, an auto used for business purposes that is not owned, leased, hired, or borrowed by the insured. **(AU)**

nonparticipating (non-par). Insurance contracts on which no policy dividends are paid because there is no contractual provision for the policyowner to participate in the surplus. *See also* **participating. (G)**

nonparticipating provider. (1) A provider who has not signed a contract with a health plan. (2) A medical or health care provider who is not certified to participate in the Medicare program. **(H)**

nonparticipating provider indemnity benefits. Coverage where services provided by nonparticipating providers are reimbursed under an indemnity basis. **(H)**

nonprofit insurers. Insurers organized under special state laws, usually exempting them from some taxes imposed on regular insurers, to supply medical expense reimbursement insurance, usually on a service basis. Blue plans (i.e., Blue Cross and Blue Shield) in most states are an example. **(H)**

nonproportional reinsurance. *See* **aggregate excess of loss reinsurance.** Nonproportional reinsurance is a term for the first instance cited under that entry. **(R)**

nonqualified plan. A benefit type of plan, such as a retirement plan, which may be discriminatory, need not be filed with the IRS, and does not provide a current tax deduction for contributions. **(PE)**

nonrenewal. Termination of insurance coverage at an expiration date or anniversary date. This action may be taken by an insurer who refuses to renew, or by an insured who rejects a renewal offer. **(G)**

nonresident agent. An agent licensed in a state where he does not live. **(G)**

notice of cancellation. Written notice by an insurer of intent to cancel insurance, or written notice by an insured requesting cancellation. **(G)**

notice of loss. Notice to an insurer that a loss has occurred. Notice of loss is a condition of most policies, and it is frequently required within a given time and in a particular manner. **(G)**

nonvalued policy. A policy that is not valued—that is, when the policy is written, the amount to be paid in the event of a loss is not stated. Most property policies are nonvalued. **(G)**

noon clause. A provision in an insurance contract stating that the insurance coverage starts at noon, standard time, at the location of the insured's property. Most property policies have now been changed so that the effective time is 12:01 am; thus, the noon clause is not often encountered. **(PR)**

normal retirement. Retirement at an age specified by the pension plan as being the normal or standard age for retirement. *See also* **mandatory retirement** . **(PE)**

normal retirement benefit. An employee's early retirement benefit from a plan, or the benefit payable at the time of his normal retirement age, whichever is greater. The value of the benefits is determined without regard to medical and/or disability benefits. **(PE)**

not otherwise classified. *See* NOC. **(LA, WC)**

not taken. Policies applied for and issued but rejected and not paid for by the proposed owner. **(G)**

notice to company. Written notice to an insurer of the occurrence of an event on which a claim is to be based. **(G)**

nuclear energy contamination. *See also* **mutual atomic energy reinsurance pool** and **radioactive contamination insurance. (LA, PR)**

nuisance value. An amount that an insurance company will pay to settle a claim not because it is a valid claim but because the company considers it worth that amount to dispose of it. **(G)**

numerical rating. An underwriting method of determining the extra rate to be charged for a substandard insured. Standard is rated 100. Various impairments are assigned various numerical values. The sum of 100 plus the values of the ratings of the impairments indicates the table to use in determining the rate of the policy. **(LI)**

nurse fees. A provision in a medical expense reimbursement policy calling for reimbursement for the fees of nurses other than those employed by the hospital. **(H)**

nursing home. A licensed facility that provides general nursing care to those who are chronically ill or unable to take care of necessary daily living needs. May also be referred to as a long-term care facility. **(H)**

O

ABBREVIATIONS AND ACRONYMS

OAA. Old Age Assistance, a form of public assistance. *See also* **public assistance. (G)**

OASDHI. *See* Old Age, Survivors, Disability, and Health Insurance. **(G)**

OBRA. *See* Omnibus Budget Reconciliation Act. **(H)**

OL&T. *See* owners, landlords, and tenants liability insurance. **(LA)**

OSHA. *See* Occupational Safety and Health Act. **(G)**

PRESENTATION OF TERMS

object. In boiler and machinery insurance, the name of the vessel insured; the object of insurance. This term is not used in newer equipment breakdown protection forms. **(PR)**

obligatory reinsurance. *See* **automatic reinsurance. (R)**

obligee. Broadly, anyone in whose favor an obligation runs. This term is used most frequently in surety bonds, where it refers to the person, firm, or corporation protected by the bond. The obligee under a bond is similar to the insured under an insurance policy. In the case of a construction bond, the person for whom the building is being built is the obligee. **(S)**

obligor. Commonly called the principal. One bound by an obligation. In the case of a construction bond, the contractor is the principal. **(S)**

occupancy. This refers to the type or character of use of the property in question. The type of occupancy has a bearing on its desirability and also affects the rate for the policy. **(PR)**

occupational accident. An accident arising out of or occurring during the course of one's employment and caused by hazards inherent in or related to that employment. **(G)**

occupational disease. (1) Impairment of health caused by continued exposure to conditions inherent in a person's occupation or a disease caused by an employment or resulting from the nature of an employment. **(H)**. (2) Sickness or disease arising out of or during the course of employment. State compensation laws provide coverage for this type of loss. **(WC)**

occupational hazard. A condition in an occupation that increases the peril of accident, sickness, or death. **(H, LI, WC)**

occupational manual. A book listing occupational classifications for various types of work. **(H, LI, WC)**

Occupational Safety and Health Act (OSHA). A federal statute that establishes safety and health standards on a nationwide basis. The act is enforced by Labor Department safety inspectors and also provides for the recordkeeping of statistics relevant to work injuries and illnesses. **(G)**

occurrence. An event that results in an insured loss. In some lines of insurance, such as liability, it is distinguished from accident in that the loss does not have to be sudden and fortuitous and can result from continuous or repeated exposure that causes bodily injury or property damage neither expected nor intended by the insured. **(G)**

occurrence coverage. A policy form providing liability coverage only for injury or damage that occurs during the policy period, regardless of when the claim is actually made. For example, a claim made during the current policy year could be charged against a prior policy period, or may not be covered, if it arises from an occurrence before the effective date. *See also* **claims-made coverage. (LA)**

ocean marine insurance. A general term used to indicate all types of insurance associated with coverage on vessels and their cargoes. **(OM)**

odds. The probable frequency of incidence of a given occurrence in a statistical sample. It is expressed as a ratio to the probable number of nonoccurrences or as a decimal fraction of the total occurrences. For example, a probability of .25 equals odds of three to one against the occurrence. A probability of .75 equals odds of three to one in favor of the occurrence. *See also* **probability, law of large numbers,** and **degree of risk. (G)**

off premises. A clause in a property insurance contract extending coverage away from the premises described in the policy. The amount of coverage away from the premises is usually restricted to a percentage of the total coverage on the premises (e.g., 10%). **(PR)**

offer. The terms of a contract proposed by one party to another. In property and casualty insurance, submitting an application to the company is usually considered an offer. In life insurance, the application plus the initial premium constitutes an offer. **(G)**

offeree. One to whom an offer is made. **(G)**

offeror. One who makes an offer. **(G)**

office burglary and robbery policy. A special policy designed for offices. It usually consists of several crime coverages on office equipment and supplies that are purchased as a package. There is relatively low limit for each coverage and very little flexibility in that the policyholder must buy the complete package. **(C)**

office visit. Services provided in the physician's office. **(H)**

officers and directors liability insurance. A type of insurance that protects the officers and directors of a corporation against damages resulting from negligent or wrongful acts that may harm the corporation or its stockholders. **(LA)**

offset rider. A rider in a health insurance policy designed to reduce the benefit by a portion of the Social Security benefits received. **(H)**

Old Age, Survivors, Disability, and Health Insurance. The system of social insurance benefits for the aged, surviving dependents, and disabled workers set up by the Social Security Act of 1935, plus amendments and additions. *See also* **social insurance** and **Social Security**. **(G)**

old line. A term without a precise meaning but generally applied to nonfraternal insurers operating on a legal reserve basis. The origin of the term is in doubt but it seems to have come into use at the time of the competition between the new fraternal insurers and the commercial insurers to indicate the fact that the fraternals were newcomers. **(LI)**

Omnibus Budget Reconciliation Act. A federal law that extends the minimum COBRA continuation of group health care coverage from 18 to 29 months for qualified beneficiaries who are disabled at the time of qualification. **(H)**

omnibus clause. An agreement in most automobile liability policies and some others that, by its definition of insured, extends the protection of the policy to others within the definition without the necessity of specifically naming them in the policy. An example would be a policy that covers the named insured and those residing with him. **(G)**

omnibus risk. A structure housing a number of tenants engaged in a variety of businesses. **(PR)**

open access. Allows a participant to see another participating provider of services without a referral. Also called **open panel. (H)**

open cover. A reinsurance facility under which risks of a specified category are declared and insured. **(R)**

open debit. A life and health insurance debit (territory) currently without an agent. **(H, LI)**

open-end investment company. An investment company managed by professional investment advisors who invest in stocks and bonds on behalf of shareholders. Also known as a mutual fund. **(PE)**

open enrollment period. A period during which members can elect to come under an alternate plan, usually without providing evidence of insurability. **(H)**

open panel. *See* open access. **(H)**

open perils. Insurance against loss of or damage to property arising from any cause except those that are specifically excluded. *See also* **all-risk insurance** and **named perils. (G, PR)**

open policy. An insurance contract in which the terms of the policy are not fixed at the inception nor is an expiration date specified, but limits of liability are set forth for the protection it offers. No deposit premium is required, but monthly reports are made and sent with premiums due at that time, and certificates of insurance are issued to indicate the property covered. An open policy is commonly used to cover goods in transit. **(IM, PR)**

open rating. A system whereby a state allows an insurer to use rates without prior approval. **(G)**

open stock burglary policy. *See* **mercantile open stock burglary coverage. (C)**

option. A choice of methods of receiving policy dividends, nonforfeiture values, death benefits, or cash values. **(LI)**

optional benefits. *See* elective benefits. **(H)**

optional modes of settlement. The different options from which the beneficiary can choose to receive the proceeds from a life insurance policy. **(LI)**

optionally renewable. A contract of health insurance in which an insurer reserves the unrestricted right to terminate coverage at any anniversary or, in some cases, at any premium due date. It may not do so in between. **(H)**

ordinary agency. A life insurance agency that handles only ordinary life. *See also* **ordinary life insurance. (LI)**

ordinary construction. A building in which floors are on wood joists, in which the interior finish usually conceals space where fire can spread, and in which there is little protection of stair shafts. **(PR)**

ordinary life pension trust. A pension plan funded by means of a trust that provides death benefits through the purchase of ordinary or whole life insurance contracts for covered employees. The trust pays the insurance premium until the employee reaches retirement age and accumulates the additional sums necessary to purchase the retirement benefits, using the paid-up value of the life insurance policies. **(PE)**

ordinary life policy. A whole life policy for which premiums are paid continuously as long as the insured lives. Same as **straight life policy.** *See also* **whole life insurance. (LI)**

ordinary payroll. A business interruption term that refers to the entire payroll expense for all the employees of an insured except officers, executives, department managers, employees under contract, and other important employees. This payroll can be excluded or limited from business interruption forms, reducing the amount of insurance an insured is required to carry. **(PR)**

ordinary register. The record book in a combination insurer or agency containing data on the ordinary policies in an agent's account. **(LI)**

other insurance. The existence of other contracts covering the same interest and perils. *See also* **concurrent insurance. (G)**

other insurance clause. A provision found in almost every insurance policy except life and sometimes health stating what is to be done in case any other contract of insurance embraces the same property and/or hazards. *See also* **nonduplication of benefits** and **apportionment. (G)**

other structures. Structures such as a garage or storage shed that are separated from an insured dwelling by a clear space, or are connected only by a fence or utility line. Dwelling and homeowner policies provide coverage for other structures. **(PR)**

outage insurance. A type of insurance that covers against loss of earnings due to the failure of machinery to operate as the result of an insured peril causing damage to the premises. *See also* **extra expense insurance. (PR)**

outcomes measurement. A method of keeping track of a patient's treatment and the responses to that treatment. **(H)**

outline of coverage. A document presented to applicants for life or health insurance that provides a brief description of proposed coverages, premiums, benefits, limitations, and exclusions. It generally warns an applicant that it is a summary only and encourages the applicant to read the actual policy or certificate carefully. An outline of coverage may include various disclosures and may inform the applicant of certain rights, such as the right to a free look—that is, the right to return the policy and receive a full refund of premium within a stipulated period if not satisfied for any reason. **(H, LI)**

out of area (OOA). Treatment given to a member outside of the normal area. **(H)**

out-of-pocket costs. The amounts the covered person must pay out of his own pocket. This includes such things as coinsurance and deductibles. **(H)**

out-of-pocket limit. The maximum coinsurance an individual will be required to pay, after which the insurer will pay 100% of covered expenses up to the policy limit. **(H)**

outpatient. A patient who is not a bed patient in the hospital where he is receiving treatment. **(H)**

outstanding premiums. Premiums due but not yet collected. **(G)**

overage insurance. Health insurance issued at ages above the usual limit, which is generally 65. **(H)**

overhead expense insurance. Insurance that covers such things as rent, utilities, and employee salaries when a business owner becomes disabled. The insurance benefit is generally not a fixed amount but pays the amount of expenses actually incurred. **(H)**

overinsured. A term used to describe the condition that exists when an insured has purchased coverage for more than the actual cash value or replacement cost of a subject of insurance. It is also used to describe a situation in which so much insurance is in force as to constitute a moral or morale hazard, such as having so much disability income insurance in force that it becomes profitable to be disabled. **(G)**

overlapping insurance. Coverage from two or more policies or insurers that duplicates coverage of certain risks. *See also* **concurrent insurance. (G)**

overline. (1) The amount of insurance or reinsurance exceeding an insurer's or reinsurer's normal capacity, inclusive of automatic reinsurance facilities. (2) A commitment by an insurer or reinsurer above and beyond normal facilities or capacities. **(G)**

overriding commission. (1) A commission that an agent or broker may receive on any business sold in his exclusive territory by sub-agents. Also sometimes called overwriting or overriding. (2) An allowance paid to a ceding company over and above the acquisition cost to allow for overhead expenses, often including a margin for profit. **(G)**

over-the-counter drugs (OTC). A drug that can be purchased without a prescription. **(H)**

owners and contractors protective liability policy. A policy that protects an insured against losses caused by the negligence of a contractor or subcontractor that he hires. Also sometimes referred to as independent contractors insurance. **(LA)**

owners, landlords, and tenants liability insurance (OL&T). Coverage for an insured against legal liability for bodily injury or property damage caused to others by negligence and arising out of the ownership, maintenance, or use of the premises designated in the policy and all operations necessary or incidental to those premises. A form of premises and operations liability insurance designed to cover premises where the public is invited. The OL&T form has largely been replaced by the **commercial general liability coverage form. (LA)**

ownership. All rights, benefits, and privileges under life insurance policies are controlled by their owners. Policy owners may or may not be the insureds. Ownership may be assigned or transferred by written request of the current owner. **(LI)**

ownership of expirations. An agreement by an insurer that certain information regarding the details of a policy, usually a property or liability form, will be revealed to no agent or broker other than the originating agent. **(G)**

ownership provision. A provision that a policy may be owned by someone other than the insured. **(LI)**

P

PD. *See* physical damage. **(AU)**

P&I. *See* protection and indemnity insurance. **(OM)**

PIA. Professional Insurance Agents. An association of independent agents involved in educational programs, consumer efforts, and government and industry affairs pertaining to the insurance industry. **(G)**

PILR. *See* property insurance loss register. **(PR)**

PML. *See* probable maximum loss. **(PR)**

PPO. *See* preferred provider organization. **(H, LI)**

PRESENTATION OF TERMS

package policy. Any insurance policy including two or more lines or types of coverages in the same contract. Personal and commercial package policies are very common today. In fact, most policies sold are package policies. **(G)**

paid business. Insurance for which the application has been signed, the medical examination completed, and the settlement for the premium tendered. **(H, LI)**

paid claims. Amounts paid to providers on the basis of the health plan. **(H)**

paid claims loss ratio. Paid claims divided by total premiums. **(H)**

paid-for. Insurance on which the premium has been paid. **(G)**

paid-in capital. The amount paid for the stock sold by a corporation. **(G)**

paid-in surplus. Surplus paid in by stockholders, as contrasted with surplus earned through the operations of a business. **(G)**

paid losses. The amount actually paid in losses during a specified period, not including estimates of amounts that will be paid in the future for losses that occurred then. **(G)**

paid-up additions (or adds). *See* dividend additions. **(LI)**

paid-up insurance. Insurance on which all premiums are paid but that has not yet matured by either death or endowment. An example would be a limited payment life policy for which the premium-paying period is over. **(LI)**

pair and set clause. A clause stating that if a part of a pair or set is lost or damaged, the measure of the loss shall be a reasonable and fair proportion of the total value of the set, giving consideration to the importance of the article. The insurer is under no obligation to pay for the total loss of a set when one part is lost, damaged, or destroyed. **(IM)**

par. Abbreviation for participating. *See* **participating.** **(G)**

parasol policy. Another name for the difference in conditions policy. *See* **difference in conditions. (LA)**

parcel post insurance. Coverage to protect an insured against damage to or loss of parcels while they are in the care of the United States Post Office Department. Packages can be insured by either the United States Post Office or by private insurance companies. **(IM)**

parent company. The senior company in a group or fleet of insurers. *See also* **fleet of companies. (G)**

parol. A legal term that refers to oral statements as distinguished from written statements. **(LE)**

parol evidence rule. This rule states that a written instrument or contract cannot be modified by an oral agreement. It is based on the concept that written contracts should contain all of the facts and agreements between the parties and, therefore, prevents contemporaneous oral declarations from being included in the contract. **(LE)**

partial disability. A condition in which, as a result of injury or sickness, the insured cannot perform all of the duties of his occupation but can perform some. Exact definitions vary from policy to policy. **(H)**. *See also* **permanent partial disability** and **temporary partial disability. (G, H, WC)**

partial hospitalization services. Additional services provided to mental health or substance abuse patients that provide outpatient treatment as an alternative or follow-up to inpatient treatment. **(H)**

partial loss. A loss covered by an insurance policy that does not completely destroy or render worthless the insured property. **(G)**

participant. An employee or former employee who is eligible to receive benefits from an employee benefit plan or whose beneficiaries may be eligible to receive benefits from the plan. **(H, LI, PE)**

participating (par). (1) Insurance that pays policy dividends. In other words, it entitles a policyowner to participate in allocations of the insurer's surplus. In life insurance there are several options available for the use of such dividends. (2) Insurance that contributes proportionately with other insurance on the same risk. **(G)**

participating provider. A health care provider approved by Medicare to participate in the program and receive benefit payments directly from carriers or fiscal intermediaries. **(H)**

participating reinsurance. *See* pro rata reinsurance. **(R)**

participation. The number of employees enrolled, compared with the total number eligible for coverage. Many times, a minimum participation percentage is required. **(H)**

particular average. Refers to a partial loss that must be borne entirely by the individual owning the property, which has been damaged or lost. In many cases, it is used synonymously with the term *partial loss*. *See also* **free of particular average. (OM)**

partnership entity. The partnership considered as an entity and not in terms of its individual partial owners. **(G)**

partnership insurance. Life or health insurance sold to a partnership, usually for guaranteeing business continuity in case of the death or disability of one of the partners. For instance, two partners might buy life insurance on each other so that in the event of one partner's death, the other can use the insurance proceeds to purchase the deceased partner's share of the business from the heirs. **(H, LI)**

party-in-interest. Any of the parties to an employee benefit plan, including individuals serving as a fiduciary or counsel, or employees of an employee benefit plan; or any person providing service to the plan; or the employer who establishes the plan; or an employee organization whose members are covered by the plan; or an owner of 50% or more of a company that establishes an employee benefit plan. **(PE)**

party wall. A common wall between two buildings. **(G)**

past service benefit. A term used in pension or retirement insurance policies to refer to credit given an employee for the amount of time the person was employed before the effective date of the retirement plan. Example: An insured starts a pension plan on January 1, 1980. It states that all eligible employees will be given credit for their length of service or employment prior to that date. **(LI)**

past service liability. The monetary value at the start of a pension plan of all annuity credits vested before the effective date. **(PE)**

Paul v. Virginia. The 1869 United States Supreme Court decision holding that insurance is not commerce and, hence, not subject to regulation by the federal government. This was the ruling decision with respect to insurance regulation until the SEUA case in 1944, which reversed that decision but which was later modified by Public Law 15. *See also* **Southeastern Underwriters Association** and **Public Law 15. (G)**

pay. An abbreviation for *payment* (e.g., 20-pay life policy). **(LI)**

pay-as-you-go. *See* **current disbursement. (LI)**

payee. The person receiving money. **(G)**

paymaster robbery insurance. Coverage against loss by the robbery of a payroll from a custodian. **(C)**

payment bond. A bond furnished by a contractor that guarantees that he will pay for the labor and materials used in a particular project. It relieves the owner of the project from possible liability because of nonpayment by the contractor. *See also* **labor and material bond. (S)**

payor benefit. A rider or provision often found in juvenile policies under which premiums are waived if the person paying the premium, usually one of the parents, becomes disabled or dies while the child is still a minor. **(LI)**

payroll audit. An examination of an insured's payroll record by a representative of the insurer to determine the final premium due on a policy for the latest policy year. **(LA, WC)**

payroll deduction insurance. A term used to describe a plan whereby an employer is authorized by an employee to deduct insurance premiums for an individual life insurance policy that he has purchased from an insurer. The employer pays the insurer the amount deducted on a periodic basis. **(LI)**

peak season endorsement. An endorsement that provides increased amounts of coverage on inventories during peak seasons, beginning and ending on dates specified in the endorsement. **(PR)**

peer review. Review of health care provided by a medical staff with training equal to that of the staff providing the treatment. **(H)**

peer review organization (PRO). Groups of physicians who are paid by the federal government to conduct preadmission, continued stay, and services reviews provided to Medicare patients by Medicare-approved hospitals. **(H)**

penalty. The limit of an insurance company's liability under a fidelity bond. **(S)**

Pension Benefit Guaranty Corporation (Pen Ben). A nonprofit corporation within the Department of Labor that insures participants in and beneficiaries of covered plans against the loss of benefits arising from a premature termination of a retirement plan. **(PE)**

pension plan. A qualified retirement plan established by an employer for the benefit of its employees and their beneficiaries. The design can provide for either a specific benefit (defined benefit plan) or a specific contribution (defined contribution plan). **(PE)**

pension trust fund. A fund consisting of money contributed by the employer, and, in some cases, the employee, to provide pension benefits. **(PE)**

per capita. Literally "by heads." Distribution among survivors by persons on a share-and-share-alike basis. The term is often used in beneficiary designations. *See also* per stirpes. **(LI)**

per diem business interruption. A type of business interruption policy that provides a stated amount to be paid for each day that the business is interrupted as the result of an insured peril. **(PR)**

per risk excess reinsurance. Reinsurance in which the retention and the cession apply per risk rather than per accident, per event, or on an aggregate basis. **(R)**

per stirpes. Literally "by branches." Distribution of property between or among two or more beneficiaries with the provision that if one dies before the insured, the beneficiary's heirs shall have the beneficiary's full share distributed among them. *See also* per capita. **(LI)**

percent subject. *See* amount subject. **(PR)**

percentage participation. A provision in a health insurance contract stating that the insurer will share losses in an agreed proportion with the insured. An example would be an 80/20 participation where the insurer pays 80% and the insured pays the 20% of losses covered under the contract. Often erroneously referred to as coinsurance. **(H)**

percentage test. A coverage test for a qualified plan in which a formula is used to determine whether a plan benefits at least 70% of the lower paid employees. **(PE)**

performance bond. A bond that guarantees the faithful performance of a contract. *See also* **contract bond. (S)**

peril. The cause of a possible loss. *See also* **hazard** and **risk. (G)**

perils of the sea. A term that appears in most ocean marine contracts. It refers to such perils as collision, sinking, stranding, and burning. **(OM)**

period. *See* term. **(G)**

period of restoration. The period during which business income coverage applies. It begins on the date that direct physical loss occurs and interrupts business operations, and ends on the date that the damaged property should be repaired, rebuilt, or replaced with reasonable speed. **(PR)**

permanent and total disability. Total disability from which the insured does not recover. When used as a definition in a policy (usually a life insurance policy rider), permanent disability is presumed after a stated period, commonly six months. **(H)**

permanent life insurance. A term loosely applied to life insurance policy forms other than group and term, usually cash value life insurance, such as endowments and whole or ordinary life policies. **(LI)**

permanent partial disability. A condition in which the injured party's earning capacity is impaired for life, but he is able to work at reduced efficiency. **(H, WC)**

permanent total disability. A condition in which the injured party is not able to work at any gainful employment for the remaining lifetime. **(H, WC)**

permit bond. A bond guaranteeing that a person who has been issued a permit will comply with the laws and ordinances regulating the privilege for which the permit was issued. A house movers' permit bond is an example. **(S)**

persistency. (1) The tendency or likelihood of insurance business not lapsing or being replaced by another insurer's product; an important underwriting factor. **(G)**. (2) The staying quality of insurance policies (i.e., the renewal quality). High persistency means that a high percentage of policies stay in force to the end of the period coverage, whereas low persistency means that a high percentage of policies lapse for non-payment of premiums. **(LI)**

personal articles floater (PAF). Originally an inland marine policy. It can be sold as a separate policy or attached to an existing property insurance policy, such as a homeowners form. The PAF is used for listing items to be covered, such as furs and jewelry, with an amount shown for each item. This is usually an open perils (all risk) form. *See also* floater. **(IM, PR)**

personal assets. Wealth and things of value accumulated and owned by an individual. These would include real estate, cash, investments, and other items of value. **(G)**

personal auto policy. A revised edition of the family auto policy, with simplified wording used in the policy provisions. It is the most common auto insurance policy sold today. **(AU)**

personal effects floater. A policy covering personal effects usually carried by tourists. It can be written on either an open-perils (all risk) or specified-peril form. It covers worldwide but excludes coverage at the insured's residence, because it provides travel coverage only. **(IM)**

personal injury. Injury other than bodily injury arising out of false arrest or detention, malicious prosecution, wrongful entry or eviction, libel or slander, or violation of a person's right to privacy committed other than in the course of advertising, publishing, broadcasting or telecasting. *See also* **advertising injury. (LA)**

personal injury protection (PIP). The formal name usually given to no-fault benefits in states that have enacted mandatory or optional no-fault automobile insurance coverages. PIP usually includes benefits for medical expenses, loss of work income, essential services, accidental death, and funeral expenses. **(AU)**

personal liability supplement. This form is used to provide personal liability insurance. It may be attached to a dwelling policy or written as a separate policy. **(LA)**

personal lines. This term is used to refer to insurance for individuals and families, such as private passenger automobile insurance and homeowner policies. *See also* **business insurance** and **commercial lines. (G)**

personal property. Any property of an insured other than real property. Homeowners policies protect the personal property of family members, and commercial forms are used to protect many types of business personal property of an insured. **(PR)**

personal property floater. A broad form policy covering all personal property worldwide, including at the insured's home. Similar coverage is available by endorsement as part of the special homeowners policy form. **(PR)**

personal property of others. Property, other than real property, that is not owned by an insured. Liability forms have traditionally excluded coverage for property of others in an insured's care, custody, or control. Modern homeowner forms and commercial property forms provide some coverage for property of others. **(G)**

personal surety. An individual, as opposed to an insurance company or other corporate institution, acting as a surety or guarantor. **(S)**

personal theft policy. *See* broad form personal theft policy. **(C)**

personalty. Movable personal property items, as opposed to realty, such as land, buildings, and mineral rights. **(LE)**

pharmacy and therapeutics (P&T) committee. A panel of physicians—usually from different specialties—who advise a health plan regarding the proper use of prescription drugs. **(H)**

physical damage. (1) A term indicating damage from such perils as collision, comprehensive, fire, and theft or any damage to the vehicle itself. **(AU)**. (2) A generic term indicating actual damage to property. **(PR)**

physical exam and autopsy. A standard health insurance policy provision that allows the insurer at its own expense to examine the insured when a claim is pending, and in the event of death, to perform an autopsy where not prohibited by law. **(H)**

physical hazard. Any hazard arising from the material, structural, or operational features of the risk itself apart from the persons owning or managing it. **(G)**

physical therapist. A trained medical person who provides rehabilitative services and therapy to help restore bodily functions, such as walking, speech, the use of limbs, and so forth. **(H)**

physician contingency reserve (PCR). A portion of the claim that is deducted and withheld by the health plan before payment is made to the physician. It serves as an incentive for proper quality and utilization of health care. A portion of this reserve may be returned to the physician or to pay claims where the plan needs additional funds. It is also sometimes called *withhold*. **(H)**

physicians and surgeons equipment form. A form used to cover equipment, materials, supplies, and office furniture of individuals in the medical and dental professions. **(IM)**

physicians and surgeons professional liability insurance. Malpractice insurance for physicians and surgeons. *See* **malpractice. (LA)**

physician's current procedural terminology (CPT). This terminology includes medical services and procedures performed by physicians and other providers of health care. The health care industry uses it as a standard for describing services and procedures. **(H)**

pilferage. Petty theft, particularly theft of articles in less than package lots. This term is associated with the insuring of cargo under an inland marine insurance form. **(G)**

piracy. Unlawful seizure of a ship and/or its cargo on the high seas. Commonly covered by ocean marine contracts. **(OM)**

place of service. This designates where the actual health services are being performed, whether it be a home, hospital, office, or clinic. **(H)**

plain language laws. Mandatory state law that requires policies to be written in everyday language so that the laws are easily understood. Technical terms with their technical meanings are used only where required by law or where a substitution would be misleading. **(G, LE)**

plaintiff. The party who brings a legal action against another, called the defendant. **(LE)**

plan, excess. A retirement plan designed around the benefits of Social Security. **(PE)**

plan, formal. A retirement plan set forth in writing under which contractual and legally enforceable rights are granted to the participating employees. **(PE)**

plan, funded. All plans under which funds are deposited to provide for retirement benefits. **(PE)**

plan, informal. A retirement system under which the employer has no legal obligation and the employee has no legal rights. These plans have no standard of benefits to be paid, and have no special method of funding. **(PE)**

plan, insured. A retirement plan under which some kind of benefits are guaranteed by an insurance carrier. **(PE)**

plan, offset. A retirement plan in which each employee's standard benefit is reduced by a portion of the Social Security benefits the employee will receive. **(PE)**

plan, point-of-service. This health care plan allows a choice of whether to receive services from either a participating or nonparticipating provider. **(H)**

plan, qualified. A retirement plan under which contributions by the employer are allowed as a deduction from taxable income and that provides that the deposits for employees' future benefits are not to be considered as taxable income to them in the year when they are made. **(PE)**

plan sponsor. An employer or other entity that establishes or maintains a retirement plan for its employees or members. **(PE)**

plan, unfunded. Any pension plan that follows a pay-as-you-go method. *See* **funding, disbursement. (PE)**

plan, uninsured. Any pension plan that is not funded through insurance products. **(PE)**

plan, unqualified. Any pension plan that does not meet the qualifications for special tax advantages as set forth in the IRS Tax Code. **(PE)**

plan year. A calendar, policy, or fiscal year on which the records of the plan are kept. **(PE)**

plate glass insurance policy. *See* **comprehensive glass insurance policy** and **glass coverage form. (PR)**

pluvious insurance. Another name for **rain insurance. (PR)**

point-of-service plan. This plan allows a choice of whether to receive services from a participating or nonparticipating provider. **(H)**

Poisson's Law. *See* **Theory of Probability. (G)**

policy. The written statement of a contract effecting insurance, or certificates thereof, by whatever name called, and including all clauses, riders, endorsements, and papers attached thereto and made a part thereof. **(G)**

policy anniversary. The anniversary of the date of issue of a policy, as shown in the policy declarations. **(G)**

policy conditions. *See* **conditions. (G)**

policy date. *See* **effective date. (G)**

policy dividend. The return of a portion of the premium paid on a participating policy. It represents the difference between the gross premium charged and the actual cost assessed against the policy by actuarial formula. **(G)**

policy fee. (1) A one-time charge added to the first premium to help defray acquisition costs; now illegal in many states. (2) A flat, per policy charge that does not change with the size of the policy and thus serves as a form of quantity discount. Various insurers call it by other names, such as quantity discount factor and quantity adjustment fee. **(LI)**

policy loan. A loan made by an insurer to a policyowner of a part or all of the cash value of the policy assigned as security for the loan. This is one of the usual nonforfeiture values. **(LI)**

policyowner. (1) The person who has ownership rights in an insurance policy and who may or may not be either the policyholder or the insured. (2) Often used loosely to refer to the policyholder and/or the insured. *See also* **insured. (G)**

policy period (or term). The period during which the policy contract affords protection (e.g., six months or one or three years). **(G)**

policy proceeds. The amount actually paid on a life insurance policy at death or when the insured receives payment at surrender or maturity. It includes any dividends left on deposit and the value of any additional insurance purchased with dividends; and it excludes any loans not repaid, plus unpaid interest on those loans. **(LI)**

policy reserve. (1) *See* **unearned premium reserve. (H)**. (2) A reserve that exists because of the concept that each policy has a pro rata share of the total reserve established for all policies. **(LI)**

policy summary. A document that summarizes the coverages, benefits, limitations, exclusions, cost, and terms of a proposed life insurance policy. Cost and benefit information usually includes annual premiums, guaranteed amounts payable at death, guaranteed cash surrender values at the end of various years, life insurance cost indexes, and (if applicable) dividend information. In many jurisdictions, policy summaries are required to be delivered to applicants in connection with any solicitation or replacement transaction. **(LI)**

policy term. *See* policy period. **(G)**

policy year. The period between policy anniversary dates. **(G)**

policy year experience. The measure of premiums and losses for each 12-month period a policy is in force. Losses occurring during this 12-month period are assigned to the period regardless of when they are actually paid. **(G)**

policyholder. (1) The person in actual possession of an insurance policy. (2) Often used loosely to refer to the policyowner and/or insured. *See also* **insured. (G)**

policyholder's surplus. The amount over and above liabilities available for an insurer to meet future obligations to its policyholders. In the case of a mutual insurer, it is the whole equity section of the balance sheet. In the case of a stock insurer, the equity section is divided into two parts, stockholder's surplus and policyholder's surplus. **(G)**

policywriting agent. An agent who has the authority to prepare and effect an insurer's policy. **(G)**

pollution liability coverage form. Commercial form providing pollution insurance on a claims made basis and also including coverage for clean-up costs. *See also* **limited pollution liability coverage form. (LA)**

pollution liability extension endorsement. An endorsement to general liability insurance that removes part of the pollution exclusion, creating liability coverage for pollution injury or damage. **(LA)**

pool (association or syndicate). An organization of insurers or reinsurers through which particular types of risks are written, with the premiums, losses, and expenses shared in agreed amounts among the insurers belonging to the pool. A pool is often the entity to write large values, such as those on commercial aircraft. **(G)**

pool (risk pool). A separate account that includes entries for income and expenses. It is used when a number of groups are put together for the purposes of combining their premium and paying their losses. **(H)**

pooling. A method of reinsurance similar to quota share, where every member assumes a share of each risk written by every other member. Provisions of the pooling agreement may include a maximum limit to be borne by any member. **(R)**

portfolio. (1) The securities in which the assets of a company or a retirement plan are invested. **(PE)**. (2) All of the insurer's in-force policies and outstanding losses, respecting described segments of its business. Also, the total securities owned by an insurer. **(G)**

portfolio entry. Part of the mechanics of instituting a reinsurance treaty. It may be arranged on various bases, such as new and renewal business or business in force, any and all of which are referred to as the portfolio entry. **(R)**

portfolio reinsurance. (1) A transfer of the portfolio of an insured via a cession of reinsurance. (2) A form of reinsurance under which the reinsurer assumes a percentage of the entire book of the ceding company's business either in a particular class or in all classes. **(R)**

portfolio return. Reassumption by a ceding company of a portfolio that has formerly been reinsured. **(R)**

portfolio runoff. Continuing the reinsurance of a portfolio until all ceded premiums are earned. **(R)**

position schedule bond. *See* name position bond and name schedule bond. **(C)**

postdated check plan. A premium-paying arrangement under which the policyowner gives the insurer a series of checks, each dated ahead of the date on which premiums fall due for a year or more. The insurer then presents each check on its date. This plan has become less common and mostly been replaced by preauthorized electronic bank withdrawal. **(LI)**

postmortem dividend. A policy dividend allotted after the death of an insured. It is sometimes called a mortuary dividend. **(LI)**

pour over trust. A revocable living trust that serves as a receptacle for distributions from employee benefit plans. **(EP, PE)**

power interruption insurance. This coverage indemnifies the insured in the event of loss due to the interruption of power supplied by a public utility and caused by any of the perils insured against. **(PR)**

power of agency. *See* agent's authority. **(G)**

power of appointment. The right or authority given by a donor to a donee that allows the donee to select the ultimate beneficiary of property or a gift. **(EP)**

power of attorney. (1) The authority given to one person or corporation to act for and obligate another to the extent set forth in the agreement creating the power. (2) The authority given to the chief administrator of a reciprocal insurance exchange who is called an attorney in fact by each subscriber. *See also* attorney in fact and reciprocal insurance exchange. **(G)**

power plant insurance. This policy insures electricity generating plants against loss caused by certain specified perils. **(PR)**

practical nurse. A licensed individual who provides custodial type care, such as help in walking, bathing, feeding, and so forth. Practical nurses do not administer medication or perform other medically related services. **(H)**

preadmission authorization. A cost containment feature of many group medical policies whereby the insured must contact the insurer before a hospitalization and receive authorization for the admission. **(H)**

preadmission certification. Before being admitted as an inpatient in a hospital, certain criteria are used to determine whether the inpatient care is necessary. **(H)**

preauthorization check plan. A premium-paying arrangement by which the policyowner authorizes the insurer to draft money from his bank account for the payments. This is usually done on a monthly basis. **(LI)**

precedent. In common law, previous cases are used to prove the present case. These cases are called precedence. **(LE)**

precertification authorization. A cost containment technique that requires physicians to submit a treatment plan and an estimated bill before providing treatment. This allows the insurer to evaluate the appropriateness of the procedures, and lets the insured and physician know in advance which procedures are covered and at what rate benefits will be paid. **(G)**

preemptive right. A current stockholder's right to maintain proportionate ownership in a corporation through the exercising of this right to purchase new issues of stock before the general public. **(G)**

preexisting condition. A physical condition that existed before the effective date of a policy. In many health policies, these are not covered until after a stated period of time has elapsed. **(H)**

preferred provider organization (PPO). An organization of hospitals and physicians who provide, for a set fee, services to insurance company clients. These providers are listed as preferred, and the insured may select from any number of hospitals and physicians without being limited, as with a health maintenance organization. Coverage is 100%, with a minimal copayment for each office visit or hospital stay. *See also* **health maintenance organization. (H, LI)**

preferred risk. Any risk considered to be better than the standard risk on which the premium rate was calculated. **(G)**

prelicensing education requirement. Statutory requirement of many states that an applicant for an insurance license must complete a specified education program before being eligible for the license. **(G)**

preliminary term. The period of a short-term insurance issued to cover a risk to a date that the policyowner wishes to establish as the anniversary date for future premiums. **(G)**

preliminary term. A reserve system in life insurance under which the entire first year's premium is used for acquisition costs. The effect is to reduce the first year's premium, making it more attractive to the prospective buyer. **(LI)**

premises. The particular location of property or a portion thereof as designated in a policy. **(G)**

premises and operations liability insurance. Liability coverage for exposures arising out of an insured's premises and business operations. One of the two major sublines of general liability. *See also* **products and completed operations insurance. (LA)**

premises burglary. A burglary that occurs on an insured premises. Various commercial insurance forms distinguish between coverage provided on and off an insured premises. Premises burglary coverage may be written separately or as part of a broader package of crime coverages. **(C)**

premises theft—outside robbery coverage form. A commercial crime coverage form that protects against loss of property, other than money and securities, by theft on the premises or robbery outside the premises. Separate crime coverage forms have been largely replaced by newer crime policies that provide multiple coverage options in a single policy. **(C)**

premium. The price of insurance protection for a specified risk for a specified period. **(G)**

premium adjustment form. A form wherein a deposit premium is charged at the beginning of the policy period, periodic reports of exposures are made by the insured during the policy term or at the end of it, and premiums are adjusted as reports are received or at the end of the policy period. **(PR)**

premium advance. *See* deposit premium. **(G)**

premium and dispersion credit plan. A method of allowing certain credits to large commercial property risks with two or more locations. These credits are based on the fact that there are several dispersed locations that represent a reduced hazard. Efficiency of management in loss prevention, plus expense savings in handling large amounts of insurance under one policy are also considered. **(PR)**

premium base. *See* subject premium. **(R)**

premium deposit. *See* deposit premium. **(G)**

premium discount. (1) A discount allowed on premiums paid in advance of one year and based on projected interest to be earned. (2) A discount allowed on certain workers' compensation and general liability policies to allow for the fact that larger premium policies do not require the same percentage of the premium for basic insurer expenses, such as policywriting. The discount percentage increases with the size of the premium. This is not available in all states. **(G)**

premium, earned. *See* earned premium. **(G)**

premium load. A universal life term, also called a front-end load, that refers to the percentage of premium deducted from each premium payment to help cover expenses. Some policies provide for a no-load feature. **(LI)**

premium loan. A loan made by the insurance company to the insured, with the cash value of the policy as security, to pay a premium due. **(G)**

premium notice. A form notice from an insurer or agency to a policyowner that a premium will be due on a given date. **(G)**

premium, pure. *See* pure premium. **(G)**

premium rate. The price per unit of insurance. An example would be a property insurance rate of 10 cents per $100 of the value of the property to be insured. **(G)**

premium receipt. The receipt given a policyowner for the payment of a premium. **(G)**

premium receipt book. The policyowner's record of premium paid, usually used for a weekly payment or monthly debit ordinary policy. **(LI)**

premium refund. A special provision that allows a beneficiary to collect the face amount of a policy plus all the premiums that have been paid. **(LI)**

premium return. *See* return premium. **(G)**

premium, unearned. *See* unearned premium. **(G)**

premiums written. *See* written premiums. **(G)**

prepaid legal service plan. A type of employee benefit whereby benefits are provided by the employer for certain legal services. **(PE)**

prepayment of premiums. Payment by an insured of future premiums through paying the present (discount) value of future premiums or having interest paid on the insured's deposit. **(G)**

prescription medication. A drug that can be dispensed only by prescription and that has been approved by the Food and Drug Administration. **(H)**

present interest. Current use and enjoyment of personal property. **(EP)**

present value. (1) The amount of money that future amounts receivable are currently worth. For example, a life insurance policy may provide for payments to be made monthly for 10 years. The present value of that money would be less than the total amount of the monthly payments for 10 years because of the amount of interest that a present lump sum could earn during the term that the payments otherwise would have been made. **(G)**. (2) The present amount equivalent to an amount or series of amounts payable or receivable in the future adjusted for the time value of money (through discounts for interest). **(LE, PE)**

pressure vessel. Any type of vessel or container designed to hold liquids or gases under pressure. **(PR)**

presumed negligence. *See* res ipsa loquitur. **(LE)**

presumption of agency. A legally binding agency relationship that exists when, in fact, no formal agency agreement is in effect. If an insurer acts to give the appearance of agency, perhaps by furnishing letterhead and applications before a person has been licensed and appointed, an agency relationship exists under the law, and the insurer may be legally bound by the acts of a person acting as agent. **(G)**

presumptive disability. A disability involving loss of sight, hearing, speech, or any two limbs, which is presumed to be a permanent and total disability. In such cases, the insurer does not require the insured to submit to periodic medical examinations to prove continuing disability. **(H)**

pretext interview. An interview in which the party gathering information refuses to reveal his identity, pretends to be someone else, misrepresents the true purpose of the interview, or pretends to represent someone who is not in fact represented. In most cases, federal and state laws prohibit pretext interviews in connection with insurance-related consumer reporting. They are permitted only in connection with investigations into suspected material misrepresentation, fraud, or criminal activity. **(G)**

prevailing charge. Used to determine Medicare benefit amounts, this usually means the typical charge in the area where the patient lives. *See also* **allowable charge** and **customary charge. (H)**

preventive care. This type of care is best exemplified by routine physical examinations and immunizations. The emphasis is on preventing illnesses before they occur. **(H)**

prima facie. Literally means "at first view." It refers to evidence that is, according to law, sufficient to establish or prove a point, unless successfully rebutted by other evidence. **(LE)**

primary beneficiary. The beneficiary named as first to receive proceeds or benefits from a policy when they become due. **(LI)**

primary care. Basic health care provided by doctors who are in the practice of family care, pediatrics, and internal medicine. **(H)**

primary care network (PCN). This is a group of primary care physicians who provide care to those members of a particular health plan. **(H)**

primary care physician. Some health insurance plans require members to select and seek treatment from a primary physician who either renders treatment or refers the member to an appropriate specialist within the approved health care network. **(H)**

primary coverage. (1) This is the coverage that pays expenses first, without consideration of whether there is any other coverage. *See also* **coordination of benefits (H)**. (2) Insurance coverage that covers from the first dollar, perhaps after a deductible, as distinguished from excess coverage, which pays only after some primary coverage has been exhausted. *See also* **excess insurance. (G)**

primary insurance amount (PIA). A Social Security calculation that serves as the principal element determining the amount of various Social Security benefits. **(EP)**

primary insurer. The company that originates business, (i.e., the ceding company). **(R)**

principal. The individual or corporation whose performance is guaranteed in suretyship. **(S)**

principal sum. The amount payable in one sum in the event of accidental death or certain accidental dismemberments. When a contract provides benefits for both accidental death and accidental dismemberment, each dismemberment benefit is an amount equal to the principal sum or some fraction thereof. Examples would be half the principal sum for loss of one arm or half the principal sum for the loss of one leg. **(H, LI)**

prior approval rating forms. A term used to indicate that an insurer must have rate changes formally approved by the state insurance department before it can use them. **(G)**

prior authorization. A cost containment measure that provides full payment of health benefits only when the hospitalization or medical treatment has been approved in advance. **(H)**

priority. A term meaning retention in some foreign reinsurance markets. **(R)**

private carrier. A transportation company that contracts to carry goods for specific customers, as opposed to a common carrier, which carries goods for anyone who wishes to use its service. **(IM)**

private passenger automobile. Four-wheeled motor vehicles of the private passenger, station wagon or van type, designed for use on public highways and subject to motor vehicle registration. **(AU)**

pro rata. (1) Distribution of the amount of insurance under one policy among several objects or places covered in proportion to their value or the amounts shown. (2) Distribution of liability among several insurers with policies on a risk, usually in the proportion that the amount of coverage in each policy bears to the total amount of coverage in all policies. **(G)**

pro rata cancellation. The termination of an insurance contract or bond with the premium charge being adjusted in proportion to the exact time the protection has been in force. *See also* **short rate cancellation. (G)**

pro rata distribution. A provision, also known as the pro rata distribution clause, used in the writing of certain blanket policies. Its purpose is to divide the amount of insurance carried under a single item in the policy form among the several subjects of insurance, in the proportion that the value of each subject of insurance bears to the total value of all property covered under that single item in the policy form. **(G)**

pro rata liability clause. Provides that losses will be paid in the proportion that the amount of the policy bears to the entire amount of insurance on all policies covering the loss. This provides for insurance companies to appropriately share in the loss when more than one policy exists yet prevents the insured from collecting in total from several insurance companies and making a profit. **(G)**

pro rata liability rule. *See* limit of liability rule. **(PR)**

pro rata rate. A rate charged for a period of coverage shorter than the normal period. For example, if an insured had coverage for only one quarter of a year, the premium would be only one quarter of the annual premium. **(G)**

pro rata reinsurance. A generic term describing all forms of reinsurance in which the reinsurer shares a pro rata portion of the losses and premiums of the ceding company. Also called share and participating reinsurance. Pro rata reinsurance includes quota share reinsurance and surplus reinsurance. *See also* **excess of loss reinsurance. (R)**

probability. The likelihood or relative frequency of an event expressed in a number between zero and one. The throw of a die is an example. The probability of throwing five is found by dividing the number of faces that have a five (1) by the total number of faces (6). That is a probability of one-sixth or one divided by six, which is .17. *See also* **degree of risk, law of large numbers,** and **odds. (G)**

probable maximum loss (PML). The maximum amount of loss that one would expect under ordinary circumstances, such as fire departments responding or sprinklers working. *See also* **amount subject. (PR)**

probate. The process of paying debts, taxes, expenses, and disposing of property in accordance with a testator's will and state laws. **(EP, LE)**

probate bond. A bond required by a probate court to protect the administration of an estate or the assets of one person being cared for by another, such as assets in the hands of an executor or guardian. Probate bonds fall within the classification of fiduciary bonds. **(S)**

probationary period. A period of time between the effective date of a health insurance policy and the date coverage begins for all or certain physical conditions. **(H)**

proceeds. The amount payable by a policy, usually in reference to the face amount of a life insurance policy, payable at the death of the insured. **(LI)**

producer. A term applied to an agent, solicitor, or other person who sells insurance. **(G)**

product failure exclusion. *See* business risk exclusion. **(LA)**

product recall insurance. Insurance that indemnifies the insured for the cost of recalling products known or suspected to be defective. **(LA)**

products and completed operations insurance. A major general liability subline that provides coverage for an insured against claims arising out of products sold, manufactured, handled, or distributed, or operations that are complete. Claims are covered only after a product has been sold and possession relinquished, or operations have been completed or abandoned by the named insured. Manufacturers and contractors have a need for this coverage. *See also* **premises and operations liability. (LA)**

professional corporation. An artificial person or entity, governed by charter, engaged in a business that provides a professional service to the public, such as medicine or law. **(G)**

Professional Insurance Agents Association. A trade association of mutual insurance agents. **(G)**

professional liability insurance. (1) *See* **malpractice insurance** for the definition applicable to the healing arts. (2) *See* **errors and omissions insurance** for the definition applicable to those in professions such as law and accounting. **(LA)**

professional partnership. An association of two or more individuals who operate and manage a business that provides a professional service to the public, such as medicine or law. **(G)**

profit commission. *See* **contingent commission. (G)**

profit-sharing plan. A plan under which some of the profits of a company are set aside for distribution to qualified employees. The plan may provide for immediate distribution, or distribution upon death, disability, termination, or attainment of a specific retirement age. Such plans are subject to special tax exemption if they meet the requirements of the Internal Revenue Code. **(PE)**

profits and commissions insurance. A kind of insurance with which a salesperson or a sales agent whose income is tied to profits or commissions on certain property can insure against loss of income due to the destruction of the property. **(PR)**

prohibited list. A list of types of business or types of risks that an insurance company will not insure. Also called the undesirable list, the do not solicit list, and other designations. **(G)**

prohibited risk. Any class of business that an insurance company will not insure under any condition. **(G)**

promulgate. (1) To develop, publish, and put into effect insurance rates or forms. (2) To make public, by publishing or announcing, the fact that a statute or rule of court is a legal order or direction enforceable by law, and that violation of such is punishable as provided by law. **(G, LE)**

proof of loss. A formal statement made by a policyowner to an insurer regarding a loss. It is intended to give information to the insurer to enable it to determine the extent of its liability. **(G)**

property damage liability insurance. Protection against liability for damage to the property of another, including loss of the use of the property, as distinguished from liability for bodily injury to another. In most cases, it is written along with bodily injury liability protection. **(LA)**

property insurance. Insurance that indemnifies a person with an interest in physical property for its loss or the loss of its income producing abilities. **(PR)**

Property Insurance Loss Register (PILR). A computerized record of all fire losses greater than $500 established by the American Insurance Association (AIA). The PILR enables companies to determine undisclosed duplicate insurance coverage and patterns of losses on submitted risks. **(PR)**

property other than money and securities. Under commercial crime insurance coverages, any tangible property other than money and securities that has intrinsic value, such as merchandise, supplies, raw materials, and office equipment. **(C)**

proposal bond. *See* bid bond. **(S)**

proration of benefits. The adjustment of health insurance policy benefits by reason of the existence of other insurance covering the same contingency. **(H)**

prospect. The term commonly used to refer to a potential buyer of insurance. **(G)**

prospecting. The act of looking for prospects (i.e., potential insurance buyers). **(G)**

prospective loss costs. *See* loss costs. **(LA, PR)**

prospective payment system. A system of Medicare reimbursement for Part A benefits that bases most hospital payments on the patient's diagnosis at the time of hospital admission. **(H)**

prospective rating. A method used to calculate the rate and premium for a specified future period, based in whole or in part on the loss experience of a prior specified period. *See* **experience rating. (G)**

prospective rating plan. A plan that uses a formula for determining premiums for a specified period, based in whole or in part on the loss experience of the previous period. **(G)**

prospective reserve. A life or health insurance reserve that, it is estimated, will be sufficient to pay future claims when probable future premiums, interest, and survivorship benefits are added to it. **(H, LI)**

prospective reimbursement. A system in which hospitals or other health care providers are paid annually according to rates of payment that have been established ahead of time. **(H)**

protected risk. A property risk that is within the geographical area protected by a fire department. **(PR)**

protection. (1) A term used interchangeably with *coverage* to denote insurance provided under the terms of a policy. (2) The fire-fighting facilities in the area where a risk is located. **(G)**

protection and indemnity (P&I) insurance. Coverage that provides protection for a ship owner against loss of life, illness, or injury to the passengers or crew, plus property damage to the cargo, piers, and docks caused by the insured's negligence. **(OM)**

protection class. The grading of fire protection, determined by the grading schedule of cities and towns, for a given area. This designation is used for all fire rating except for dwellings, in which case the dwelling class is used. **(PR)**

protective liability insurance. *See* **owners and contractors protective liability. (LA)**

prototype plan defined. A standard retirement plan made available by the sponsoring organization to an employer to use without charge. **(PE)**

provider. Any individual or group of individuals that provide a health care service, such as physicians and hospitals. **(H)**

provisional premium. *See* deposit premium. **(G)**

provisional rate. Tentative rates, premiums, or commissions that are subject to subsequent adjustment. *See* **commission** and **premium**. **(G)**

provisions. Statements contained in an insurance policy that explain the benefits, conditions, and other features of the insurance contract. **(G)**

proximate cause. The effective cause of loss or damage. It is an unbroken chain of cause and effect between the occurrence of an insured peril or a negligent act and resulting injury or damage. **(LE)**

public adjuster. An insurance adjuster who represents an insured on a fee basis in claims settlement. *See also* **independent adjuster**. **(G)**

public assistance. The federal and state system for providing welfare payments to the aged, blind, and disabled and to families with dependent children. *See also* **social insurance**. **(G)**

public employees dishonesty coverage. Commercial crime coverage written for public entities to cover losses of money, securities, or other property caused by employee dishonesty. Coverage may be written on a per loss or per employee basis. **(C)**

Public Law 15. A Congressional Act of 1945 exempting insurance from federal antitrust laws to the extent that it is regulated properly by states. This law was passed after the reversal of the *Paul v. Virginia* case by the SEUA decision. **(G)**

public liability insurance. A general term applied to forms of third-party liability insurance with respect to both bodily injury and property damage liability. It protects the insured against suits brought by members of the public. **(LA)**

public official bond. A surety bond under which the company (surety) guarantees that the principal (public official) will faithfully perform his official duties and will account for all funds entrusted to his care. **(S)**

punitive damages. Damages awarded over and above compensatory damages to punish a negligent party because of wanton, reckless, or malicious acts or omissions. Also known as **exemplary damages. (LE)**

pure endowment. An endowment is payable if the designated person is alive at the end of the endowment period but not payable if the person is not alive at that time. This type of policy is not often used today. **(LI)**

pure loss cost ratio. (1) The ratio of reinsurance losses incurred to the ceding company's subject premium. (2) The ratio of the re-insurance losses incurred and allocated, less expenses to the ceding company's gross earned premium. **(R)**

pure mortality cost. *See* mortality cost. **(LI)**

pure premium. A term used in insurance rate making. It refers to the portion of the total premium that is needed to pay expected losses. It does not take into account money needed for other company expenses. **(G)**

pure risk. Uncertainty as to whether a loss will occur. Under a pure risk situation, there is no possibility for gain. *See also* **speculative risk. (G)**

pyramiding. (1) A term sometimes applied to an alleged practice of some consumer credit organization under which lenders add new credit insurance coverage for consolidation loans without canceling the old, thus producing a situation of overinsurance for the amount of the loan outstanding. (2) The term also applies to liability insurance in which the limits of liability in several policies may apply and, in effect, pyramid into higher amounts of insurance being available than was originally intended. **(G)**

Q

Q schedule. A schedule of the business expenses of a life insurer required by the New York State Code to be filed to determine compliance with the state's limitation on total expenses. This limitation has the effect of setting a ceiling on commissions. **(LI)**

quadruple indemnity. A multiple indemnity form similar to double indemnity and triple indemnity. *See also* **multiple indemnity. (LI)**

qualified Medicare beneficiary (QMB). A person whose income is below the federal poverty guidelines. For such persons, the state is required to pay the Medicare Part B premiums plus any deductibles or copayments. **(H)**

qualified plan. A retirement plan that has been filed with and approved by the IRS, that does not discriminate as to participation, and for which the contributor (usually the employer) receives a tax deduction for plan contributions and investment income is tax deferred until paid out. **(PE)**

qualifying event. An occurrence (e.g., death, termination of employment, or divorce) that triggers an insured's protection under COBRA, which requires continuation of benefits under a group insurance plan for former employees and their families who would otherwise lose health care coverage. **(H)**

qualifying terminal interest property (QTIP). A trust that may contain marital deduction property, as determined by the executor at some future time. All trust income goes to the surviving spouse. **(EP)**

quality assurance. Activities involving a review of quality of services and the taking of any corrective actions to remove any deficiencies. **(H)**

quantity discount. A premium discount given for the purchase of a policy with a larger face amount. *See also* **policy fee. (LI)**

quarantine benefit. A benefit paid for loss of time resulting from the quarantining of an insured by health authorities. **(H)**

quarantine indemnity. *See* quarantine benefit. **(H)**

quasi contract. A legal doctrine for situations in which there is no specifically drawn contract. It prevents unjust enrichment or injustice by treating the situation as if a contract actually had been in effect. **(LE)**

quasi-insurance institutions. A term sometimes applied to government institutions created to carry out social insurance arrangements that have some, but not all, the characteristics of insurers. An example is the United States Department of Health and Human Services. **(G)**

quick assets. Assets that are quickly convertible into cash. **(G)**

quid pro quo. Latin for "this for that," or "one thing for another." In insurance it could refer to the consideration in an insurance contract that calls for the exchange of values by both parties to the contract in order for it to be a valid contract. *See also* **consideration. (G)**

quota share insurance. Property insurance that shares according to some percentage, or quota, with other policies covering the same risk. **(PR)**

quota share reinsurance. A form of pro rata reinsurance indemnifying the ceding company with a fixed percentage of any loss on each risk covered in the contract and paid for with the same percentage of the premium, with an allowance made for the writing company's expenses. **(R)**

R

ABBREVIATIONS AND ACRONYMS

RHU. Registered Health Underwriter. **(H)**

RIMS. *See* Risk and Insurance Management Society, Inc. **(G)**

PRESENTATION OF TERMS

rabbi trust. An irrevocable trust often used with an informally funded nonqualified deferred compensation whereby plan assets are subject to the claims of creditors and thus current taxation to the employee is avoided. **(PE)**

radioactive contamination insurance. Coverage that may be added to a property policy to cover certain risks, where there is neither a nuclear reactor nor nuclear fuel on the premises but where there might be occasional exposure to contamination damage from other material on the insured's premises. Liability losses caused by nuclear reaction and radioactive contamination are excluded from most insurance contracts and are usually covered under policies issued by pools created for this purpose. See also **mutual atomic energy reinsurance pool. (PR)**

radius of operation. Usually used to determine rates for automobiles owned by a business. Beyond a certain number of miles in radius (e.g., 50), the rate is increased. **(AU)**

railroad protective liability. A protective liability coverage written in favor of a railroad on behalf of those who are conducting operations on or adjacent to railroad property. **(LA)**

railroad retirement. A system that provides retirement and other benefits, including eligibility for Medicare, for railroad workers. **(H)**

railroad sidetrack agreement. *See* sidetrack agreement. **(LA)**

railroad subrogation waiver clause. A provision in a property insurance contract that the contract shall be valid even though the insured has an agreement with the railroad waiving subrogation against the railroad. Usually used in connection with a railroad sidetrack agreement. **(LA)**

railroad travel policy. A form of accident insurance policy sold in railroad stations by ticket agents or by vending machines. *See also* **travel accident insurance. (H)**

rain insurance. A type of coverage that protects an insured against losses caused by cancellation of an outdoor event because of rain. The policy usually covers loss of income. The rain, hail, snow, or sleet usually must exceed a certain amount and must occur during a stated period, either before or during the event. **(PR)**

rate. (1) The cost of a given unit of insurance. For example, in ordinary life insurance, it is the price of $1,000 of the face amount. In disability income insurance, it is usually the price per $10 or per $100 of monthly benefits. In property insurance, it is the rate per $100 of value to be insured. The premium, then, is the rate multiplied by the number of units of insurance purchased. **(G)**. (2) The percentage or factor applied to the ceding company's subject premium to produce the reinsurance premium or the percentage applied to the reinsurer's premium to produce the commission. *See also* **premium. (R)**

rate card. A pocket-sized card issued by an insurer giving rates for various coverages. It is carried by an agent or sales representative for quotation purposes. **(G)**

rate discrimination. The use of different rates for insureds or risks of the same class and general characteristics. Rate discrimination is prohibited by all state insurance laws. **(G)**

rate manual. A manual containing rates for various coverages, information and instructions for field underwriting, insurer's rules for the guidance of agents, and, in the case of life insurance rate manuals, cash amount forfeiture values and dividend scales (if any). **(G)**

rate of natural increase (or decrease). The birth rate minus the death rate. If there were no migration, this would equal the rate of population increase (or decrease). **(G)**

rated. Coverages issued at a higher rate than standard because of impairment of the insured. Usually used as an adjective in such expressions as "rated risk," "rated policy," and "rated up." **(LI)**

rated up. *See* rated. **(LI)**

rating bureau. A private organization that classifies and promulgates manual rates and, in some cases, compiles data and measures the hazards of individual risks in terms of rates in geographic areas, the latter being true especially in connection with property insurance. **(G)**

rating class. The rate class into which a risk has been placed. *See also* class. **(G)**

rating, experience. *See* experience rating. **(G)**

rating, merit. *See* merit rating. **(G)**

rating process. The steps used to determine a premium rate for a particular group on the basis of the amount of risk that group presents. Items that generally go into the rating process include age, sex, type of industry, benefits, and administrative costs. **(H)**

rating, retrospective. *See* retrospective rating. **(LA, WC)**

rating, schedule. *See* schedule rating plan. **(LA, PR)**

ratio test. A coverage test for a qualified plan in which a percentage of lower paid employees benefiting from the plan must equal 70% of the higher paid employees from the plan. **(PE)**

readjustment income. (1) The income needed after the death or disability of a wage earner to allow the family time to adjust to a new, lower standard of spending. (2) The insurance coverage that provides readjustment income. **(LI)**

realty. Real property, such as land, buildings, and mineral rights, as opposed to personalty (i.e., movable personal property items). **(LE)**

reasonable and customary charges. The charge for medical services that refers to the amount approved by the Medicare carrier for payment. Customary charges are those that are most often made by a provider for services rendered in that particular area. **(H)**

reassured. The company that purchases reinsurance. *See* **ceding company. (R)**

rebate. A portion of the agent's commission returned to an insured or anything else of value given an insured as an inducement to buy. The payment of policy dividends, retroactive rate adjustments, and reduced premiums that reflect the savings of direct payment to an agent or home office are not usually considered to be rebates. In most cases, rebates are illegal, both for the agent or insurer to give and for an insured to receive. **(G)**

recapture. The action of a ceding company taking back from a reinsurer insurance previously ceded. **(R)**

recapture of products. *See* products recall. **(LA)**

recidivism. This term refers to how often a patient returns to an inpatient hospital status for the same reason. **(H)**

recipient. Anyone designated by Medicaid as being eligible to receive Medicaid benefits. **(H)**

recipient location. A location that accepts the insured's products or services. One of the four types of dependent properties for which business income coverage may be written. **(PR)**

reciprocal insurance exchange. An unincorporated group of individuals, called subscribers, who mutually insure one another, each separately assuming his share of each risk. Its chief administrator is an attorney in fact. **(G)**

reciprocity. A system of placing reinsurance on a reciprocal basis so that a ceding company will give a share of its reinsurance to a reinsurer who is able to offer reinsurance in return. **(R)**

recording agent. The name by which a policywriting agent is known in the property insurance business. **(PR)**

recruiting. The hiring of insurance agents, or the process of looking for, interviewing, and hiring agents. It is also used to mean the process of locating and hiring any type of employee. **(G)**

recurrent disability. Disability resulting from the same or a related cause as a prior disability. **(H, LI)**

recurring clause. A health insurance policy provision defining the duration of time during which the recurrence of a condition will be considered a continuation of a prior period of disability or confinement. **(H)**

red-lining. Discriminating unfairly against a risk solely because of its location. An example would be refusing to insure a risk because the building is located in a depressed area or location. Sometimes these areas are referred to as blackout areas. **(PR)**

reduced paid-up insurance. A form of insurance available as a nonforfeiture option. It provides that the cash value of the policy be used as a single premium to purchase paid-up insurance in whatever amount the cash value will provide, which will be less than the original face amount in most cases. *See also* **nonforfeiture values. (LI)**

reduction. A decrease in the benefits in an insurance policy because of a specified condition. For example, benefits may be reduced because a disability is caused by a specific condition. **(G)**

reduction of risk. Taking steps to reduce the probability or severity of a possible loss. For example, installing alarms and sprinkler systems to reduce the risk of fire loss to a building. One of the four major risk management techniques. *See* **risk management. (G)**

referral. Occurs when a physician or other health plan provider receives permission to consult another physician or hospital. **(H)**

referral provider. The person or provider to whom a participating provider has referred a member of the plan. **(H)**

refund annuity. A form of annuity that provides for a cash or install-ment refund to the beneficiary if the annuitant dies before having drawn benefits equal to the total consideration that he paid on the policy. **(AN)**

refund life annuity. An annuity paying installments as long as the insured lives and installments after death to the beneficiary until the amount paid equals the principle sum of insurance. **(AN)**

regional office. A suboffice of a home office that is equipped to handle all lines of business in a particular territory or region. Some companies use the term *branch office*. **(G)**

register. A record of all policies charged to a debit account. **(LI)**

registered mail insurance. Coverage for loss of money and securities sent through the post office by registered mail. **(IM)**

registered nurse (RN). A licensed professional with a four-year nurs-ing degree. Able to provide all levels of nursing care, including the administration of medication. **(H)**

registered representative. A person who has met the qualifications set by law or regulation to sell securities to the public. **(G)**

registered tonnage. For warships, the weight or displacement. For commercial vessels, the cubic capacity of enclosed space. One ton oc-cupies 100 cubic feet. **(OM)**

regular stock option (RSO) plan. An executive stock option plan whereby key executives have the right to purchase company stock at a predetermined price. When the option is exercised, it is taxable as compensation to the executive. **(PE)**

Regulatory Information Retrieval Service (RIRS). A database product developed by the National Association of Insurance Commissioners in conjunction with state insurance departments that lists regulatory actions (e.g., suspensions, revocations, fines, penalties, cease and desist orders, and consent orders) against insurance firms and individuals. **(G)**

rehabilitation benefits. Physical and/or vocational rehabilitation benefits provided to an injured person following a work-related injury, and intended to restore the person to a point where gainful employment is possible. **(WC)**

rehabilitation clause. Any clause in a health insurance policy, particularly a disability income policy, that is intended to assist the disabled policyholder in vocational rehabilitation. **(H)**

rehabilitation of insurer. Action undertaken by a state Insurance Department to restore an impaired or insolvent insurer to sound financial standing. *See also* **liquidation of insurer. (G)**

rehearing. A second hearing by a court. Its purpose is to call the court's attention to an error or omission that may have occurred in the court's first consideration of the claim. **(LE)**

reimbursement. Payment of an amount of money upon the occurrence of a loss covered by the policy. **(G)**

reinstatement. (1) Restoration of a lapsed policy. (2) Restoration of the original amount of a type of policy that reduces the principal amount by the amount of claims. **(G)**. (3) Putting back into effect a catastrophe reinsurance coverage that has been reduced by the payment of a reinsurance loss as the result of one catastrophe. This is usually effected by the payment of a reinstatement premium. **(R)**

reinsurance. A type of insurance that involves acceptance by an insurer (i.e., the reinsurer) of all or a part of the risk of loss covered by another insurer (i.e., the ceding company). It is a way for an insurer to avoid having to pay for large or catastrophic losses. **(R)**

reinsurance assumed. (1) *See* **cession.** (2) The premium for an assumption of reinsurance. **(R)**

reinsurance, automatic. *See* **automatic reinsurance. (G)**

reinsurance broker. An individual or organization that places reinsurance for the ceding companies who are its customers. **(G)**

reinsurance ceded. *See* **cession. (R)**

reinsurance credit. Credit taken on its annual statement by a ceding company for reinsurance premiums ceded and losses recoverable. **(R)**

reinsurance, excess. *See* excess of loss reinsurance. **(R)**

reinsurance, facultative. *See* facultative reinsurance. **(R)**

reinsurance, pooling. *See* pooling. **(R)**

reinsurance premium. The consideration paid by a ceding company to a reinsurer for the reinsurance afforded by the reinsurer. **(R)**

reinsurance, quota share. *See* quota share reinsurance. **(R)**

reinsurance, spread loss. *See* spread loss reinsurance. **(R)**

reinsurance, stop-loss. *See* stop-loss reinsurance. **(R)**

reinsurance, surplus. *See* surplus reinsurance. **(R)**

reinsurer. An insurer that assumes all or a part of the insurance or reinsurance written by another insurer. **(R)**

rejection. (1) Refusal by an insurer to underwrite a risk. (2) Sometimes used to refer to the refusal or denial of a claim by an insurer. **(G)**

relation of earnings to insurance. A health insurance provision used in noncancellable and guaranteed renewable contracts stating that, if at the beginning of a disability the insured's total disability income exceeds his earned income, the benefits will be reduced proportionally, and premiums for any excess coverage will be refunded. **(H)**

relative value schedule. A surgical schedule that basically compares the value of one surgical procedure to another and establishes the surgical fee to be paid. **(H)**

relative value unit. Sometimes used instead of dollar amounts in a surgical schedule, this number is multiplied by a conversion factor to arrive at the surgical benefit to be paid. **(H)**

release. (1) To give up, abandon, and discharge a claim or an enforceable right of one person against another. (2) The name of the instrument evidencing such an act. For example, if a claim representative obtains a release from a claimant, this means that the claimant has given up all further rights against the insurance company. **(G)**

remainder. The amount of a risk to be reinsured after deducting the amount the ceding company is keeping in its own account. **(R)**

remand. Usually used in appellate courts whereby the appellate court refers the case back to the original court for further action. **(LE)**

remittitur. Process by which an excessive jury verdict is reduced by the court. *See also* **additur. (LE)**

removal. Removing property to protect it from loss. Most personal and commercial property forms cover damage to property at another location when it has been removed from the premises to protect it from loss by a peril insured against. **(PR)**

renewable term. Term insurance that may be renewed for another term without evidence of insurability. **(LI)**

renewal. (1) The reestablishment of the in-force status of a policy, the term of which has expired or will expire unless it is renewed. **(G)**. (2) The automatic reestablishment of in-force status effected by the payment of another premium. **(H, LI)**

renewal certificate. A short-form certificate that is used to renew a policy. It refers to the original policy, keeping all of its provisions, but does not restate all of its insuring agreements, exclusions, and conditions. **(G)**

renewal commission. A commission paid on premiums subsequent to the first-year commission. **(G)**

renewals. (1) The premiums paid for renewed policies. (2) The commissions paid on renewal premiums. **(G)**

rent insurance. *See* **rental value insurance. (PR)**

rental value insurance. A form of property insurance that provides indemnity (1) for the loss of the rental value of property when the owner or tenant is deprived of the use of the property because it has been damaged by an insured peril, or (2) for the loss by the owner-landlord of the rent that would have been payable by a tenant of the property, under the terms of the lease or by statute, when he is relieved of liability for the payment of rent during a period of untenantability due to an insured peril. **(PR)**

replacement. A new policy written to take the place of one currently in force. **(G)**

replacement cost. The cost of replacing property without a reduction for depreciation. By this method of determining value, damages for a claim would be the amount needed to replace the property using new materials. *See also* **actual cash value. (PR)**

replacement cost insurance. Insurance that provides that loss will be paid on a replacement cost basis. *See also* **replacement cost. (PR)**

reporting form. The form for a periodic report to an insurer by an insured that covers the fluctuating values of stocks of merchandise, furniture and fixtures, and improvements and betterments. Premiums are adjusted annually, on the basis of the average values insured during the policy period. An insured with fluctuating inventories might use this form. **(PR)**

representation. A statement made on an application for insurance that the applicant represents as correct to the best of his knowledge and belief. *See also* **warranty. (LE)**

representative. An agent or sales representative. **(G)**

res ipsa loquitur. Literally translated, this expression means "facts speak for themselves." Under this doctrine, an individual is presumed to be negligent if the circumstances of injury are under his complete and exclusive control, and if it can be shown that the injury or damage could only have occurred if the individual were negligent. **(LE)**

rescission. (1) Repudiation of a contract. A party whose consent to a contract was induced by fraud, misrepresentation, or duress may repudiate it. A contract may also be repudiated for failure to perform a duty. (2) The termination of an insurance contract by the insurer when material misrepresentation has occurred. **(G, LE)**

reserve. (1) An amount representing actual or potential liabilities kept by an insurer to cover debts to policyholders. (2) An amount allocated for a special purpose. Note that a reserve is usually a liability and not an extra fund. On occasion, a reserve may be an asset, such as a reserve for taxes not yet due. **(G)**

reserve, unearned premium. *See* unearned premium reserve. **(G)**

residence employee (or domestic). A person who performs full- or part-time services of a household nature. **(WC)**

residence premises. In homeowners insurance, the dwelling, other structures and grounds, or that part of any other building where the named insured lives. **(LA, PR)**

resident agent. An agent domiciled in the state where he writes insurance. **(G)**

residual disability. The form of disability that becomes defined as partial disability when an insured has returned to work immediately following a period of total disability. **(H)**

residual income. A clause used with disability income policies that provides for benefits to be paid when the insured can do some but not all of his normal duties. For example, if the insured suffers a disability that causes him to lose a third of his earning power, the residual disability clause would provide one-third of the benefit that the policy would provide for total disability. **(H)**

residual markets. Various insurance markets outside of the normal agency-company marketing system. Residual markets include government insurance programs, specialty pools (aviation risks and nuclear risks), and shared market mechanisms (assigned risk plans). **(G)**

Resource Based Relative Value Scale (RBRVS). This is a classification system used to determine how physicians will be compensated for services provided under Medicare benefits. **(H)**

respite care. Normally associated with hospice care, respite care is a benefit to family members of a patient whereby the family is provided with a break or respite from caring for the patient. The patient is confined to a nursing home for needed care for a short period of time. **(H)**

respondeat superior. Originally the law said that, under certain circumstances, a master was liable for the wrongful acts of a servant. In today's usage, this expression refers to the fact that, under certain circumstances, a principal is responsible for the wrongful acts of its agents or an employer for those of its employees. Under this doctrine, if an employee negligently injures a customer during the course of employment, the employer could be held liable. **(LE)**

restoration of benefits. A provision in many major medical plans that restores a person's lifetime maximum benefit amount in small increments after a claim has been paid. Usually, only a small amount ($1,000 to $3,000) may be restored annually. **(H)**

retainer clause. A clause stating how much a company placing reinsurance intends to retain. **(R)**

retaliatory law. A state law that says that agents from another state applying for a license to operate in the state in question will be accorded the same treatment as agents residing in the retaliatory state are given in the foreign state. **(LE)**

retention. (1) The portion of the premium that is used by the insurance company for administrative costs. **(H)**. (2) The amount of liability retained by the ceding company and not reinsured. *See also* **cession**. **(R)**

retention of risk. Assuming all or part of a risk instead of purchasing insurance or otherwise transferring the risk. One of the four major risk management techniques. *See* **risk management**. **(G)**

retirement annuity. A form of annuity contract that is entered into before a selected retirement age with the consideration paid in installments until that age is reached. It is a form of deferred annuity. **(LI)**

retirement income policy. An adaptation of an endowment at a selected retirement age in which the annuity benefit is a percentage of the face amount of life insurance in force before retirement age, usually 10%; for example, for each $1000 of insurance, a $10 per month annuity installment is payable. Under this type of policy, the cash value will exceed the face amount in the later policy years, and if death occurs before the selected retirement age, the death benefit would be the face amount or the cash value, whichever is greater. **(LI)**

retroactive conversion. The conversion of a term life insurance policy to a cash value form as of the original date of issue of the term policy, rather than as of the time the conversion is made. In other words, the cash value policy will have already attained the age of the former term policy. **(LI)**

retroactive date. Date on a claims made liability policy that triggers the beginning period of insurance coverage. A retroactive date is not required. If one is shown on the policy, any claim made during the policy period will not be covered if the loss occurred before the retroactive date. **(LA)**

retrocession. The transaction whereby a reinsurer cedes all or part of the reinsurance it has assumed to another reinsurer. **(R)**

retrocessionaire. The reinsurer of a reinsurer (rare). **(R)**

retrospective premium. The final premium in a retrospective rating plan. *See* **retrospective rating. (G)**

retrospective rate derivation (RETRO). A rating system whereby the employer becomes responsible for a portion of the group's health care costs. If health care costs are less than the portion the employer agrees to assume, the insurance company may be required to refund a portion of the premium. **(H)**

retrospective rating. A plan for which the final premium is not determined until the end of the coverage period and is based on the insured's own loss experience for that same period. It is subject to a maximum and minimum. A plan of this type can be used in various types of insurance, especially workers' compensation and liability, and is usually elected by only very large insureds. *See also* **basic premium. (G)**

return commission. A commission that is paid back by the agent if a policy is canceled before its normal expiration date. This situation arises because the commission was based on the full annual premium, and if the policy is canceled before it is earned, a pro rata portion of the commission must be returned. **(G)**

return of cash value. A provision or rider on a life insurance policy stating that if death occurs during a certain period (often, 20 years), the policy will pay an amount, in addition to the face amount, that is equal to the cash value of the policy as of the date of death. This is really a form of increasing term insurance and is used as a sales tool. **(LI)**

return of premium. (1) A rider or provision in a health insurance policy agreeing to pay a benefit equal to the sum of all the premiums paid, minus claims paid, if claims over a stated period do not exceed a fixed percentage of the premiums paid. **(H)**. (2) A rider on a life insurance policy providing that, in the event of the death of the insured within a specified period, the policy will pay, in addition to the face amount, an amount equal to the sum of all premiums paid to date. This is a form of increasing term insurance and is used as a sales tool. **(LI)**. (3) A portion of the premium returned to a policyowner as a result of cancellation, rate adjustment, or a calculation that an advance premium was in excess of the actual premium. *See also* **pro rate** and **short rate. (G)**

revenue. *See* premium. **(H)**

reversionary annuity (or insurance). A contract providing annuity benefits only if the annuitant is living upon the death of the insured, such as the wife upon the death of her husband. Although labeled an annuity, this contract is actually a form of life insurance on the life of the person whose death will initiate the benefit. **(AN)**

revocable beneficiary. The beneficiary in a life insurance policy in which the owner reserves the right to revoke or change the beneficiary. **(LI)**

revocable trust. A type of trust instrument in which the grantor maintains control over the trust assets and can revoke the trust. *See also* irrevocable trust. **(EP, LE)**

rider. An attachment to a policy that modifies its conditions by expanding or restricting benefits or excluding certain conditions from coverage. *See* **waiver** and **endorsement. (G)**

riot. A peril covered by the extended coverage (EC) or direct reference in some policies. It is violent action by two or more people. State laws vary as to how many people it takes to constitute a riot. **(PR)**

risk. (1) Uncertainty as to the outcome of an event when two or more possibilities exist. *See also* **pure risk** and **speculative risk.** (2) A person or thing insured. *See also* **hazard** and **peril. (G)**

risk analysis. The process of determining which benefits to offer and premium to charge a particular group. **(H)**

Risk and Insurance Management Society, Inc. (RIMS). An association of risk managers and insurance buyers, organized for educational purposes to promote the risk management concept. RIMS attempts to foster closer relationships among buyers, to make the insurance needs of businesses known, and to promote better relations among all interested parties within the insurance industry. **(G)**

risk appraiser. An employee of a life insurer who screens the applications submitted. He may accept or reject an applicant, or propose an alternative policy or premium. **(LI)**

risk-based capital ratio. A ratio used to set capital standards for insurance companies, on the basis of the company's size and risk profile. **(G)**

risk control insurance. *See* reinsurance. **(H)**

risk, degree of. *See* degree of risk. **(G)**

risk management. Management of the pure risks to which a company might be subject. It involves analyzing all exposures to the possibility of loss and determining how to handle these exposures through such practices as avoiding the risk, reducing the risk, retaining the risk, or transferring the risk, usually by insurance. **(G)**

risk pool. *See* pool. **(H)**

risk premium insurance. *See* yearly renewable term. **(LI)**

risk retention groups. Liability insurance companies owned by their policyholders. Membership is limited to people in the same business or activity that exposes them to similar liability risks. The purpose is to assume and spread liability exposure to group members and to provide an alternative risk financing mechanism for liability. **(G)**

river marine. The part of ocean marine insurance that addresses itself to the insuring of craft which work on inland waterways. **(OM)**

robbery. The felonious taking, either by force or fear of force, of the personal property of another. **(C)**

robbery and safe burglary coverage form. There are two variations of this commercial crime coverage. Form D covers property other than money and securities against inside or outside loss or damage by robbery, and against inside loss or damage by safe burglary. Form Q covers money and securities against loss by robbery or safe burglary inside the premises, and loss by robbery outside the premises. Separate crime coverage forms have been largely replaced by newer crime policies that provide multiple coverage options in a single policy. **(C)**

rollover contribution. A contribution that consists of a distribution from a qualified plan that is deposited (rolled) in another qualified plan to postpone current taxation of the distribution. **(PE)**

Roth IRA. A type of individual retirement account for which contributions are not tax deductible but distributions may be tax free if certain conditions are met. **(PR)**

rule against perpetuities. A trust is not valid unless individual beneficiaries become vested in the trust property within 21 years. **(EP, LE)**

running down clause. This is an additional coverage which can be added to an ocean marine hull policy to provide protection to the insured against liability for damage to another ship caused by collision. **(OM)**

runoff. A termination provision in a reinsurance contract stipulating that the reinsurer shall remain liable for loss under each reinsured policy in force until its expiration date. **(R)**

S

ABBREVIATIONS AND ACRONYMS

SAA. *See* Surety Association of America. **(G)**

SAP. *See* statutory accounting principles. **(G)**

SEC liability. The Federal Securities Act of 1933 and the Federal Securities Exchange Act of 1934 place very stringent obligations on those offering stock issues to the public to disclose full information on the offering. If misrepresentations, intended or not, are made, liability can attach to them. **(G)**

SEGLI. Service Employees Group Life Insurance, which is issued to members of the armed forces while they are in the service. After separation it is convertible to individual policies from certain private insurers. **(LI)**

SEUA. *See* Southeastern Underwriters Association. **(G)**

SIMPLE. *See* savings incentive match plan for employees. **(PR)**

SIR. *See* self-insured retention. **(G)**

SMP. *See* special multi-peril. **(LA, PR)**

SNF. skilled nursing facility. **(H)**

PRESENTATION OF TERMS

sacrifice. Cargo that is thrown overboard in order to save the rest of the cargo and the ship. *See* jettison. **(OM)**

safe burglary. The taking of property from within a locked safe or vault by a person unlawfully entering the safe or vault, as evidenced by visible marks of forced entry upon its exterior, or the complete removal of a safe from the premises. **(C)**

safe depository coverage. Two commercial crime coverage forms are available for firms other than financial institutions that rent safe deposit boxes to others. One covers an insured's legal liability for loss or damage, whereas the other covers direct losses regardless of liability. Both cover customers' property on the insured's premises while in a safe deposit box or vault, or while being deposited or removed from such containers. Separate crime coverage forms have been largely replaced by newer crime policies that provide multiple coverage options in a single policy. **(C)**

safe driver plan. A system in which points are assigned for traffic violations and certain accidents, and each point adds a percentage surcharge to the rating factor. It is similar to merit rating. Also called a safe driver incentive plan. **(AU)**

safety consultant. *See* engineer. **(LA, PR)**

safety responsibility law. *See* financial responsibility law. **(G)**

salary savings insurance (deductions or allotment). Insurance issued to an individual employee whose employer agrees to deduct the premiums from the insured's paychecks and submit them to the insurer. **(LI)**

sales representatives. *See* special agent. **(LI)**

salvage. (1) Property taken over by an insurer to reduce its loss. **(G)**. (2) Property recoverable by salvagers under maritime law. **(OM)**

salvage corps. An organization whose duties are limited to preventing further damage to property during or after a fire. They are established by property insurance companies. **(PR)**

savings bank life insurance. Life insurance sold by mutual savings banks. Allowed only in a few states, such as New York, Connecticut, and Massachusetts. **(LI)**

savings incentive match plan for employees (SIMPLE). A type of qualified retirement plan available to certain small employers who do not maintain any other qualified plan. Employee participation is voluntary, but employer contributions are mandatory. **(PR)**

schedule. (1) A list of the items covered by an insurance policy with their descriptions and valuations. **(IM)**. (2) A list of individual items covered under one policy, such as various buildings and contents.**(PR)**

schedule bond. *See* name schedule bond and position schedule bond. **(C)**

schedule policy. An insurance contract that lists separate kinds of property, separate locations, or separate insurance coverages with the amount of insurance applying to each. **(PR)**

schedule Q. *See* Q schedule. **(LI)**

schedule rating plan. (1) Applying debits or credits within established ranges for various characteristics of a risk that are either below or above average according to an established schedule of items. (2) Under liability and automobile insurance, the schedule rating plan has been designed to allow credits and debits for various good or bad features of a particular risk. An example in automobile schedule rating would be allowing credits for driver training classes or fleet maintenance programs. **(AU, LA, PR)**

schedule (surgical). A list of specified amounts payable for surgical procedures, dismemberments, ancillary expenses, and the like in hospital and medical reimbursement policies. **(H)**

scheduled premium variable life insurance. A whole life policy that features a fixed, level premium and a minimum guaranteed face amount. The performance of the policy is dependent on the separate account. **(LI)**

seasonal risk. A risk that is present only during certain parts of the year. Examples might be manufacturing concerns, such as canners that have operations only during the summer and seasonal dwellings, such as cottages used for vacations. **(G)**

seaworthiness, implied. *See* implied seaworthiness. **(OM)**

second injury fund. Special funds set up by some states to pay all or part of the compensation required when a partially disabled employee suffers a subsequent injury. Because the compound effect of two injuries can be greater than the effect of the same two injuries in isolation, employers might be reluctant to hire handicapped persons if they had to bear the full burden for a second injury. Second injury funds relieve employers of some of this burden. The passage of the Americans with Disabilities Act has essentially made second injury funds obsolete. Consequently, a number of states have eliminated their funds or are considering doing so. However, they are still in operation in some states. **(WC)**

second surgical opinion. A cost containment technique to help patients and insurance companies determine whether a recommended procedure is necessary, or whether an alternative method of treatment could accomplish the same result. Some health policies require a second surgical opinion before specified procedures will be covered, and many policies pay for the second opinion. **(H)**

second surplus reinsurance. Reinsurance accepted by a second reinsurer in a surplus treaty. It is the amount that exceeds the total of the original insurer's net retention and the full limit of the first surplus treaty. *See also* **surplus reinsurance. (R)**

secondary beneficiary. The second person named to receive benefits upon the death of an insured if the first named beneficiary is not alive or does not collect all the benefits before his own death. *See also* **contingent beneficiary. (LI)**

secondary care. Medical services provided by physicians who do not have first contact with patients. Examples would be such specialists as urologists and cardiologists. *See also* **primary care** and **tertiary care. (H)**

secondary coverage. Coverage that provides payment for charges not covered by the primary policy or plan. *See also* **coordination of benefits. (H)**

Section 125 plan. A plan that provides flexible benefits. This plan qualifies under the IRS code that allows employee contributions to be met with pretax dollars. **(H)**

Section 302 stock redemption. A total stock redemption that qualifies as a capital transaction and not a dividend distribution. **(PE)**

Section 303 stock redemption. A partial stock redemption permitted under Section 303 of the IRC for the purpose of providing funds for estate settlement costs. **(PE)**

secular trust. An irrevocable trust that provides for current taxation of deferred compensation assets and a degree of security in an informally funded plan. **(EP)**

securities. Evidences of a debt or of ownership, such as stocks, bonds, and checks. **(G)**

Securities Act of 1933. A federal law that requires full and fair disclosure and the use of a prospectus in the sale of securities. **(G)**

securities deposited with others coverage form. A commercial crime coverage form that protects against loss by theft, disappearance, or destruction of securities that have been deposited with others, such as a bank, trust company, or stock broker. Separate crime coverage forms have been largely replaced by newer crime policies that provide multiple coverage options in a single policy. **(C)**

Securities Exchange Act of 1934. A federal law that requires the registration of companies and agents with the federal government if they are selling securities. **(G)**

selection. The choosing by an underwriter of risks acceptable to an insurer. **(G)**

selection of risk. A phrase used in reinsurance referring to the practice of ceding poorer business to a reinsurer while retaining good risks. **(R)**. *See also* **selection. (G)**

self-administered trusteed plan. A retirement plan in which contributions are paid to a trustee who invests the money, accumulates the earnings and interest, and pays benefits to eligible employees. **(PE)**

self-funded plan. Plan of insurance in which an employer that has fairly predictable claim costs pays the claims, rather than an insurance company. *See also* **administrative services only. (H, LI)**

self-inflicted injury. An injury to the body of the insured inflicted by himself. **(H)**

self-insurance. Making financial preparations to meet pure risks by appropriating sufficient funds in advance to meet estimated losses, including enough to cover possible losses in excess of those estimated. Few organizations are large or dispersed enough to make this a sound alternative to insurance. **(G)**

self-insured retention (SIR). The portion of a risk or potential loss assumed by an insured. It may be in the form of a deductible, self-insurance, or no insurance. **(G)**

self-reinsurance. The creation of a fund by an insurer to absorb losses beyond its normal retention. It is used in place of buying reinsurance. **(R)**

selling price clause. *See* **market value clause. (PR)**

separate account. An account established or maintained by an insurance company under which the income, gains, and losses of that specific account are credited or charged without consideration of the income and investment results of the other assets of the insurance company. Separate accounts are used to fund variable contracts and provide the participant with a hedge against inflation. **(PE)**

separate account. An investment company (usually a unit investment trust) registered with the SEC that owns and holds assets for the benefit of participants in variable contracts. Because of the investment risk, insurers are required to keep their variable contract portfolios separate from their fixed investment portfolios. **(AN, LI)**

service area. The area where a health plan can provide services, as allowed by state agencies or by the certification of authority,. **(H)**

service benefits. Medical expense benefits provided by service associations whereby benefits are identified in terms of days of coverage instead of monetary values. **(H)**

service plans. Plans of insurance in which benefits are the actual services rendered, rather than a monetary benefit. *See* **Blue Cross** and **Blue Shield. (H)**

settlement. (1) Usually, a policy benefit or claim payment. It is an agreement between both parties to the policy contract as to the amount and method of payment. **(G)**. (2) Conclusion of litigation by the mutual agreement of the parties involved before the final verdict; certain settlements must be court approved. **(LE)**

settlement options. The various methods for the payment of the proceeds or values of a life insurance policy that may be selected in lieu of a lump sum. **(LI)**

share reinsurance. *See* pro rata reinsurance. **(R)**

Sherman Antitrust Act. An antitrust law from which insurance is exempted to the extent that it is regulated by state law. **(G)**

shock loss. A catastrophic loss so large that it has a material effect on the underwriting results of a company. **(G)**

shoppers guide. A consumer publication that describes the type of coverage being offered and provides general information to help an applicant for life or health insurance compare different types of policies and reach a decision about whether the proposed coverage is appropriate. Also known as buyers guide. **(H, LI)**

short rate cancellation. A cancellation procedure in which the premium returned to the insured is not in direct proportion to the number of days remaining in the policy period. In effect, the insured has paid more for each day of coverage than if the policy had remained in force for the full term. *See also* **pro rata cancellation. (G)**

short rate premium. The premium required for issuing a policy for a period less than its normal term. **(G)**

short-term disability income policy. A disability income policy with benefits payable for a short term, usually less than two years, as opposed to a long-term disability income policy. **(H)**

short-term disability insurance. A group or individual policy usually written to cover disabilities of 13 or 26 weeks' duration, though coverage for as long as two years is not uncommon. *See also* **long-term disability insurance. (H)**

short-term policy. A policy written for a shorter period than is normal for that type of policy. **(G)**

sickness. Includes physical illness, disease, and pregnancy, but does not include mental illness. **(H)**

sickness insurance. A form of health insurance against loss by illness or disease. It does not include accidental bodily injury. **(H)**

sidetrack agreement. Any agreement between a railroad and a customer who is served by a railroad sidetrack built on the customer's premises. Among other things, it provides that the customer hold the railroad harmless for losses resulting from certain types of accidents. **(LA)**

sidetrack insurance. *See* sidetrack agreement. **(LA)**

simple probability. *See* probability. **(G)**

simplified employee pension plan (SEP). A plan for which the employer contributes a specific amount into an eligible employee's IRA on behalf of the employee. **(PE)**

sine qua non rule. This rule says that a person's conduct is not held to be the cause of a loss if the loss would have occurred anyway. **(LA)**

single carrier replacement. A situation in which one carrier replaces several other carriers who had been providing services. **(H)**

single interest policy. Insurance protecting the interest of only one of the parties with an insurable interest in a property, such as insurance protecting a mortgagee but not a mortgagor or protecting a seller but not a buyer. **(PR)**

single limit. Any insurance coverage that is expressed as a single amount of insurance, or a single limit of liability. *See also* **split limit. (G)**

single premium funding method. A method of accumulating money for future payment of pension benefits under which the money required to pay for each year's accumulated benefits is paid to an insurance company or paid to the trust fund annually. **(PE)**

single premium policy. A life insurance policy paid for in one single premium in advance rather than in annual premiums over a period of time. **(LI)**

single premium whole life. A whole life policy that is paid with a single premium payment at the time of purchase. *See also* **continuous premium whole life** and **limited payment whole life. (LI)**

sinkhole collapse. The peril of a sudden sinking or collapse of land into underground empty spaces created by the action of water on limestone or similar rock formations. This peril is now covered by the latest commercial property forms. Other forms of earth movement continue to be excluded in most cases. **(PR)**

sistership exclusion. A products insurance exclusion that denies coverage for the withdrawal and recall of products from the market. **(LA)**

skilled nursing care. Daily nursing and rehabilitative care that is performed only by or under the supervision of skilled professional or technical personnel. Skilled care includes administering medication, medical diagnosis and minor surgery. **(H)**

skilled nursing facility (SNF). A facility designed to qualify for treatment to Medicare-eligible people. Included is treatment for rehabilitation and other care, such as 24-hour nursing coverage, physical, occupational, and speech therapies. **(H)**

slander. A spoken statement about someone that is personally injurious to the individual. *See also* **defamation** and **libel. (LE)**

sliding scale commission. A commission adjustment under a formula whereby the actual commissions paid by a reinsurer to a ceding insurer varies inversely with the loss ratio, subject to a maximum and minimum. **(R)**

slip. A paper submitted by a broker to the underwriters at Lloyd's of London that identifies syndicates accepting the risk and notes the extent of their participation. **(G)**

slow-burning construction. *See* **mill construction. (PR)**

small group pooling. The combining into one pool of several small group business; used especially for computing more accurate premium rates for members of the pool. **(H)**

smoke damage. Damage caused by the smoke from a fire in contrast to damage caused by the actual combustion. **(PR)**

Social Health Maintenance Organization (SHMO). A demonstration project funded by the Department of Health and Human Services that combines the delivery of acute and long-term care with adult day care services and transportation. **(H)**

solicitor

social insurance. Compulsory insurance legislated to provide minimum economic security for large groups of people, particularly those with low incomes. It is primarily concerned with the costs and loss of income resulting from sickness, accidental injury, old age, unemployment, and the premature death of the head of a family. *See also* **legislated coverages** and **Social Security. (G)**

Social Security. (1) The programs provided under the United States Social Security Act of 1935, plus amendments and additions thereto. It is now called Old Age, Survivors, Disability, and Health Insurance. (2) Any government program that provides economic security for portions of the public (e.g., social insurance, public assistance, family allowances, and grants-in-aid). **(G)**

Social Security rider. An optional disability income rider that provides an additional benefit depending on the amount of disability benefits payable by Social Security. *See also* **all or nothing rider** and **offset rider. (H)**

Social Security tax. A tax paid by workers and employers on wages earned. The taxes support the benefit programs under the Social Security System. **(H)**

Society of Chartered Property and Casualty Underwriters. The society of people who have been awarded the CPCU (Chartered Property and Casualty Underwriter) designation. Its primary purpose is the continuing education of its members. It also encourages insurance research. **(G)**

Society of Insurance Research. An organization that encourages insurance research and promotes the exchange of ideas and methods of research. **(G)**

sole proprietorship. A business enterprise owned by one person who is its manager and employee. **(G)**

sole proprietorship insurance. Life and health insurance that handles the business continuity problems peculiar to a sole proprietorship. For instance, such insurance could be used to enable the heirs of the sole proprietor to bring the value of the business back to the level where it was prior to the death of the owner. **(H, LI)**

solicitor. An individual appointed and authorized by an agent to solicit and receive applications for insurance as the agent's representative. Solicitors are not usually given the power to bind coverage but are required to be licensed. **(G)**

solvency. With regard to insurers, having sufficient assets (capital, surplus, and reserves) and being able to satisfy financial requirements (investments, annual reports, and examinations) to be eligible to transact insurance business and meet liabilities. **(G)**

sonic boom. Noise, pressure, and shock waves resulting from an aircraft or missile exceeding the speed of sound. At one time, property damage caused by sonic boom was excluded under most property forms. Modern commercial property forms and homeowner policies now cover losses by sonic boom. **(PR)**

Southeastern Underwriters Association (SEUA). A property insurance rating organization that was the defendant in the 1944 United States Supreme Court decision declaring insurance to be commerce and thus subject to regulation by federal law. This pronouncement was later modified by Public Law 15. *See also* **Public Law 15. (G)**

special acceptance. A specific agreement by a reinsurer to accept a risk that would not be automatically included within the terms of a reinsurance contract. **(R)**

special agent. An insurer's representative in a territory. He services the insurer's agents and in general is responsible for the volume and quality of the business written in that territory. In the property and liability fields, this person is a special agent or marketing representative, and in the life field this person is known as a sales representative. **(G)**

special auto policy. An automobile policy with a single limit of liability applying to bodily injury and property damage and a corresponding limit applying to medical payments. Broad physical damage coverage could be added to it. This policy, which was designed for private passenger vehicles, has become obsolete. *See* **personal auto policy. (AU)**

special building form. A form that provides open-perils (all risk) coverage on commercial buildings, subject to certain exclusions. It was once the broadest coverage available on buildings but has been largely replaced by the **building and personal property coverage form. (PR)**

special coverage form. Any of the commercial or personal lines property forms that provide coverage on an open-perils (all risk) type basis. These forms provide the broadest coverage and do not list covered perils, but they do include a lengthy list of exclusions. *See also* **open peril** and **named peril. (PR)**

special multi-peril (SMP). A business policy that combined into one contract the coverages normally purchased under several. Property and liability coverages were mandatory, Crime and boiler and machinery were optional. Many other options and endorsements allowed the SMP to be tailor made for each policyholder. It has been largely replaced by new commercial forms. *See* **commercial package policy. (LA)**

special personal property form. A form that provides open-perils (all risk) coverage on the personal property (contents) of commercial risks with certain exclusions. It was once the broadest coverage available on commercial contents but has been largely replaced by the **building and personal property coverage form. (PR)**

special power of appointment. A donee is authorized to appoint interest in property to specific individuals to the exclusion of others. **(EP)**

specific insurance. A policy that describes specifically the property to be covered. This is in contrast to a policy that covers on a blanket basis all property at one or more locations without specific definitions. In the case of overlapping coverages, specific insurance is considered the primary one. **(PR)**

specific rate. A rate applying to an individual piece of property. **(PR)**

specific reinsurance. *See* **facultative reinsurance (R)**

specified causes of loss. A commercial automobile physical damage coverage for loss by the specified perils of fire, lightning, explosion, theft, windstorm, hail, earthquake, flood, vandalism, or the sinking, burning, collision, or derailment of any conveyance transporting a covered auto. Comprehensive coverage is slightly broader. **(AU)**

specified disease policy. *See* **dread disease policy. (H)**

specified perils. *See* **named perils. (PR)**

speculative risk. Uncertainty as to whether a gain or loss will occur. An example would be a business enterprise where there is a chance that the business will make money or lose it. Speculative risks are not normally insurable. *See also* **pure risk. (G)**

spendthrift clause. A clause in most life insurance policies that prevents the creditors of a beneficiary from claiming any of the benefits before the beneficiary actually receives the money. The purpose of this clause is to keep those to whom he is in debt from taking legal action to require the insurer to pay the proceeds directly to them. **(LI)**

split-dollar coverage. An arrangement of disability income insurance in which the employer and employee each pay a portion of the premium.

The employer purchases coverage for the sick pay or paid disability leave provided as an employee benefit. The employee pays for disability coverage beyond what the employer provides as a benefit. **(H)**

split-dollar life insurance. An arrangement, usually between an employer and an employee, in which the employer and the employee's beneficiary share the death benefits and the premiums may be split between the employer and the employee. **(LI)**

split life insurance. A combination of installment annuity and term insurance under which the amount of annuity consideration (premium) paid determines the amount of one-year renewable term insurance an annuitant can purchase and place on the life of anyone designated. **(LI)**

split limit. Any insurance coverage that is expressed in different amounts for different types of losses. For example, automobile liability of 50/100/50 means bodily injury limits of $50,000 per person, $100,000 per accident, and a property damage limit of $50,000 per accident. *See also* single limit. **(G)**

sponsor plan. An employer that establishes or maintains a plan for its employees; or an employee organization that establishes or maintains a plan for the employees of the organization; or in the case of a plan established and maintained by two or more employers, the committee, board of trustees, or relatives of the parties who establish or maintain the plan. **(PE)**

spread loss reinsurance. (1) The working cover subject to a prospective rating plan. (2) A form of excess reinsurance wherein each year's premium rate is determined by the amount of the ceding insurer's excess losses for a specified number of preceding years. A form of experience rating. **(R)**

sprinkler leakage insurance. Insurance against damage done by the accidental discharge of water from an automatic sprinkler system, as contrasted with discharge because of heat from a fire. **(PR)**

sprinkler leakage legal liability insurance. Insurance that covers the legal liability of an insured who has a sprinkler leakage loss that damages the property of others, such as on a floor below or in adjoining premises. **(LA, PR)**

stacking of limits. Applying the limits of more than one policy to an occurrence, loss, or claim. In some cases, courts have required a stacking of limits when multiple policies, or multiple policy periods, cover an occurrence. **(LE)**

staff model HMO. This is an HMO where physicians are employed and all premiums are paid to the HMO, which then compensates the physicians on a salary and bonus arrangement. **(H)**

Stamping Bureau. *See* Audit Bureau. **(G)**

Standard Annuity Table. The 1937 Standard Annuity Table; a mortality table widely used for annuities. **(PE)**

standard class rate (SCR). This is a rate that is arrived at by using a base rate per participant multiplied by a factor to allow for group demographic information. **(H)**

standard exception. In workers' compensation insurance, certain classes of employees are classified separately for rating, rather than being included in the main classification for a risk. Examples would be clerical office employees, outside sales representatives, draftsmen, drivers, chauffeurs, and their helpers. **(WC)**

standard fire policy. *See* New York standard fire policy. **(PR)**

standard limit. *See* basic limit. **(G)**

standard policy. (1) Coverage that has identical provisions regardless of the issuing insurer. Many common policies are standardized. (2) Insurance issued to a standard risk. **(G)**

standard premium. Most often used in connection with retrospective rating for workers' compensation and general liability insurance. It is the premium of which the basic premium is a percentage and is developed by applying the regular rates to an insured's payroll. *See also* **retrospective rating** and **basic premium. (LA, WC)**

standard provisions. (1) Provisions prescribed by state law that must appear in all policies issued in that jurisdiction. (2) Provisions adopted by the NAIC to apply to group life insurance as minimum protection. They are required by law in most states. (3) Formerly, a set of prescribed provisions regulating the operating conditions of a health insurance policy required by law in most jurisdictions between about 1912 and 1950. They are now superseded by uniform provisions for individual accident and health insurance policies which contain an NAIC model bill. These have been enacted in virtually all jurisdictions. **(H, LI)**

standard risk. A risk that is on a par with those on which the rate has been based in the areas of health, physical condition, and morals. An average risk, not subject to rate loadings or restrictions because of poor health. **(LI)**

state agent. An outmoded term meaning an agent who has an exclusive territory of one or more states. Also, an obsolete term for special agent. *See* **special agent. (G)**

state associations of insurance agents. Each state may have one or more associations of insurance agents. These organizations are made up of individual agents who have joined forces to discuss common problems and promote the American agency system. **(G)**

state death taxes. A tax imposed by states on beneficiaries who receive property from a decedent. **(EP)**

state fund. A fund set up by a state government to finance a mandatory insurance system, such as workers' compensation, nonoccupational disability benefits, or, in Wisconsin, state-offered life insurance. Such a fund may be monopolistic (i.e., purchasers of the type of insurance required must place it in the state fund), or it may be competitive (i.e., an alternative to private insurance if the purchaser desires to use it). **(G)**

stated amount. An agreed amount of insurance that is shown on the policy and that will be paid in the event of total loss regardless of the actual value of the property. **(PR)**

statement blank. *See* **convention blank. (G)**

statement of policy information. For universal life policies, this document is prepared at the end of each year giving complete information on all transactions affecting the policy, such as premium paid, current death benefit, interest credited, loans outstanding, monthly charges, and cash surrender value. **(LI)**

statement of values. Sometimes property is written using a blanket rate and one single limit of liability applying to all locations. To determine the blanket or average rate, a rating bureau or company requires an insured to submit a declaration of the amounts of value at each separate location on a statement of values form. **(PR)**

statewide average weekly wage (SAWW). A statistical computation that is periodically updated and is used to determine compensation benefit amounts. Many benefits are set forth as a percentage of the SAWW. **(WC)**

statute of frauds. A statute stating that certain contracts must be in writing in order to be enforceable. An example would be any contract involving the sale of real estate. **(LE)**

statute of limitations. The time limit set by law during which a person must bring legal action on a case. **(LE)**

statutory. Required by or having to do with law or statute. **(G)**

statutory accounting principals (SAP). Those principals required by statute that must be followed by an insurance company when submitting its financial statement to the state insurance department. Such principles differ from generally accepted accounting principles (GAAP) in some important respects. For one thing, SAP requires that expenses must be recorded immediately and cannot be deferred to track with premiums as they are earned and taken into revenue. **(G)**

statutory earnings (or losses). Earnings or losses shown on the NAIC convention blank, in contrast to earnings or losses that would be shown if generally accepted accounting procedure statements were used. **(G)**

statutory reserve. A reserve, either specific or general, required by law. **(G)**

step-rate premium. Premium is increased at times specified in the policy, on the basis of a predetermined attained age, or number of policy years in force. **(LI, H)**

stock. Merchandise for sale or materials in the process of manufacture, as distinguished from furniture, fixtures, or equipment. **(PR)**

stock bonus plan. A type of profit-sharing plan whereby contributions to the plan and benefits derived from the plan are in the form of the company's stock. **(PE)**

stock insurer. An incorporated insurer with capital contributed by stockholders, to whom the earnings are distributed as dividends on their shares. *See also* **mutual insurer. (G)**

stock option plan. Surviving stockholders have the option to purchase or not purchase the shares of a deceased stockholder. **(G)**

stock purchase agreement. A formal buy-sell agreement whereby each stockholder is bound by the agreement to purchase the shares of a deceased stockholder and the heirs are obligated to sell. **(G)**

stock redemption agreement. A formal buy-sell agreement whereby the corporation is bound by the agreement to purchase the shares of a deceased stockholder and the heirs are obligated to sell. **(G)**

stop loss. Any provision in a policy designed to cut off an insurer's losses at a given point. In effect, a stop loss agreement guarantees the loss ratio of the insurer. **(G)**

stop-loss insurance. This is a type of reinsurance that can be taken out by a health plan or self-funded employer plan. The plan can be written to cover excess losses over a specified amount either on a specific or individual basis, or on a total basis for the plan over a period of time such as one year. **(H)**

stop-loss reinsurance. (1) A form of reinsurance under which the reinsurer reinsures the ceding insurer for an amount by which the latter's incurred losses in a calendar year for a specified class of business exceed a specified loss ratio. (2) *See* **aggregate excess of loss reinsurance. (R)**

storekeepers burglary and robbery insurance. A type of package crime policy designed for a storekeeper that provides coverage on seven different crime hazards. A specific amount of coverage is purchased and the limits apply separately to each of the coverages. There is very little flexibility in that the insured must buy the package. *See also* **broad form storekeepers insurance. (C)**

storekeepers liability policy. A single-limit package policy covering bodily injury and property damage liability claims in the operation of the storekeeper's business. It includes limited coverage on contractual and products liability. **(LA)**

straight life policy. (1) A whole life policy that stretches the premium payments over the insured's lifetime (to age 100). Also known as continuous premium whole life. **(LI)**. (2) *See* **ordinary life policy. (LI)**

stranded. A term used to describe a ship that has run aground. **(OM)**

strict liability. Usually used when referring to products coverage. The liability that manufacturers and merchandisers may be subject to for defective products sold by them, regardless of fault or negligence. A claimant must prove that the product is defective and therefore unreasonably dangerous. *See also* **absolute liability. (LA)**

strike-through clause. A clause providing that, in the event of the insolvency of a ceding insurer, the reinsurer continues to be liable for its share of losses, which will then be payable directly to the insured rather than to the liquidator of the insolvent ceding insurer. *See also* **insolvency clause. (R)**

structured settlement. Method of paying insurance claim settlements in periodic payments, usually after an initial payment for immediate expenses. The funds are placed into an investment vehicle from which periodic payments of a fixed amount are made for a certain period of time or for the remainder of the claimant's life. **(G)**

subagents. Agents reporting to other agents or general agents, and not directly to the company. **(G)**

subbroker. An intermediary from whom another intermediary obtains reinsurance business to be placed. **(R)**

subchapter S corporation. A corporate form of business in which all profits and losses are shared by the stockholders and thus the corporation is taxed on an individual basis as opposed to corporate taxation. **(G)**

subject premium (base premium, premium base, or underlying premium). A ceding company's premium to which the reinsurance premium rate (factor) is applied to produce the reinsurance premium. In other words, the reinsurance premium is a percentage of the ceding company's premium. **(R)**

sublimit. Any limit of insurance that exists within another limit. For example, special classes of property may be subject to a specified dollar limit per occurrence, even though the policy has a higher overall limit; a health insurance policy may limit certain benefits to fixed dollar amounts or maximum amounts per day, even though the overall coverage limit is higher. **(G)**

submitted business. Applications for insurance submitted to an insurer but not yet acted upon by it. **(G)**

subordination. Putting below in importance. Sometimes the creditors of a contractor will subordinate their interests in the obligations owed them until a construction project is completed. This has the effect of increasing the contractor's working capital. **(S)**

subrogation. (1) The right of one who has taken over another's loss to also take over the other person's right to pursue remedies against a third party. It is never used in life insurance and seldom in health. **(LE)**. (2) The right of a surety, in its name or in the name of the obligee under a bond, to pursue a course of action against the principal or any other party liable for a loss paid by the surety. **(S)**

subrogation clause. A clause giving an insurer the right to pursue any course of action, in its own name or the name of a policyowner, against a third party who is liable for a loss which has been paid by the insurer. One of its purposes is to make sure that an insured does not make any profit from his insurance. This clause prevents collecting from both the insurer and a third party. It is never part of a life insurance policy. **(G)**

subrogation release. A release taken by an insurer upon indemnifying an insured. It contains a provision specifying that the insurer will be subrogated to the rights of recovery that the insured has against any person responsible for the loss. **(G)**

subrogation waiver. A waiver by the named insured giving up any right of recovery against another party. Normally an insurance policy requires that subrogation (recovery) rights be preserved. In commercial property insurance, a written waiver of subrogation rights is permitted if it is executed before the loss occurs. **(PR)**

subscriber. This term has two meanings: first, it refers to a person or organization who pays the premiums, and second, to the person whose employment makes him eligible for membership in the plan. **(H)**

subscriber contract. An agreement that describes the individual's benefits under a health care policy. **(H)**

subscription policy. A policy to which two or more insurers may subscribe, indicating in the policy the share of the risk to be borne by each insurer. **(G)**

subsidence. Movement of the land on which property is situated. A structure built on a hillside may slide down the hill as a result of earth movement caused by heavy rains. This is different from earthquake damage. **(PR)**

substandard risk. (1) A risk not measuring up to underwriting standards. It may still be written but usually at a surcharged premium. **(G)**. (2) *See* **impaired risk. (H, LI)**

sue and labor clause. A provision permitting and requiring an insured to take all practical measures to protect any salvage, without prejudicing any right to claim against the insurer. The intent of this clause is to make sure the insured does not fail to use proper care to preserve the property. One effect of it is that in case of a total loss an insurer may pay the loss plus the cost of salvage. **(OM)**

summary annual report. A summary of a qualified plan's operation that is required to be given to each participant annually. **(PE)**

summary plan description. This is a recap or summary of the benefits provided under the plan. It is used most often with employees covered by self-funded plans. **(H)**

superbill. A form that specifically lists all of the services provided by the physician. It cannot be used in place of the standard AMA form. **(H)**

Superintendent of Insurance. The title of the head of a state or provincial insurance department used in some jurisdictions. In most states the title *Commissioner* is used. **(G)**

superseded suretyship rider. An endorsement or provision on a new bond under which the new bonding company assumes liability for claims that cannot be recovered from the prior bond because its discovery period has ended. The discovery period of a bond is normally one year, during which it will cover any loss which occurred during the term of the bond. **(S)**

supplemental actuarial value. The actuarial present value of all benefits expected to be provided in the future under a plan reduced by the actuarial present value of a future annual actuarial values (including any participants' contributions), with respect to the participants included in the valuation of the plan. **(PE)**

supplemental contract. A rider usually relating to the method of settlement of the proceeds of a life insurance policy. **(LI)**

supplemental dental plan. *See* dental plan, supplemental. **(H)**

supplemental extended reporting period. An optional maxi tail or full tail that extends for an unlimited period of time after expiration of a claims-made liability policy, and covers claims made after the policy period. **(LA)**

Supplemental Medical Insurance (SMI). Part B of Medicare. It is a voluntary program that generally covers physician's services and various outpatient services. A premium is charged for electing Part B coverage. **(H)**

supplementary payments. A provision in most liability policies under which the insurer agrees to pay defense costs, premiums on various bonds, interest accruing after a judgment, and other reasonable expenses in addition to the limit of liability. **(LA)**

supplemental services. Additional services that can be purchased over and above the basic coverage of a health plan. **(H)**

surety. One who guarantees the performance or faithfulness of another. A surety can be either a corporation or an individual, but it is usually an insurance company. **(S)**

Surety Association of America (SAA). An association of bonding companies that establishes rules and regulations, rates and rating plans, and forms and collects information on rating that is supplied to members. **(S)**

surety bond. A bond guaranteeing that a principal will carry out the obligation for which he is bonded. A surety bond is most often issued to a contractor, a person seeking a license or permit, or someone involved in a court case. **(S)**

Surety Bond Guarantee Program. A federal Small Business Administration (SBA) program for minority contractors. The SBA agrees to back the surety company in the event of loss under a construction contract bond. **(S)**

suretyship. The means by which one person or entity, the surety, guarantees another entity, the obligee, that a third entity, the principal, will or will not do something. It differs from insurance by being a three-party contract, but most sureties today are insurers. **(S)**

surgical insurance benefits. A form of health insurance against loss due to surgical expenses. **(H)**

surgical schedule. Usually part of a basic medical expense plan that itemizes various surgical procedures and the monetary benefit allocated to each procedure. **(H)**. *See also* schedule. **(H)**

surgi-center. A separate facility (from a hospital) that provides outpatient surgical services. **(H)**

surplus. (1) The amount by which assets exceed liabilities. **(G)**. (2) A reinsurer's portion of a risk, that part which remains after deducting the retention established by the ceding company. **(R)**

surplus lines. A risk or a part of a risk for which there is no market available through the original broker or agent in its jurisdiction. Therefore, it is placed with nonadmitted insurers on an unregulated basis, in accordance with the surplus or excess lines provisions of the state law. **(G)**

surplus reinsurance. (1) A form of pro rata reinsurance wherein the reinsurer accepts that part of each risk written in excess of a specified retention. The part reinsured is usually a multiple of the retention. *See also* lines. (2) The amount of any risk that exceeds the net line retained by the ceding company. The reinsurer receives premiums and contributes to the payment of losses in proportion to its share of the risk. **(R)**

surplus release. The use of admitted reinsurance on a portfolio basis to offset extraordinary drains on policyholder's surplus. *See also* portfolio reinsurance. **(R)**

surplus share. *See* surplus reinsurance. **(R)**

surplus to policyholders. *See* policyholder's surplus. **(G)**

surrender. To give up a whole life policy. The insurer pays the insured the cash value that the policy has built up if it is surrendered. **(LI)**

surrender value. *See* cash surrender value. **(LI)**

survivor. The beneficiary of an annuity contract—that is, the annuitant's survivor. **(AN)**

survivorship annuity. *See* reversionary annuity. **(LI)**

survivorship benefits. Funds available to pay an annuitant who survives longer than statistically expected from premiums paid by annuitants who died before they had collected amounts equal to their contributions. **(LI)**

swap maternity. A provision granting immediate maternity coverage in a group health insurance plan but terminating coverage on pregnancies in progress upon termination of the plan. The term *swap* means providing the coverage at the beginning of the policy where it is not usually provided, but not providing it after the end of the policy where it usually is provided. **(H)**

switch maternity. A provision for group health maternity coverage on female employees only when their husbands are included in the plan as dependents. **(H)**

syndicate. A group of insurers or underwriters who join to insure property that may be of such total value or high hazard that it can be covered more safely or efficiently on a cooperative basis. *See also* **pool**. **(G)**

T

3-D policy. *See* dishonesty, disappearance, and destruction policy. **(C)**

TDB. *See* temporary disability benefits. **(G)**

TEFRA. *See* Tax Equity and Fiscal Responsibility Act. **(H, LI)**

TIRB. Transportation Insurance Rating Bureau. **(IM)**

TPA. *See* third-party administrator. **(H, LI)**

PRESENTATION OF TERMS

T tables. The factors used to properly fund retirement benefits for employees of varying types of industries incorporating the ideas of interest, mortality, and turnover. **(PE)**

Table 2001. An IRS table used to determine the cost of pure death protection under split-dollar life insurance plans and some other plans. **(L)**

tabular. Of or pertaining to a table. Tabular cost is the cost of mortality, morbidity, or other claims, according to the valuation tables and assumptions used by the insurer. **(G)**

tabular plan. A retrospective rating plan that uses tables to furnish the various values for the rating formula. **(G)**

tail. This term has been used to describe both the exposure that exists after expiration of a policy and the coverage that may be purchased to cover that exposure. On occurrence forms, a claims tail may extend for years after policy expiration, and the losses may be covered. On claims made forms, tail coverage may be purchased to extend the period for reporting covered claims beyond the policy period. *See* **mini, midi, maxi tail. (LA)**

target benefit plan. A qualified plan that is a combination of a defined benefit and defined contribution plan whereby an employer is required to fund a specific targeted benefit for plan participants. Target benefit plans impose defined contribution limitations for plan funding. **(PE)**

target risk. (1) Certain high-value bridges, tunnels, and fine art collections that are excluded from an automatic reinsurance contract to permit specific handling of the capacity problem and to release the reinsurer from the potential heavy accumulation of liability on any one risk. (2) A large, hazardous risk on which insurance is difficult to place. (3) A large, attractive risk that is considered a target for competing insurance companies. **(G)**

tariff rate. A rate established by a rating organization that comes from the tables, schedules, and rules found in the tariff of rates. **(G)**

taxable estate. Is equal to the adjusted gross estate less the marital deduction property and any charitable deductions. **(EP, LE)**

tax basis. Money that has yet to be taxed, usually part of a qualified plan benefit or distribution. **(PE)**

Tax Equity and Fiscal Responsibility Act. A federal law intended to prevent group term life insurance plans from discriminating in favor of key employees. It also amends the Social Security Act to make Medicare secondary to group health plans. **(H, LI)**

tax factor (or tax multiplier). A factor applied in retrospective rating to an insurance premium to increase it to cover state premium taxes. **(LA, WC)**

tax-free rollover. The tax-free transfer of assets from one qualified retirement plan to an IRA or annuity, and vice versa. **(PE)**

tax-sheltered annuity (TSA). An annuity program under which contributions reduce the taxable income of participating employees, and the benefits are not taxable until distributed. **(LI)**

Teachers Insurance and Annuity Association. An organization selling life and health insurance and annuities to college and university staff members. **(H, LI)**

temporary agent. A person who is licensed to act as an agent for a brief period (usually 90 days) without taking a written examination. Temporary licenses are commonly granted to allow someone to continue the business of an agent who has died, become disabled, or entered active military service. **(G)**

temporary disability benefits (TDB). Legislated benefits payable to employees for nonoccupational disabilities under TDB laws in certain states. *See also* **disability benefits law. (H)**

temporary partial disability. A condition where an injured party's capacity is impaired for a time but is able to continue working at reduced efficiency and is expected to fully recover. **(H, WC)**

temporary total disability. A condition where an injured party is unable to work at all while he recovering from injury but is expected to recover. **(H, WC)**

ten-day free look. A notice, placed prominently on the face page of the policy, advising the insured of his right to examine a health policy and, if dissatisfied, return the policy within ten days for a full refund of premium and no further obligation. **(H)**

ten-year funding. Primarily for older individuals, this type of funding requires that premiums be payable for 10 years even though retirement is permitted within 10 years. **(PE)**

tenancies for years. Ownership of real property for a specific period. **(LE)**

tenants in common. Where two or more persons have undivided ownership and possession of real property, but (unlike joint tenancy) each owner may transfer or dispose of their share of ownership. *See also* **fee simple** and **joint tenancy. (LE)**

tenants improvements and betterments. Property affixed to an owner's building by the lessee or tenant that may not be legally removed at the end of the rental period. **(PR)**

tenants policy. A homeowners form that is specifically designed for people who rent. **(PR)**

1035 exchange. A nontaxable exchange of life insurance policies and annuities as provided under section 1035(a) of the Internal Revenue Code. **(LI)**

tertiary care. Services provided by such providers as thoracic surgeons, intensive care units, neurosurgeons, and so forth. **(H)**

term. The period of time for which a policy or bond is issued. **(G)**

term insurance. The type of life insurance policy that provides protection only for a specified period. A common policy period would be one year, five years, 10 years, or until the insured reaches age 65 or 70. It does not build up any of the nonforfeiture values associated with whole life policies. *See also* **decreasing term insurance, increasing term insurance, term insurance,** and **whole life insurance. (LI)**

term rule. The provision in a rating manual that states the periods for which coverages run and which discounts, if any, apply to the rates or premiums of policies issued for more than one year. **(G)**

terminal funding. A form of retirement funding whereby an employer sets aside a single sum of money when the participant retires. This sum will fund the individual's retirement benefit. **(PE)**

terminally ill. A term that refers to the status of a person who will normally die within 6 months of a specific illness or sickness. Often refers to the terminally ill requirement for hospice care. **(H)**

termination. The time the coverage under an insurance policy ends, either because its term has expired or because it has been canceled by either party. **(G)**

termination. The cessation of premium paying for a whole life or endowment policy before the agreed upon time. This ends the coverage, and the insured receives one of the nonforfeiture values. The cessation of a policy that does not or has not yet developed a cash value is termed a lapse. **(LI)**

territorial limitation. *See* geographical limitation. **(G)**

tertiary beneficiary. A beneficiary designated as third in line to receive proceeds or benefits if the primary and secondary beneficiaries do not survive. **(LI)**

testamentary capacity. The testator satisfies the necessary requirements imposed by law for the purpose of making a will; the ability to form a valid will. **(EP)**

testamentary transfer. Transfer of the assets of an estate according to the provisions of the deceased person's last will and testament. *See also* inter vivos transfer. **(LE)**

testamentary trust. A trust created after the grantor's death, according to the provisions of the deceased person's last will and testament. *See also* inter vivos trust. **(EP, LE)**

testing exclusion. In boiler and machinery insurance, a provision that excludes coverage for any object while it is being tested. **(PR)**

thaisoi. An ancient Greek benevolent society that was a step in the evolution of life and health insurance. **(H, LI)**

theatrical floater. An inland marine form used to cover theatrical properties, such as costumes and scenery. **(IM)**

theft. The act of stealing. It includes such acts as larceny, burglary, and robbery. **(C)**

theft, disappearance, and destruction coverage Form.
A commercial crime coverage form covering money and securities
against the causes of loss described in its title. Separate crime coverage
forms have been largely replaced by newer crime policies that provide
multiple coverage options in a single policy. **(C)**

theory of probability. The mathematical principle upon which
insurance is based. *See also* **degree of risk, law of large numbers, odds,**
and **probability. (G)**

therapeutic alternatives. Alternate drug products that may be different in chemical content but provide the same effect when administered to patients. **(H)**

therapeutic equivalence. Different drugs that will control a symptom or illness exactly the same as other drugs used to control that
illness. **(H)**

third-party administration (TPA). Organizations that administer
qualified plans by providing accounting and actuarial services as well
as filing of various reports required by the IRS and the Department of
Labor. **(PE)**

third-party administrator (TPA). A firm that provides administrative services for employers and other associations with group insurance
policies. In addition to being the liaison between the employer and the
insurer, the TPA is also involved with certifying eligibility, preparing reports required by the state, and processing claims. TPAs are being used
more and more with the increase in employer self-funded plans. **(H, LI)**

third-party beneficiary. A person who is not a party to a contract
but who has legally enforceable rights under the contract. It might be a
life insurance beneficiary or a mortgagee. **(G)**

third-party insurance. A term for liability insurance. Liability always
involves a third party—that is, the one who has suffered a loss—in addition to the insurer and the insured. *See also* **liability insurance. (LA)**

third-party payor. This refers to any organization such as Blue Cross/
Blue Shield, Medicare, Medicaid, or commercial insurance companies
that is the payor for coverages provided by a health plan. **(H)**

three-fourths value clause. A clause stating that the maximum
loss the insurer will pay is three-fourths of the actual cash value of the
property. It is rarely used today. **(IM, OM, PR)**

threshold level. The point at which the insured may bring tort action
under a modified no-fault auto plan. Many of these plans prohibit tort

action for pain and suffering unless medical bills exceed some figure (e.g., $1,000) or disfigurement or death occurs. **(AU)**

thrift plan. Any type of retirement plan in which an employee savings feature is added. **(PE)**

ticket policy. *See* transportation ticket Policy. **(H)**

ticket reinsurance. A notation on a separate sheet of paper attached to a daily report setting forth the details of any reinsurance that has been effected. **(R)**

time element insurance. Insurance that covers expenses consequent to damage or destruction by an insured peril that continue over a period of time. The amount paid depends on the length of time during which the expenses accumulate. An example would be business interruption insurance, which pays for the loss of earnings during the time it takes to repair the property. **(PR)**

time limit on certain defenses. One of the uniform individual accident and sickness provisions required by state law to be included in every individual health policy. It sets a limit on the number of years after a policy has been in force that an insurer can use as a defense against a claim the fact that a physical condition of the insured existed before the policy was issued but was not declared at that time. **(H)**

time limits. The limits of time within which notice of a claim and proof of a loss must be submitted. **(G)**

time of payment of claims provision. A health insurance provision that requires that claims be paid immediately upon receipt of proofs of loss. Some states specify a number of days in place of the word *immediately*. **(H)**

title insurance. Insurance that indemnifies the owner of real estate in the event that his clear ownership of property is challenged by the discovery of faults in the title. **(G)**

Title XIX benefits. *See* Medicaid. **(H)**

tobacco sales warehouses coverage form. A commercial property coverage form used to insure tobacco warehouse operations. Tobacco is covered only while in the warehouse and only for a limited period before, during, and after the regular auction season. **(PR)**

tontine policy. A kind of policy that came into use after the Civil War. It was a high-premium contract that paid dividends to those participants who were still living at the end of a stated period, at the expense of those who had died or let their policies lapse. It is almost the opposite of insurance and is no longer allowed by law. **(LI)**

tort. A private wrong, independent of contract and committed against an individual, that gives rise to a legal liability and is adjudicated in a civil court. A tort can be either intentional or unintentional, and it is mainly against liability for unintentional torts that one buys liability insurance. **(LE)**

tortfeasor. A person who has committed a tort. **(LE)**

total disability. A degree of disability from injury or sickness that prevents the insured from performing the duties of any occupation from remuneration or profit. The definition in any given case depends on the wording in a covering policy. **(H)**

total loss. A loss of sufficient size so that it can be said there is nothing left of value (i.e., the complete destruction of the property.) The term is also used to mean a loss requiring the maximum amount a policy will pay. **(G)**

towing costs. Optional automobile coverage that pays the cost up to a fixed amount for the towing of a disabled automobile. **(AU)**

trailer interchange agreement. An arrangement whereby one trucker transfers a trailer containing a shipment to a second trucker for continued transportation. **(AU)**

trailer interchange coverage. Coverage for the legal liability of truckers for loss or damage to nonowned trailers and equipment that are in the insured's possession under a written trailer interchange agreement. **(AU)**

transacting insurance. The solicitation, inducement, and preliminary negotiations effecting a contract of insurance and the subsequent carrying on of business pertaining to it. The exact definition will vary somewhat according to the state laws regulating insurance. **(G)**

transfer of risk. Shifting all or part of a risk to another party. Insurance is the most common method of risk transfer, but other devices, such as hold harmless agreements, also transfer risk. One of the four major risk management techniques. *See* **risk management. (G)**

transit policy. A policy that provides coverage for loss to property while it is being transported. **(IM)**

transportation expenses. Automobile coverage for transportation expenses incurred by the named insured when an auto is damaged in

271

an accident. Coverage begins after a waiting period and is subject to a daily limit and maximum dollar limit. **(AU)**

transportation insurance. Usually an open form policy that covers the insured's property in the course of transportation. It can include all modes of transportation, including ocean vessels, required to carry the property from the originating location to the final destination. **(IM, OM)**

transportation ticket policy. An accidental death and dismemberment and disability benefit policy issued with a common carrier ticket and limited to the risks of travel and the duration of the trip for which the ticket has been purchased. The name is derived from the fact that it was originally issued in the form of an extra stub on a travel ticket. **(H)**

traumatic injury. An injury to a person's physical body caused by an outside source, as distinct from physical disability caused by sickness or disease. **(G)**

travel accident insurance. A form of health insurance limiting coverage to accidents occurring while the insured is traveling. **(H)**

treatment facility. Any facility, either residential or nonresidential, that is authorized to provide treatment for mental illness or substance abuse. **(H)**

treaty reinsurance. A contract of automatic reinsurance setting forth the conditions for reinsuring a class or classes of business. *See also* **facultative reinsurance. (R)**

trend factor. The factor applied to rates that allows for such changes as increased cost of medical providers, the cost of new and expensive medical technology, and so forth. **(H)**

trespasser. An individual who goes onto another person's property without any legal right to do so. The only duty that the owner of the property owes a trespasser is not to intentionally harm or set a trap for him. **(LE)**

triage. A method of ranking sick or injured people according to the severity of their sickness or injury to ensure that medical and nursing staff facilities are used most efficiently. **(H)**

trial work period. An incentive for a disabled worker under Social Security to attempt a return to work. The individual may work nine months in a five-year period without loss of Social Security disability income benefits. **(H)**

TRICARE. The Department of Defense's managed health care program for active duty military, active duty service families, retirees and their families, and other beneficiaries. **(H)**

trigger. *See* coverage trigger. **(LA)**

trip transit insurance. A type of policy that provides coverage for goods in transit for a specified trip and by a specified mode of transportation. **(IM)**

triple indemnity. *See* multiple indemnity. **(LI)**

triple option. A plan where employees have their choice among different types of providers such as HMO, PPO, or basic indemnity plan. Usually, their choice depends on how much they want to pay for the coverage. **(H)**

triple protection. A form of life insurance that is usually a combination of whole life and twice as much term insurance. The term portion applies until a stated date. Such a policy might be used to provide maximum protection to an individual at an earlier age when the need for insurance is greater but the ability to pay is less. **(LI)**

truckers coverage form. A commercial automobile insurance coverage form used to insure truckers who are engaged in the business of transporting goods for others. **(AU)**

truckers liability. *See* motor cargo policy—carriers form and Interstate Commerce Commission Endorsement. **(IM)**

true group insurance. Group insurance issued under a master contract with certificates of insurance that are not policy contracts issued to persons included in the group. This would be in contrast to franchise or wholesale group insurance, under which a covered person is issued an individual policy contract. **(H, LI)**

trust. A legal arrangement whereby property is held and managed by a trustee for the benefit of beneficiaries. **(EP)**

trust agreement. (1) A supplemental agreement attached to and made a part of a life insurance policy setting forth the manner in which the proceeds are to be paid, in lieu of having them paid in a lump sum or under one of the other installment settlement options in the policy itself. (2) An agreement or instrument under which a corpus (fund/property) is given over to the management of the trustee named in a trust instrument for the benefit of the beneficiaries of the trust. (3) A written agreement between two parties—the employer and the trustee—setting forth the provisions of a pension plan. **(EP, LI, PE)**

trust and commission clause. A provision found in some property, ocean marine, and inland marine policies enabling a person to insure his interest in the property of another. **(IM, OM, PR)**

trustee. A person appointed to manage the property of another. **(G)**

trustees. Those persons who, by entering into trust agreement with the employer, assume the impartial supervision of a retirement plan. They may be employees, a trust company, or outside individuals. **(PE)**

trust fund plans. A type of qualified plan in which contributions are made to a plan trustee or a corporate trustee. The trustee in turn will provide retirement benefits for plan participants. **(PE)**

tuition fees insurance. An adaptation of business interruption coverage. It protects a school against the indirect loss of tuition fees that may result from a fire or other peril covered by the policy that closes the school. **(PR)**

turnkey insurance. Insurance coverage that includes general liability for contractors and architects errors and omissions. **(LA)**

turnover. The number of persons hired within a stated period to replace those leaving or dropped; also, the ratio of this number to the average workforce maintained. In pension plans, turnover refers to the ratio of participants who leave employment through quits, discharge, and so forth to the total of participants at any age or length of service. **(PE)**

24-hour care coverage. A health insurance concept that blends occupational and nonoccupational benefits to provide round-the-clock coverage for injuries or diseases whether or not they are work-related. **(H, WC)**

twisting. Misrepresenting a policy or making incomplete comparisons of policies to induce a policyowner to change or replace an existing policy. **(G)**

U

UAB. Underwriters Adjustment Bureau. **(G)**

UAC. Underwriters Adjusting Company. **(G)**

UCD. *See* unemployment compensation disability insurance. **(H)**

UJF. *See* unsatisfied judgment fund. **(AU)**

UL. *See* Underwriters Laboratories, Inc. **(G)**

U&O. *See* use and occupancy. **(PR)**

USAIG. United States Aircraft Insurance Group. **(AV)**

USGLI. *See* United States Government Life Insurance. **(LI)**

PRESENTATION OF TERMS

ultimate net loss. The total sum that the insured or any company as its insurer, or both, becomes legally obligated to pay either through adjudication or compromise, including such things as legal, medical, and investigative costs. **(G)**

umbrella liability policy. A coverage basically affording high limit coverage in excess of the limits of the primary policies as well as additional liability coverages. These additional coverages are usually subject to a substantial self-insured retention. The term *umbrella* is derived from the fact that it is a separate policy over and above any other basic liability policies the insured may have. **(LA)**

umpire. For property coverage, if a company and a claimant fail to agree on the amount of loss, each may appoint an appraiser, and these in turn select an umpire. A decision by any two of the three is binding. **(G)**

unallocated benefit. A benefit providing reimbursement of expenses up to a maximum but without any schedule of benefits as such. **(H)**

unallocated claim (or loss) expense. Expenses of loss adjustment that cannot be charged specifically to any claim. Examples would be claim department salaries and office overhead. **(G)**

unallocated funds. Plan contributions are made or pooled for the benefit of all plan participants collectively. **(PE)**

unauthorized insurer. *See* nonadmitted insurer. **(G)**

underground property damage. Refers to damage to underground property, such as wires, conduits, pipes, or sewers, beneath the surface of the ground caused by the use of mechanical equipment for the purpose of grading land, paving, excavating, drilling, burrowing, filling, backfilling, or pile driving. **(LA)**

underinsurance. A condition in which not enough insurance is carried to cover the insurable value. **(G)**

underinsured motorists coverage. A coverage in an automobile insurance policy under which the insurer will pay damages up to specified limits for bodily injury damages, if the limits of liability under the liable motorist's policy are exhausted and he cannot pay the full amount for which he is liable. **(AU)**

underlying. The amount of insurance or reinsurance on a risk that attaches before the next higher excess layer of insurance or reinsurance attaches. **(R)**

underlying premium. *See* subject premium. **(R)**

underwriter. A technician trained in evaluating risks and determining rates and coverages for them. The term derives from the practice at Lloyd's of each person willing to accept a portion of the risk writing his name under the description of the risk. **(G)**

Underwriters Laboratories, Inc. (UL). A testing laboratory for manufactured items to determine their safety propensities. **(G)**

underwriting. The process of selecting risks and classifying them according to their degrees of insurability so that the appropriate rates may be assigned. The process also includes rejection of those risks that do not qualify. **(G)**

underwriting profit (or loss). (1) The profit or loss realized from insurance operations, as contrasted with that realized from investments. (2) The excess of premiums over losses and expenses (profit) or the excesses of losses over premiums (loss). **(G)**

unearned premium. That portion of the written premium applicable to the unexpired or unused part of the period for which the premium has been paid. Thus, in the case of an annual premium, at the end of the first month of the premium period, eleven-twelfths of the premium is unearned. **(G)**

unearned premium reserve. The amount shown in the insurance company's balance sheet that represents the approximate total of the premiums that have not yet been earned as of a specific point in time. *See also* **unearned premium. (G)**

unearned reinsurance premium. That part of the reinsurance premium applicable to the unexpired portion of the policy reinsured. **(R)**

unemployment compensation disability insurance (UCD). Health insurance that covers off-the-job accidents and sickness. It does not cover disability resulting from an injury or sickness covered by workers' compensation insurance. *See also* **disability benefits law. (H)**

unemployment insurance. Insurance against loss of income due to unemployment. It is funded by payroll taxes and subject to control by both the federal and state governments. Individuals who are willing and able to work qualify for this insurance by working at a job in an eligible classification, earning a minimum amount of money, and being subject to involuntary unemployment. **(G)**

unfair claim settlement practices law. State laws designed to protect the consumer against unfair practices in the reporting, investigation, payment, and final resolution of insurance claims. **(G)**

unfair trade practices law. State laws designed to protect the consumer against misleading, deceptive, monopolistic, or otherwise unfair practices in the business of insurance. **(G)**

unfunded plan. Any plan that follows a pay-as-you-go method is termed as such. *See* **funding, disbursement. (PE)**

unfunded supplemental actuarial value. The excess of the supplemental actuarial value over the actuarial asset value. **(PE)**

Uniform Billing Code of 1992 (UB-92). This code was implemented on October 1, 1993. It is a federal directive stating that a hospital must provide its patients with bills, itemizing all services included and billed on each invoice. **(H)**

uniform forms. The wording on many policy documents has been agreed upon by most companies and standardized. They are printed and distributed by rating bureaus and by certain well-known establishments and are called standard or uniform forms. **(G)**

uniform premium. A rating system that is used to calculate premiums for all insureds with no distinctions as to age, sex, or occupation. **(H, LI)**

uniform provisions. A set of provisions regarding the operating conditions of individual health policies developed in a model law recommended by the National Association of Insurance Commissioners and required, with minor variations by almost all jurisdictions, and permitted in all jurisdictions. **(H)**

uniform provisions. A set of provisions required by state law in life insurance policies. The actual wording of the provisions can vary, but the intent must be the same as the wording of the uniform provisions. **(LI)**

Uniform Simultaneous Death Act. State law stating that if the insured and beneficiary die in the same accident and it cannot be determined who died first, it will be assumed that the beneficiary died first, and all proceeds will then pass to the insured's contingent beneficiary. **(CIC)**

unilateral contract. A contract such as an insurance policy in which only one party to the contract, the insurer, makes any enforceable promise. The insured does not make a promise but pays a premium, which constitutes the insured's part of the consideration. **(G)**

uninsured motorists coverage. A coverage in an automobile insurance policy under which the insurer will pay damages to the insured for which another motorist is liable if that motorist is unable to pay because he is uninsured. This coverage usually applies to bodily injury damages only. Injuries to the insured caused by a hit-and-run driver are also covered. **(AU)**

uninsured plan. Any pension plan that is not maintained or handled through insurance products. **(PE)**

United States Aircraft Insurance Group. A group of insurers providing facilities for all forms of aviation insurance. **(G)**

United States Government Life Insurance (USGLI). A form of life insurance issued to members of the armed forces during World War I until about the end of World War II. **(LI)**

unit benefit plan. A type of pension plan providing retirement benefits as a definite amount or percentage of earnings for each year of service with the employer. If a unit of annuity is purchased each year to fund the ultimate benefit, this may also be referred to as a unit-purchase type of plan. **(PE)**

unit investment trust (UIT). An investment company that invests on behalf of investors in a portfolio of securities, such as stocks and bonds. The trust does not have a management function. It merely holds the assets. **(PE)**

universal life. A combination flexible premium, adjustable life insurance policy. The premium payer may select the amount of premium he can pay, and the policy benefits are those that the premium will purchase. Alternatively, the premium payer may change the amount of insurance and pay premium accordingly. Many believe this is the only true solution to the "buy term, invest the difference" problem. **(LI)**

unlevel commission system. A system of commissions under which the first year's commission is a higher percentage of the premium than are renewal commissions. **(G)**

unpaid premium provision. A provision in a health insurance policy that allows deduction of unpaid premiums from claims payments. **(H)**

unoccupied. Refers to property that may be furnished or have furnishings in it but is not occupied or being lived in. The standard fire policy prohibits unoccupancy beyond a specified period. This term is contrasted with *vacant*, which means that there is nothing within the building. **(PR)**

unqualified plan. Any plan that does not meet the qualifications for special tax advantages as set forth in the Tax Code. Such a plan provides only those deductions that are allowed in the course of normal business operation. **(PE)**

unreported claims. A reserve that is based on estimates and is used to set up claims that have occurred but have not yet been reported to the insurer as of the time when either the policy has expired or the insurer is preparing its annual statement. *See also* **IBNR. (G)**

unsatisfied judgment fund (UJF). Several states have laws that provide for reimbursement to a person injured in an automobile accident who has been unable to collect from the person responsible. **(AU)**

unscheduled premium payments. In universal life insurance, the policyowner can pay extra premiums in addition to the scheduled premium payment amount. These payments can be made at any time, but are subject to a minimum amount. **(LI)**

use and occupancy insurance (U&O). A term that was once used to refer to the coverages later known as business interruption insurance, and now called business income coverage. In this sense, it is obsolete. It is, however, still used to refer to such loss of earnings in boiler and machinery insurance. It is also used in some contracts that promise to pay on a valued basis, or fixed amount, for each day the insured is deprived of the use or occupancy of described property because of damage caused by a peril insured against. **(PR)**

usual, customary, and reasonable (UCR). *See* reasonable and customary. **(H)**

utilization. This refers to how much a covered group uses a particular health plan or program. **(H)**

utilization and review committee. A committee composed of medical personnel whose purpose is to monitor the health care services and supplies provided to Medicare patients. **(H)**

utilization management. This procedure or process utilizes a review coordinator to evaluate the necessity and appropriateness of various health care services. **(H)**

utilization review. A cost control mechanism by which the appropriateness, necessity, and quality of health care is monitored by both insurers and employers. **(H)**

utmost good faith. Acting in fairness and equity with a sincere belief that the act is not unlawful or harmful to others. The insurance contract requires that each party is entitled to rely on the representations of the other without attempts to conceal or deceive. **(G, LE)**

V

VEBA. Voluntary employee beneficiary association. **(H)**

V&MM, or VMM. Vandalism and malicious mischief. Damage or destruction to property that is willful. Traditionally V&MM coverage was optional on many forms or added by endorsement, but today it is automatically covered by basic commercial and homeowner forms. **(PR)**

PRESENTATION OF TERMS

vacant. A term used in property insurance to describe a building that has neither occupants nor contents. *See also* **unoccupied. (PR)**

valuable papers and records coverage. An open-perils (all risk) coverage for physical loss or damage to valuable papers and records of the insured. It includes practically all types of printed documents or records except money. **(PR)**

valuation. (1) A mathematical analysis of the financial condition of a pension plan. **(PE)**. (2) Estimation of the value of an item, usually by appraisal. **(G)**. (3) Calculation of the policy reserve in life insurance. **(LI)**

valuation assumption. An actuarial estimate of probable future experience of a pension plan with respect to rates of mortality, disability, turnover, age at hiring, age at retirement, investment yield, and so forth. **(PE)**

valuation clause. A clause stating the value of items for insurance purposes, making it a valued policy. **(G)**

valuation reserve. A reserve against the contingency that the valuation of assets, particularly investments, may be higher than what can be actually realized or that a liability may turn out to be greater than the valuation placed on it. **(G)**

value reporting form. Commercial form designed for businesses that have fluctuating merchandise values during the year. As values are reported (monthly, quarterly, or annually), the amount of insurance is adjusted. Reporting forms help eliminate problems of overinsurance and underinsurance, as well as the need to continually endorse a policy. **(PR)**

valued. Relating to an agreement by an insurer to pay a specified amount of money to or on behalf of the insured upon occurrence of a defined loss. **(G)**

valued policy. A policy stating that in the event of a total loss, a specific amount, as stated in the policy, will be paid. The effect is to eliminate the need for determining the actual cash value of an item of property in the event of a total loss. It is generally used with certain more valuable items, such as fine arts, antiques, and furs. *See also* **valued policy law. (PR)**

valued policy law. A law passed by a state legislature requiring that in the event of a total loss to a building, the insurance company must pay the face amount of a valued policy, regardless of the actual cash value of the property that was destroyed. It can have the effect of allowing the insured to recover an amount much greater than the actual cash value of the property. The intent of the law is to guard against unscrupulous insurers purposely writing in excess of the value of property in order to collect greater premiums. **(LE)**

values. Used in life insurance terminology as a shortened term for nonforfeiture values. *See* **nonforfeiture values. (LI)**

vandalism and malicious mischief. *See* V&MM. **(PR)**

variable annuity. An annuity contract in which the amount of the periodic benefit varies, usually in relation to security market values, a cost-of-living index, or some other variable factor, in contrast to a fixed or guaranteed return annuity. As a hedge against inflation, the variable annuity presents investment risks to the annuitant **(AN)**

variable contracts. Contracts such as variable annuities or variable life insurance that contain an element of risk for the investor, depending on the performance of the separate account backing the contract. Generally, these contracts are products of insurers but are regulated by both state insurance departments and the federal government. **(H, LI)**

variable life insurance. A form whose face value varies depending on the value of the dollar or securities or other equity products at the time payment is due. **(LI)**

variable universal life. A combination of the features of variable life insurance and universal life insurance under the same contract. Benefits are variable on the basis of the value of equity investments, and premiums and benefits are adjustable at the option of the policyholder. **(LI)**

vendee. A person who purchases property. **(G)**

vendor. A person who sells property. **(G)**

vested commissions. Commissions on renewal business that are paid to the agent whether or not the agent still works for the insurance company with which the business is placed. **(G)**

vested interest. A person has a right to either the present or future enjoyment of personal property. **(EP, LE)**

vested liability. The present value of a participant's retirement benefits that are nonforfeitable. **(PE)**

vesting. The attainment of a benefit right by a participant, attributable to employer contributions, that is not contingent upon a participant's continuation in specified employment. *See also* **contingent vesting, deferred vesting,** and **immediate vesting. (LI)**

viatical settlement. A written contractual agreement under which the policyholder of a life insurance contract covering the life of a terminally ill person assigns, transfers ownership, or otherwise irrevocably designates all control and rights in the contract to another person or entity in exchange for the advance payment of a portion of the death benefits. Under these arrangements, a portion of the proceeds is paid to the insured or policyholder before the death of the insured person. **(LI)**

viatical settlement company. A company or firm that specializes in negotiating viatical settlements with policyholders of life insurance contracts covering the lives of terminally ill persons. **(LI)**

vicarious liability. The law says that under certain circumstances a person is liable for the acts of someone else. For example, in matters related to an automobile, a parent might be held responsible for the negligent acts of a child. In such a case, the parent would be vicariously liable. **(LE)**

vis major. An accident for which no one is responsible (i.e., an act of God). **(G)**

vision care coverage. A health care plan usually offered only on a group basis that covers routine eye examinations and that may cover all or part of the cost of eyeglasses and lenses. **(H)**

void. A term used to describe a policy contract that is completely free of all legal effect. **(LE)**

voidable. A policy contract that can be made void at the option of one or more of the parties to it. An example would be a property insurance policy that is voidable by the insurer if the insured commits certain acts. **(G)**

voluntary compensation insurance. A coverage similar to workers' compensation that is used in circumstances in which workers' compensation coverage does not apply or is not required by law. An example would be an employer wanting to voluntarily pay compensation benefits to members of a company-sponsored athletic team, or a church wishing to cover volunteer workers. **(WC)**

voluntary employee beneficiary association (VEBA). A trust established under IRS Code 501(c)(9) that can be used to prefund health care. **(H)**

voluntary reserve. An allocation of surplus not required by law. Such reserves are often accumulated by insurers in order to strengthen their financial structure. **(G)**

voyage clause. A clause in ocean marine policies specifying the period of time or the number of trips that may be grouped together as one voyage. **(OM)**

W

WC. See workers' compensation. **(WC)**

PRESENTATION OF TERMS

wage indexing. A cost of living increase applied to Social Security benefits after a worker has achieved eligibility for benefits. **(EP)**

waiting period. The period between the beginning of a disability and the start of disability insurance benefits. *See also* **elimination period. (H)**

waiver. (1) A rider waiving (excluding) liability for a stated cause of injury or sickness. (2) A provision or rider agreeing to waive premium payments during a period of disability of the insured. (3) The act of giving up or surrendering a right or privilege that is known to exist. In property and liability fields, it may be effected by an agent, adjuster, company, employee, or company official, and it can be done either orally or in writing. **(G, LE)**

waiver of coinsurance. A provision in a property policy that the coinsurance clause will not apply if the total loss does not exceed a stated amount, such as 2% of the sum insured or the amount of $2,500, whichever is greater. The reason for such a provision is to eliminate having to do a large inventory in order to determine whether the insured has complied with the coinsurance clause, especially where very small losses are involved. **(PR)**

waiver of premium. A provision of a life insurance policy that continues the coverage without further premium payments if the insured becomes totally disabled. **(LI)**

waiver of restoration premium. (1) An agreement or decision to forego any premium for reinstatement of the face amount of coverage under an insurance policy after it has been reduced by the amount of a loss payment. (2) A provision, especially in bonds, for automatic restoration of the full amount of protection without cost to the insured. **(G)**

war clause. A provision excluding liability of an insurer if a loss is caused by war. **(H, LI)**

war risk insurance. Insurance covering damage caused by war. Most often written by ocean marine insurance companies covering vessels. **(G)**

warehouse and custom bond. A bond guaranteeing the payment of custom duties. **(S)**

warehouse-to-warehouse coverage. A clause sometimes found in inland marine coverages extending the policy to cover from the shipper's warehouse to the consignee's warehouse. **(IM)**

warehousemen's legal liability. Coverage protecting warehousemen from liability claims, common to the business of warehousing, for loss or damage to property in storage. **(LA)**

warranty. A statement made on an application that is warranted as true in all respects. If the statement is untrue in any respect, even though the untruth was not known to the applicant, the contract may be voided without regard to the materiality of the statement. Statements in life and health applications are not warranties except in cases of fraud. For other lines, the doctrine of warranty usually applies only if the statement of the applicant is material to a risk or the circumstances of a loss. *See also* **representation. (LE)**

warranty, implied. *See* implied warranty. **(LE)**

warranty policy. A policy written by a reputable company. The term is used in cases where additional coverage is needed. The additional policies all state that the reputable company's warranty policy will stay in force and that they provide coverage exactly like that of the warranty policy. **(PR)**

Warsaw Convention. An international agreement setting limits of liability on international flights with respect to payments for bodily injury and death. **(G)**

watchman warranty clause. A provision often found in a burglary or fire policy providing for a reduced premium if there is a watchman on duty. **(PR)**

watchperson. Under commercial crime insurance coverages, any person retained to have care and custody of the insured's property inside the premises, and who has no other duties. **(C)**

water damage clause. A provision affording coverage for certain specified causes of water damage (e.g., damage caused by water leakage, overflow of heating or air-conditioning systems, or plumbing). **(PR)**

water damage legal liability insurance. Coverage for an insured who suffers a water damage loss that also damages the property of others on the floor below or in adjoining premises. **(LA)**

wave damage insurance. Coverage against damage to property resulting from high waves or tides. **(PR)**

we/us/our. These words are used to refer to the insurer in many policy forms. **(G)**

wear and tear exclusion. An exclusion found in many property insurance policies. It excludes loss resulting from wear and tear, which means normal usage over time that reduces the value of the property insured. **(P)**

wedding presents floater. A form that provides temporary coverage for wedding presents, usually starting shortly before the wedding and ending shortly thereafter. **(IM)**

weekly premium insurance. (1) A policy the premium on which is collected weekly by an agent calling at the door. It is usually sold in small face amounts. (2) A form of debit or industrial life insurance. *See also* industrial life insurance. **(H, LI)**

welfare. *See* public assistance. **(G)**

wet marine insurance. Insurance provided on ocean marine forms, covering ships and their cargos. **(OM)**

while clauses. Clauses that suspend coverage while certain conditions, such as vacancy, exist. **(PR)**

whole dollar premium. In many insurance contracts today, the premiums are rounded to the nearest dollar, rather than carrying them out to the nearest cent. An amount of 51 cents or more is usually rounded up to the next dollar, and any amount less than $.51 is dropped. **(G)**

whole life insurance. Insurance that may be kept in force for a person's whole life and that pays a benefit upon the person's death, whenever that may be. All whole life policies build up nonforfeiture values, but they are paid for in 3 different ways. Under a straight or ordinary life policy, premiums are paid for as long as the insured lives. A single premium policy is paid for at one time in one premium. Between these two types there are many limited-payment plans, under which the insured pays premiums for a certain period or until reaching a certain age. *See also* **term insurance. (LI)**

wholesale group insurance. *See* franchise insurance. **(H, LI)**

widow(er)'s benefit. An early retirement benefit, at age 60, under Social Security for the surviving spouse of a covered worker. **(PE)**

will. A legally enforceable declaration of an individual's plan for the disposition of property. **(EP)**

willful injury. *See* intentional injury. **(G)**

windstorm. Wind of sufficient violence to be capable of damaging insured property. Windstorm coverage has traditionally been part of extended coverage (EC), but today it is usually included automatically as part of basic coverages. **(PR)**

Wisconsin life fund. The system of state underwritten and issued life insurance established by the state of Wisconsin and that provides life insurance for citizens who apply. Wisconsin is unique among the 50 states in this respect. **(LI)**

work and materials clause. This is a provision found in many property insurance policies stating that the insured is allowed to have the typical types of work and materials for his business. The clause makes this clear so that the policy cannot be voided later because of the increased hazard provision of the standard fire policy. **(PR)**

work program. In contract bond reinsurance, a clause specifying that reinsurance be attached at a specified level of a principal's total volume of work, rather than on the conventional basis of individual contract or bond amount. **(R)**

workers' compensation (WC). (1) A schedule of benefits payable to an employee by the employer without regard to liability, required by state law in the case of injury, disability, or death as the result of occupational hazards. (2) Insurance agreeing to pay workers' compensation law benefits on behalf of the insured employer. **(WC)**

workers' compensation catastrophe policy. Excess of loss reinsurance purchased by primary insurers to cover their unlimited medical and compensation liability under the compensation laws of the several states. **(R)**

working capital. *See* net quick assets. **(S)**

working cover. A contract covering an area of excess reinsurance in which loss frequently is anticipated. **(R)**

wrap-up. A package plan of a broad type, usually found only in large situations, which is coordinated in such a way as to be applicable to all liability risks. An example would be a wrap-up policy covering all contractors working on a specific job. **(LA)**

write. To insure, to underwrite, or to accept an application. **(G)**

written business. Insurance on which an application has been taken out but has not yet been delivered and/or the first premium has not yet been settled. **(LI)**

written premiums. The total premiums on all policies written by an insurer during a specified period, regardless of what portions have been earned. *See also* **earned premium. (G)**

wrongful abstraction. A term usually used in connection with money and securities coverage. Insurance covering wrongful abstraction protects against all forms of burglary, robbery, and stealing. **(C)**

wrongful death action. A civil court suit brought by survivors against someone believed responsible, by negligence or intention, for another's death. In a few states, actions for wrongful death have statutory minimums or maximums, but in most states they do not. **(LE)**

X-Y-Z

ABBREVIATIONS AND ACRONYMS

X table. A designation sometimes used to refer to an experimenta[l] or a draft of a table that has not developed to a point of satisfacti[on] for actual use in rating. **(G)**

XCU. Explosion, collapse, and underground damage. This term is used [in] business liability insurance to indicate that certain types of constructi[on] work involve these hazards. Many liability policies exclude them. The[y] can be added by endorsement for an additional premium charge. **(LA)**

YRT. *See* yearly renewable term. **(LI)**

PRESENTATION OF TERMS

yacht insurance. Insurance providing hull coverage and protection and indemnity liability coverage on pleasure boats. It is usually written on an open-perils (all risk) basis for hull coverage, although named-perils forms are sometimes used. **(OM)**

year plan. A calendar, policy, or fiscal year on which the records of the plan are kept. **(PE)**

yearly (or annual) renewable term (YRT). (1) Term life insurance that may be renewed annually without evidence of insurability until some stated age. (2) A form of life, and sometimes health, reinsurance in which the reinsurer assumes only the mortality risk, which is usually calculated as the face amount of reinsurance minus the terminal reserve. **(H, LI)**

years certain annuity. *See* annuity certain. **(LI)**

York Antwerp rules. A set of rules by which ocean marine general average losses are adjusted. **(OM)**

you/your. These words are used to refer to the named insured in many policy forms. **(G)**

table illustrating the ultimate experience on
according to the experienced mortality on life
panies from 1925 to 1934. The Z table was
the Commissioners' Standard Ordinary
(LI)

table
on or

in
on